New Life

Other Publications by the Authors

(Rex A E Hunt, Edited)
New Green Shoots and Other Story Sermons
(1993)

(Rex A E Hunt)
Against the Stream: Progressive Christianity Between Pulpit and Pew
(2012)

Cards, Carols, and Claus: Christmas in Popular Culture and Progressive Christianity
(Forthcoming)

(Rex A E Hunt with John W. H. Smith)
Why Weren't We Told? A Handbook on 'progressive' Christianity
(2012)

New Life

REDISCOVERING FAITH

Stories From Progressive Christians

Compiled and Edited by

John W. H. Smith & Rex A. E. Hunt

MOSAIC PRESS

Published in Australia by
Mosaic Press
508 High St
Preston Vic. 3072
Australia

Mosaic Press is an imprint of Mosaic Resources Pty Ltd

ISBN 9781743241097

First published 2013

Cataloguing-in-Publication entry is available for the National Library of Australia http:/catalogue.nla.gov.au/.

Book design by John Healy
Printed by Openbook Howden.

Abbreviations

Ps. -	The Book of Psalms
Matt. -	Matthew
Mk. -	Mark
Lk. -	Luke
Jn. -	John
Acts -	The Acts of the Apostles
Rom. -	Romans
1Jn. -	First Letter of John
Rev. -	Revelation

Contents

Contributors

Elizabeth Burns is an accredited Lay preacher in the Uniting Church in Australia. She has been actively involved in the Synod of Western Australia for almost 30 years and served as Moderator of that Synod from 1999—2002.

Richard Carter is a retired Melbourne company director with a special interest in the minerals industry. He is an active lay leader in his parish and is president and co-founder of the Progressive Christian Network of Victoria.

Gerald Christmas is a retired solicitor and from 1977—1990 was the Sydney Diocesan Registrar for the Anglican Church in Australia.

Neville Davidson a clerk of the courts for thirty-five years prior to retirement. He was active in the life of his parish until 2009 when disillusioned with orthodoxy he ceased attending church services and now refers to himself as a 'Christian in Exile'.

Ruth Doobov a retired Commonwealth senior public servant, is a member of The Uniting Church of St. James and The Centre for Progressive Religious Thought in Canberra.

Sue Emeleus a teacher from NSW who taught science, physics and Christian studies both in Australia and internationally. She is a trained counselor and chaplain as well as serving on the editorial committee of *Eremos.*

Ken Fletcher supports a wide range of continuing education programs from science to psychology, philosophy and comparative religions. Both he and his wife operate a pharmacy business.

Desley Garnett has had a varied career from microbiologist to Family Day Services Coordinator. She is currently an advisory Officer for Queensland Family Care Association. She is an active member of the Uniting Church.

Aaron Harper is currently an advisor to the Minister of Defence and has been involved in Defence budgeting for twenty years. He is actively involved with The Uniting Church of St James where he has developed a keen interest in new liturgies and prayer.

Lorna Henry is a retired teacher of German and Religion in secondary schools. She leads a monthly study group for a wide variety of church and non-church people.

Fiona McDougal is a member of St Andrew's on The Terrace and serves on the Parish Council. She is currently studying theology through distance education while working as a registered nurse at the Hutt hospital.

Gai Nowland is involved with the Nightcliff Uniting Church as a leader in progressive Christian study groups. She has also been practically involved in the community activities run by people from the parish.

Lesley Oakley is a social worker/family therapist who worked in child welfare for thirty years, much of this time as a manager in large non-government organizations.

Ian O'Reilly provides life counseling for young people as well as managing the coordination of network programs. He has worked with indigenous youth, in his role with Anglicare Northern Territory.

Frances Porter is a New Zealand writer. As an historian she has been creatively writing for approximately forty years, in particular about the role of women in society.

Adrian Pyle is the Innovation and Relationship Development Worker for the Victorian and Tasmanian Synod of the Uniting Church in Australia.

Pamela Raff has held many roles from being an ABC announcer to teaching sewing and English as a second language. She has written liturgies for the Anglican Church while representing the local parish, synod and diocesan council.

Lynne Robertson conducts Clinical Pastoral Education programs. She recently retired from her role as Field Education Coordinator for CTM and is currently writing a Supervision Training Package for the Uniting Church Assembly.

Kathleen Rowe taught technology and studies of religion in secondary schools both in Australia and New Zealand. She is currently the parish clerk of St Luke's Presbyterian Church in Auckland New Zealand.

Betty Shore was born in the USA, but has adopted New Zealand as her home since 1973. She is an advocate for quality education and social justice in Christchurch NZ.

Durham Smith is a retired Paediatric Surgeon who is the author of several books on surgery. He is also author of *"Search For Understanding"* a personal journey of faith with intellectual integrity.

Richard Smith is a scientist with extensive employment experience in CSIRO, NASA, as well as Australian and international governments. He is a lay preacher and member of the All Saints Floreat Uniting Church in Western Australia.

George Stuart an ordained Presbyterian minister who left the ministry for employment with BHP in 1975. George has continued his involvement with the Uniting Church in Newcastle where he has written over 500 sets of lyrics in modern, progressive language to well known tunes.

David Tacey a professor in psychology and postmodern theory at La Trobe University. He has written extensively on spirituality, religion and society. Although coming into conflict with the Catholic hierarchy for his outspoken views he continues to participate in parish life.

Val Webb is a microbiologist, theologian and author of numerous works on progressive theology. Having lived in the USA for more than thirty years she has now returned to Australia where she continues to write and present public presentations.

A more detailed account of the biographies of the contributors can be found in Appendix 2.

Foreword

Where is Progressive Christianity at? Four Exploratory Cameos...*

Rex A. E. Hunt

Institutional Christianity in Australia, wrapped in a rejuvenated neo-orthodoxy, or perhaps more accurately, a neo-Barthianism, is stumbling, if not showing all the signs of dying. As one of my mentors wrote way back in 1976 during the theological move from Left to Right:

> There is something about church Christianity that depresses the creativities of men (*sic*), that foreshortens their imaginative and critical powers and impels them to suspect concern with qualitative attainment, thus lulling them into or even summoning them to a preference for mediocrity *(Meland 1976:169).*

I would claim those words of Bernard Meland are still relevant today. In truth, the Australian 'institution' has been stumbling since 1788. Christianity was in the main rejected by the convicts and only slightly embraced by the free settlers in latter years, despite the very best initial efforts of evangelical Church of England chaplain, Richard Johnson. Little-known however is that prior to departure from England, Captain Arthur Phillip was instructed to "ensure that the Book of Common Prayer was read each Sunday and Holy Day", while his oath of allegiance at the foundation of the colony "included a rejection of the doctrine of transubstantiation, presumably to ensure that no taint of Romanism entered even a prison colony" *(Breward 1988:2).*

This has led some to conclude that in Australia, Christianity has always been rather a casual affair. At best, the nation was only ever superficially christianised *(Wilson 1982:6).*

Statistics suggest Australian church attendance is less now per head of population than during the 1950s and 1960s *(Kaldor 1987:21-26, Hughes et. al. 1995:7).* Of those who do attend, there are many more women than men, and more older people than young people. Those same statistics also reveal church attendance is not the total 'religion' story for Australians. It is but one dimension—an institutional dimension—of the Australian religious landscape.

In their latest Report based on the 2011 Census, the ABS declares:

> although Christian religions are still predominant in Australia, there have been increases in those reporting an affiliation to non-Christian religions, and those reporting 'No Religion' *(ABS. 'Religious Affiliation', 2013).*

Among those indicating 'No Religion', the increase was most evident among younger people, with 28% of people aged 15-34 reporting they had no religious affiliation *(ABS. 'Religious Affiliation', 2013).*

Where is progressive Christianity at? There are some claims those same young people have stopped listening to Christianity completely. The ABS does not have separate statistics of those who call themselves 'progressive Christian'. However, all indicators point to the presence of a growing number in the Census count. When national church officials make back-handed comments about 'progressives' in official communications, you know that 'growing number' is rattling their cages!

oo0oo

Within the current 'mainline/oldline' theological climate in Australia at least two different streams of thought are found. The first stream—the more dominant and holding the most number of cards in nearly all theological colleges and, more than likely, church councils—is supported by those who **guard the tradition** (or "a right understanding of the Faith" *(Thompson 2011:17).* This is usually called neo-orthodoxy, where Karl Barth is still recognised as its principal theologian, and the Fourth gospel its 'christological' favourite. The second stream—progressive—is fewer in number but growing and networking globally. This stream **challenges the tradition** *(Hunt 2012)*, and where the Westar Institute and its various Seminars are acknowledged as being part of its contemporary leadership, with the Synoptics plus Thomas, their favourite gospels.

The former see the latter as intellectually questionable, 'edgy revisionist', or heretical, open to cause 'schism' in the church. Two theological worldviews in conflict, where the task of "contemplating *church doctrine* has outranked the task of contemplating life itself" *(Vosper 2012:197)*. As Gregory Jenks also says in one of his cameo entries in *Why Weren't We Told?*: "at the heart of this controversy is the question of truth; *not simply what is true, but who determines what is true*?" *(Jenks 2013:39.* Emphasis added*).* Is so-called 'truth' settled by the church's fourth and fifth century creeds, or is 'truth' something that might yet be clarified by new research that is independent of, but not in any sense controlled by, the church?

Creeds, such as the Nicene Creed, were first debated in 325CE under the divine Emperor Constantine who was seeking a conflict-free Empire, and later refined somewhat in 381CE at Constantinople. The divine Emperor Theodosius intervened in church affairs and "by the sheer weight of imperial power... brought to a premature end a debate that was still vital and full of possibilities" *(Freeman 2009:204)*—creeds are clusters of beliefs. Let me be quite clear: this was not a dialogue among fundamentally different but mutually respectful alternative perspectives. The power of the state was deployed against 'perceived enemies' to root out all differences. Indeed, it was an expression of an insidious form of control! Power and politics, sword and the removal of financial sponsorship, exterminated any different points of view or practice.

Generally speaking, the neo-orthodox garments that surround much religious discussion have tended toward a more literal interpretation of Bible and tradition, coupled with the objectiveness of God's 'otherness'. Its claims include: Jesus is God incarnate, begotten of the Father, born of a virgin, a person of the doctrine of the Trinity, who died on the cross in place of all humanity, who all ought to die because of their sins, was raised up on the third day, ascending into heaven to be with God the Father. Added to all this is the separation of church from society—seen as deeply flawed by such theologians of a past era as Paul Tillich, Hans Kung, Johann Baptist Metz and Langdon Gilkey—and as an under-current: Jesus as an apocalyptic prophet.

In reality, the human Jesus does not matter. Jesus needs to be the full incarnation of God in human form in order to be the unsurpassable revelation of God. A human Jesus will not do! And those who 'search' for the historical/human Jesus, especially those associated with or shaped by the Jesus Seminar, are of a very questionable kind!

Some of the garments that wrap progressive thought suggest: the historical Jesus was a human being, a wandering secular or peasant Galilean sage, who belonged more to the 'wisdom' stream than the 'priestly' stream of Judaism. He taught wisdom in aphorisms and parables. What we see in these wisdom fragments is the Cynic's style of making social critique, and a person who approached life with amazement, wonder, and awe.

Theology is a human enterprise—an imaginative construction and reconstruction. Such an enterprise implies that our interests, training, social interactions, environmental location, and assumptions, as well as our habits, experiences, and customs, will all influence and help shape that theological task.

Gordon Kaufman, former Harvard Divinity School theologian, claimed traditional Christian theology from the mid-third century on, was developed from *within* a Christian world-picture. Thus *belief* was seen as a prerequisite to any proper understanding of the human condition and God. But, he argued, there needed to be a change in approach:

> Instead of asking, What are the principal doctrines or ideas prescribed by tradition for Christians to believe, and how should we interpret these today? it now becomes necessary to direct attention to questions like, How does one articulate a worldview… [a] Christian picture of the world, and how does one assess its significance for human life today. *(Kaufman 1993:40).*

Where is progressive Christianity at? Refocusing religious reflection as advocated by Kaufman raises a different agenda from that followed by neo-orthodox theologians. Progressive thought claims Christianity has never been about only one, unchanging, singular vision of the world. It is not just a history of creeds and 'right belief'. It is also the story of a people who sometimes cobbled together creeds out of beliefs, but who also questioned, altered, and discarded those same creeds. *(Cox 2011).*

As both Val Webb *(Webb 2013)* and Harvey Cox have reminded us, there is a sharp theological distinction between *faith* and *belief*. Faith is relational.

It is about trust and the way we live. Belief is primarily a cognitive function. Beliefs are more propositional than existential. I really warm to the analogy of a post in the middle of a paddock, as told by Canadian progressive, Gretta Vosper:

> The post represents the fundamentals of Christianity. Around the post are those who adhere to the faith. Some are holding on to it. Some are close, but not touching. Some are at quite a distance, and some can barely see the post at all. But all of them use it as a frame of reference for their lives. *(Vosper 2008:52).*

Then Vosper gets personal:

> This analogy was offered by a colleague at a denominational event to suggest that, despite the great distance between me and the post, I still belonged. Its telling was a gesture of kindness. But I am uncomfortable with it, for it assumes the post *will* never and *should* never be moved, much less *removed*. Its permanence is assumed...
>
> *(Vosper 2008:52).*

Traditions must always be challenged. They need questioning 'space' so they can develop, grow, and mature. If left unchallenged and bound up they will surely die. Scholarship is not created out of thin air (the technical term is *creatio ex nihilo.*) But the motion is not a straight-line development either. There are advances and retreats, arguments and divisions, and always new disciplines washing over from other scholarly activities. Thinking theologically means more than just interpreting our given 'orthodox' biblical tradition and creedal statements. It also means being willing to think differently now than in the past. Any attempt by dogmatists to impose fourth century creeds on today's twenty-first century living is an act of abusive power!

oo0oo

Despite the dismissive comments of a conservative Sydney Anglican bishop on David Busch's *Good Friday Breakfast* on Radio National this year, 1985 was a good year for biblical studies. In that year American New Testament scholar and former Executive Secretary of the Society of Biblical Literature, Robert Funk—"a spiritual descendant of Rudolf Bultmann and Karl Barth, Reinhold Niebuhr and Paul Tillich, and the neo-orthodox movement they sponsored" *(Funk 1996:304)*—called together 30 biblical scholars and invited them to join a 'Renewed Quest' for the historical/human Jesus.

This exploration was to start with a 'sayings' data base seeking to discover a Jesus 'voice print' amid the recorded subject matter of his public discourse. But what is not always appreciated even by some progressives is that the scholars would "move outside of both church and academy in order to address a wider, public audience" as well as "examine texts outside the Christian canon of the New Testament" and draw conclusions "without regard to Christian doctrine" *(Bessler 2013:163)*.

So what sustains many progressive Christians? A quick survey of resources used include the many books and articles published by Fellows and Associates of Westar-women and men-and the development of such DVD resources as 'Living the Questions', stand out. Not exclusively, because we all can name others not associated with Westar, but certainly significantly.

A bit of a mixed bag, I believe Westar membership can be 'sorted' into at least two groups: 'integrationists' and 're-constructivists'. Among the leadership of the first group are: Marcus Borg, Hal Taussig, Stephen Patterson, and probably Dom Crossan. While leadership of the second group includes: Brandon Scott, Elaine Pagels, David Galston, Arthur Dewey and Robert Miller. By 'integrationists' I am suggesting: seeks to ***reshape*** the tradition from within rather than abandon the church—confirmed by Borg in an email exchange with a group of international progressives: "...for me, that means remaining within Christianity for the sake of changing it" *(Borg 2013)*. By 're-constructivists' I am suggesting: seeks to ***reconstruct*** if not from outside the tradition, then certainly from the borders.

Most know of the Westar Institute through its 'Jesus Seminar', but there are many other sides to this progressive intellectual centre, now located within Willamette University. It has also established The Paul Seminar, The Acts Seminar, The Bible Seminar, The Early Christianity Seminar, and the one where I served for four years—the Literacy & Liturgy Seminar. The Westar Institute and The Centre for Progressive Christianity USA, now called ProgressiveChristianity.Org are also working more closely together these days, as new resources are being commissioned and published.

Where is progressive Christianity at? From my observations progressive Christianity 'down under' seems to have sided with the 'integrationists' rather than with the more radical 're-constructivists'. Although there are a few individual exceptions! The implication of such adoption is most noticeable in the shape and content of the Sunday Morning liturgy. By 'shape' I mean: the liturgical movement still flows from confession to pardon—or the presupposition of human guilt, even when 'progressives' are shaping that liturgy. By 'content' I mean: seldom does the liturgical language go beyond the "intellectual two-step" called "latitudinarianism"—that is, preserving one's intellectual integrity by proclaiming belief beyond literalism, but continuing to use the anthropomorphic language or images of the traditional hymns, prayers, and creeds—in order to remain within the tradition. But playing that game "compromises our integrity and our religion... it is another example of keeping what we know and what we believe separated" *(Loehr 2000:9).*

oo0oo

Hal Taussig's research, and published as *A New Spiritual Home*, shows there are many different expressions of grass roots 'progressive' Christianity. While nowhere near as large a sample, the stories published in *Why Weren't We Told?* along with those in this companion collection, also confirm this trend. Local informal study groups are literally springing up all over the place, offering both discussion and community.

In one of her presentations Val Webb recounted that she had led discussions for fifteen years in her local church

> with sometimes as many as forty people, from beyond our church as well. My years of theological education equipped me to challenge biblical interpretations or theological arguments which stood on shaky ground or no longer held water; and not being ordained gave me freedom to pursue my theological evolution without the bonds of denominational confessions that hampered many of my colleagues *(Webb).*

Sometimes attempts to start such groups come under heavy cross-fire from conservative clergy and lay leaders. Access to church property has been denied them in other situations. Seeking to blame progressives for "confusing and disturbing the faith of the simple believer", outraged officials have sought to "mock and suppress such inquiry as a kind of treason against the church" *(Bessler 2013:5)*. Arguing that Christian doctrine and creeds are the norm of authentic faith—both theological norm, as well as political norm required of all participants of the church—has failed, and is no longer intellectually or morally persuasive.

In a set of Lectionary Notes published the same week as a Brisbane Anglican conservative issued a call for progressives to be expelled from the church, Greg Jenks wrote:

> The theological thought police are quick to confront deviations from approved forms of liturgy or theology. What the world needs now are more religious communities with some capacity to live with ambiguity. We need fewer fatwas and no more church edicts that divide, exclude and control the faithful. What might the world be like if the followers of Jesus were famous for our gentleness towards others, and especially those with whom we disagreed? *(Jenks 2013b)*

Where is progressive Christianity at? Despite healthy differences, the exponents of progressive Christianity are together saying: (i) we don't want our religion in the old way, (ii) we cannot give up our minds for it, and (iii) we cannot become pre-modern people. The Christian community is not a sacred grotto. Ordained clergy are not antiquities dealers.

As it says on the Canadian Centre for Progressive Christianity website:

> Progressive isn't a place. It is a state of mind and the next step from wherever you find yourself entrenched. Whether in the church, in your workplace, or in your relationships, a progressive perspective is characterized by openness, passion, creativity, and a willingness to explore beyond wherever you are at the moment.

To help support those personal journeys, there are now several major 'progressive' events offering both discussion of ideas and support, open to each and every person who wishes to explore progressive Christianity. I am referring of course to the international Common Dreams Conferences, the Common Dreams on the Road events, and related regional activities, held in Australia and New Zealand. In each case these encounters do not ruin people's faith, but reawaken it.

Progressive Christianity is committed to reconstructing a vision of faith within the contours of the best understandings of reality available. To do so, progressive Christianity goes beyond the contours of Christian orthodoxy *(Bessler 2013:222)*, as well as challenging the church, laity and clergy, to be courageous—to be the community "that keeps alive the 'dangerous' memory" of the human/historical Jesus *(Johnson 2001:161)*.

For 2,000+ years, Yeshua/Jesus of Nazareth has been represented to the world in terms of later inferences drawn from his sayings and deeds, rather than in terms of what he himself said or did *(Hedrick 2004:98)*. Getting through the traditional or 'orthodox' Jesus to find the historical/human Jesus is an academic challenge that, after a few centuries, has now "arrived on the church's doorstep as the crisis of the 'historical' Jesus" *(Galston 2012:15)*. In a sense, we are in a similar situation today as others were in the first century: what to do with the homeland Jew, Jesus of Nazareth.

If we decide to order our lives in terms of the human Jesus it will be **we** who do the deciding, and **we** who take, or fail to take, the steps to carry out that decision. Not some supernatural authority, extra-human power, or prescribed creed or statement.

** A shorter version of this article was presented as part of a panel discussion on the theme 'Where is progressive Christianity at' sponsored by the Progressive Christian Network of Victoria, in Melbourne, 30 June 2013.*

Notes:

"2011 Census. Religious Affiliation". ABS. 'Religious Affiliation'. <www.abs.gov.au>

Bessler, J. A. *A Scandalous Jesus. How Three Historic Quests Changed Theology for the Better*. Salem: Polebridge Press, 2013.

Borg, M. "Where To From Here". A contribution to an online discussion between a group of international progressives. 29 June 2013.

Breward, I. *Australia. The Most Godless Place Under Heaven*. Mitcham: Beacon Hill Books, 1988.

Cox, H. *The Future of Faith*. New York: HarperCollins/Amazon e-Book, 2011

Funk, R. W. *Honest to Jesus. Jesus for the New Millennium*. New York: PolebridgePress/HarperSanFrancisco, 1996.

Galston, D. "Why I wrote Embracing the Human Jesus" in *The Fourth R* 25, 6, November December 2012, 19-20, 24.

Hedrick, C. "The 'Good News' about the historical Jesus" in Jesus Seminar (ed).

The Historical Jesus goes to Church. Santa Rosa: Polebridge Press, 2004.

Hughes, P., Thompson, C., Pryor, R., Bouma,G. D. (ed) *Believe It or Not. Australian Spirituality and the Churches in the 90s.* Melbourne. Christian Research Association, 1995.

Hunt, R. A. E. *Against The Stream: Progressive Christianity Between Pulpit and Pew*. Preston: Mosaic Press, 2012.

Jenks, G. C. "Progressive Anglicans". http://gregoryjenks.com/2013/05/30/progressive-anglicans/ 2013.

Jenks, G. C. "The Historical Jesus" in Hunt, R. A. E. & Smith, J. W. H. (ed) *Why Weren't We Told? A Handbook on Progressive Christianity*. Salem: Polebridge Press, 2013.

———————,"Pentecost 2C". GregoryJenks. http://gregoryjenks.com/2013/05/27/pentecost-2c-2-june-2013/ Posted 30 May 2013b.

Johnson, E. A. "The Word Was Made Flesh and Dwelt Among Us: Jesus Research and Christian Faith" in D. Donnelly (ed) *Jesus –A Colloquium in the Holy Land*. New York: Continuum, 2001, 146-166.

Kaldor, P. *Who Goes Where? Who Doesn't Care? Going to Church in Australia.* Homebush: West Lancer, 1987.

Loehr, D. "Salvation by Character: How UU's can find the religious center" in *Journal of Liberal Religion 1*, 2, 1-14, 2000.

Meland, B. E. *Fallible Forms and Symbols. Discourses of Method in a Theology of Culture.* Philadelphia: Fortress Press, 1976.

Smith, J. W. H. & Hunt, R. A. E. (ed) *New Life: Progressive Christianity and the Rediscovery of Faith*. Forthcoming 2013. Mosaic Press.

Thompson, G. "'Well, That's Just Your Perspective': Guarding and Declaring the Right Understanding of the Faith in a Relativist Culture" in *Uniting Church Studies 17*, 2, December 2011, 17-32.

Vosper, G. *Amen. What Prayer Can Mean in a World Beyond Belief.* Toronto: HarperCollins, 2012.

——————, *With or Without God. Why the Way we Live is More Important than What we Believe*. Toronto: HarperCollins, 2008.

Webb, V. *In Defence of Doubt. An Invitation to Adventure*. Revised and expanded edition. Melbourne: Mosaic Press, 2013.

——————, "Like Catching Water in a Net: A Personal and Theological Journey". Direct from the author. Used with permission. No date.

Wilson, B. "The Church in a Secular Society" in D. Harris, D Hynd, D Millikan. (ed) *The Shape of Belief. Christianity in Australia today*. Homebush: Lancer Books, 1982.

"Progressive Christianity" www.progressivechristianity.ca

Introduction

Embracing Life's Journey with Renewed Vigour

The influence of 'progressive' theological thought and biblical scholarship has had a profound impact on the professional life of many clergy, even if that thought was not gained in Theological College or Seminary. The 2008 book *"When Faith Meets Reason"*, edited by Charles W Hedrick records the progressive journeys of fourteen scholars and clergy as they struggled with the issue of maintaining a faith that did not negatively impact on the issue of 'intellectual integrity". These are poignant stories related by people who are attempting to make sense of their understanding of the sacred in the twenty-first century.

In the last two decades we have seen a significant increase in the effect of this scholarship in the writings of clergy such as Nolan, Meyer, Churcher, Gulley, O'Murchu, and in Australia, in the work of people like Hyde, Bodycomb, Jenks, Hunt, Leaves and Parkinson. Their journey has transformed for them their understanding of the life of Jesus of Nazareth and this is reflected not only in their writings, but also in the practice of their faith.

Many of these clergy have been influenced by writers from the Jesus Seminar, as well as scholars from the United Kingdom and New Zealand: such as Robert Funk, John Shelby Spong, Karen Armstrong, Marcus Borg, Dom Crossan, Brandon Scott, and Robert Miller. Some significant factors in the popularity of this latter group of scholars is that they have (i) taken the debate about the human/historical Jesus out of the realm of academia and into the lives of lay people, (ii) are prepared to examine texts outside the Christian canon of the New Testament, and (iii) draw their conclusions without regard to Christian doctrine.

Similarly, many lay people have, for years, questioned the traditional orthodox views and beliefs. Some have in frustration, left their faith communities. For those who questioned the virgin birth in the light of current knowledge about genetics, or the concept of a resuscitated body in the knowledge of modern medical science, these writers provided a reasoned voice that dripped with intellectual integrity. Issues raised by creedal and doctrinal statements were now not only personal questions, they were questions that went to the heart of the orthodox faith. In reality these writers had become the perfect foil for the over spiritualised and over politicised image of Jesus.

In Diana Butler Bass's book *A People's History of Christianity* (2009:12 ff) she is in someway correct in her assessment that people in the 'progressive' or 'emergent' Christian movement are sparing in their use of tradition, as a means of understanding the sacred. One reason for this could be that those attracted to this movement are committed to embracing a change from a traditional interpretation of faith, because they found that this approach did not appropriately answer their concerns.

The challenge to tradition is itself often recorded as a messy and disordered type of history. The progressive challenge to tradition is also a questioning of the truths once held as being sacrosanct. This change comes not from the powerful figures of history but from those who are considered powerless to effect change. These are the voices, not of the philosophers, theologians or bishops, but of the people who everyday live with the questions that a changing world continues to present. In reality the voices that challenge tradition are in themselves the voices that create tradition and they need to be recognised and recorded as such. This book is a small attempt to explore and record the history of a challenge to tradition as a primary source in understanding the sacred.

While we now have a substantial amount of information about the impact this movement has had on the beliefs and practices of clergy, surprisingly little has been published about the impact of this new information on lay-women and men within the Christian faith. This book, which is a companion to our earlier edited collection called *Why Weren't We Told? A Handbook on progressive Christianity*, attempts in a small way to redress this imbalance.

Research

We have asked lay women and men who have been active in the progressive Christian movements in Australia and New Zealand, to record their spiritual journey and the personal impact of their newly acquired knowledge of the human or historical Jesus of Nazareth. We asked them to describe their faith development and to share the forces that impacted on their current understanding.

We were also interested in discerning whether others, particularly those close to the subject, saw the resultant change in attitude and behaviour as a positive life experience.

Finally we were interested in discovering if this new knowledge made a positive or negative impact on the individual's life. Did the new information provide them with an alternative understanding of their faith? Did it justify their questions and doubts? Were they turned away from the church to no church? All in approximately 2,500 words!

Our questionnaire forms *Appendix 1* of this book.

A progressive Christianity is not new. In one form or another it has been around for one hundred and seventy years or more. What is new about its current expression now intentionally called 'progressive', is this open and inclusive faith is 'coming out' in unexpected ways, or resurfacing in hundreds of congregations in mainline churches around the world. That is, a dynamic grass roots movement where the initiative is often taken by a *lay person*!

So the important bits of this collection are the stories themselves. Down-to-earth, honest, gutsy, personal stories. Told by lay people who have come to 'progressive' Christianity with various life-skills and experiences: as engineers, financial advisors, medical practitioners, public servants, home makers, academics, office workers, parents, nurses, authors, scientists, poets, lawyers, carers, social workers, community workers and sociologists—all committed to the broad brush strokes within 'progressive' Christianity. Some have undertaken formal theological education. Some have been lay preachers. A couple have been ordained but later resigned. One has been refused ordination into the priesthood because of gender. Others do not wish to claim the title 'Christian'.

Their stories are recorded here because their message needs to be given a voice, if for no other reason than to encourage leaders in orthodox Christianity to listen and respond appropriately. They are shared also so others may know they are not alone when they raise their questions. These stories of encouragement, liberation and empowerment are presented to assist others still searching. They are stories that celebrate the life of the emerging… global progressive movement. As one of our contributors has written:

> I remain firmly convinced that the church should have made a far greater and more determined effort to resist the power play of conservative and fundamental Christianity in the 1960s, by taking more seriously, the scholarship available to it. If the church had embraced with radical and evangelical fervour, the challenging and liberating progressive scholarship of such writers as Bishop John A. T. Robinson, for example, then it would be enjoying greater credibility and acceptance today.

Salient Points from our Storytellers

We have structured this book with an eye to understanding something of the implications of these stories and to enhance the opportunity to use this information in study groups. Not the least of our aims is to encourage others to examine their own spiritual journeys and to be prepared to share them; so we can all learn from each other's experience in becoming faith communities of the twenty-first century.

Here we present twenty-five unique stories of people journeying in faith. These stories, which we have the privilege of presenting, display an exciting blend of a faith that enjoys and in fact expects critical analysis, yet seeks to strive to understand the sacred meaning of life. They are stories of searching for wholeness of being, which includes having an eye to the practical implications of everyday living, while recognising that the source of a sacred presence defies description.

The editors recognise that while each of these stories is quite unique there are a number of salient points that display particular characteristics from our contributors' experiences. We have defined eight such mediating factors and these are:

1. The Journey of Faith is a work in Progress

A majority of our contributors referred to their understanding of faith to be an unfinished, dynamic journey rather than having arrived at a new state of enlightenment. *Davidson* has actually titled his story as *'A Work in Progress'* and *Burns* refers to her development as a *'journey of challenge and support'* and *'a searching for meaning'*. *Christmas* actually questions whether he can refer to his journey as a *'progress'* and affirms *Davidson's* conclusion that he is, *'still a work in progress'*.

Whereas *Webb* and *Richard Smith* agree that it is the journey not the destination that is the principle issue at stake.

Both *Raff* and *Fletcher* raise the issue of living with the uncertainty of this approach as *Raff* states, *'I am comfortable with where I am even if I don't know exactly where that is'*. *Fletcher* also concludes, *'I expect my conclusions to be continually changing as I learn new facts and think through the implications of life's experiences.'* The progressive journey was a dynamic and fluid state for most of our contributors.

2. The Importance of the Community of Faith

This was a significant and consistent factor in the stories from our contributors. In the majority of the articles these communities were found within the existing framework of the Christian faith. In at least three circumstances those of *Davidson, Christmas,* and *O'Reilly* they no longer attended church communities, but had found support in group activities connected with a search for wholeness.

Our contributors stressed the importance of being able to explore their faith journey in a community that offered a safe and supportive environment, where there is a sense of belonging. This is epitomised by the sign at the front of St Andrew's on The Terrace in Wellington NZ which says, *'This is our place. This is your place.'* Often when the worship was inappropriate it was the relationships within the community that encouraged people, such as *Oakley,* to continue the struggle toward wholeness.

Shore emphasised that for her this was a crucial factor in allowing her the inclusion and acceptance she needed. For *Garnett* it was the community that allowed her to, *'feel comfortable enough to express her doubts'* and Raff looked to the community for *'love, compassion and inspiration.'*

Porter sees community as '*knowing that, one belongs to the family of things*', and Fletcher recognises the strength in community is the '*continuing communion of sharing with others*'.

The importance of an accepting, supportive community cannot be underestimated for people journeying with progressive Christianity.

3. The Importance of a Faith in Action

The importance of a practical application of faith or the 'living out' of one's beliefs was explicitly mentioned by a number of authors and implicit with others. The journey in progressive Christianity for many was only relevant when the concrete practical outcomes were apparent. This issue could be perhaps summed up by the by-line in *Gretta Vosper's "With or Without God" 'Why the Way We Live is More Important Than What We Believe.'*

It is *Porter* who makes a quite definitive statement in this regard by quoting that, '*Practice not Gnosis must be the fruit: the way we behave, particularly in striving for social justice and peace, is the fullest expression of what we believe.*' *Garnett* also emphasises the importance of the practice of faith when she writes, '*What I do and how I live is more important than a set of beliefs*'.

It is *Robertson* who makes this issue one of justice for all because faith for her is reaching out in love. She states that it is an issue of, '*equality, of feeding the hungry, caring for the vulnerable and marginalised.*'

For *Durham Smith* faith in action means to, '*engage with joy and hope in life, in work, relationships, care for others,*' but it is *Doobov* who sums this issue up succinctly by writing, '*The faith founded by Jesus needs to be practiced in community.*'

4. Embracing the Historical Jesus

Nearly all of our contributors have emphasised that a detailed understanding of the 'historical Jesus' and in most cases through the lens of New Testament scholarship that has significantly changed their understanding of the Bible and the nature of the character of the sacred source that we call God. All of our contributors through their understanding of Progressive Christianity presented an image of the divine as a compassionate loving spirit. This flies in the face of the orthodox view of a vengeful and judgmental God controlling the universe like some giant 'puppeteer'.

The net effect of this view is a deep sense of liberation illustrated so emphatically by Garnett as she states, '*I am free! I am free! Not from my sin but from having to make myself believe things my mind cannot accept.*' Unfortunately a number of our contributors, such as *Burns, Oakley* and *Tacey* were not encouraged by clergy to express their newfound freedom.

Some of our contributors experienced difficulty in deconstructing their earlier experience and this brought them into conflict with earlier beliefs. *Carter* recounts that by exploring the historical Jesus he was faced with rejecting '*the image of God*' he had previously accepted. In a similar way *Christmas* no longer regarded God as '*omnipotent, judgmental and supernatural but as a source of life not being present, not in one place, but in all humans and living things*'.

Henry came to a new image of Jesus as a result of her evolutionary journey and regarded him no longer as a divine creature, but as a '*totally God-filled human being.*'

Emeleus brings to our discussion the aspect of a 'changing' God because she now understands God not as an avenging punishing God, but as a being that, '*absorbs all that happens and is changed in the process.*'

All of these experiences and insights will provide the reader with ample information for future discussion and debate.

5. Embracing Religious Pluralism

A basic fundamental of Christian orthodoxy is the belief that there is only one way to enter into a relationship with God and that is through acceptance that Jesus brought us back by his preordained death on the cross. Those who hold to this belief often quote the words of Jesus as recorded in Jn. 14:6. The flip side is then to say that all other faiths are inferior.

Many of our contributors would argue against this fundamental. They propose that we need to keep ourselves open to the possibility that Christianity does not bring with it any greater certainty of understanding the truth than other faiths. They raise the question, is it possible that there are other 'roads home' and if so should we be exploring them?

As *Porter* concludes in relation to the issue of certainty, '*I have come to accept that my faith will always mean living with uncertainty, particularly over the mystery we name God'. George Stuart* takes this point further and suggests as progressive Christians we need to listen not only to people of other faiths but to people of no faith. He states, *'I no longer see the church's main task as proselytizing or evangelising, but entering into dialogue with other faiths and those of no religious beliefs, learning from them and sharing with them.' Burns* agrees with Stuart's last point when she writes that she finds much in common with Richard Dawkins, the internationally famous atheist.

Christmas and in particular *Webb* stress the importance of embracing doubt as a positive step in understanding our relationship with the sacred. The questions raised by people such as *Rowe*, following her study of other faiths, indicates much is to be learned from keeping ourselves open to other avenues to an understanding of the sacred.

6. Intellectual Integrity: Outcome or Initiator

A question the reader should keep in mind is, did doubts about verifying the legitimacy of the Bible stories in the light of personal knowledge and experience initiate the progressive quest? Or was it an outcome of being exposed to viable alternative information?

For many of our contributors intellectual integrity was a significant motivator in encouraging the search for a more authentic understanding of faith. These people simply are pursuing a faith that can be understood in the light of their personal knowledge and experience. Blind acceptance of creeds and doctrines or a literal interpretation of scripture in the light of twenty-first century science, could no longer be countenanced.

Davidson suggests that many people were leaving the church because *they were seeking twenty-first century answers to their questions of faith and belief, but were receiving sixteenth century answers instead.* Whereas for *Durham Smith* at an early point in his adult life he concludes, *'The religious belief I had embraced as a youth was now seriously doubted because it simply did not make sense intellectually.'*

Raff expressed the dilemma for many confronted by their own doubts and questions when she stated, *"I think that most of the time, we rely on our own intelligence, intuition whatever and just get on with life'.* Questioning for many was an almost innate activity as *Tacey* explains, *'I was progressive, critical and enquiring from the beginning of my thinking life... even as a child I asked questions about faith.' Webb* also echoes *Tacey's* words in her story. For many the intellectual journey is exciting because, it begins to make sense of the world which is be filled with wonder, but still believable to the enquiring mind. *Fletcher* claims, '*the gaining of knowledge and the relating this to our connection with nature is the exciting journey.*'

Stuart sums up the importance of the liberating impact of intellectual integrity by writing, '*Where intellectual honesty prevails and where freedom is given for people to accept their doubts as launching pads along the way to a more relevant, sensible and significant set of beliefs can be an exciting and liberating experience. I have been witness to such.*'

7. A Sense of Awe

A question often asked is, can progressive Christians seeking a rational explanation for matters of faith still have a sense of awe and wonder about so much that cannot be explained? Our contributors certainly suggest that it is possible to accommodate a search for understanding and a willingness to accept that there is so much that cannot be rationally explained. The stories we present have an exciting blend between a faith that enjoys and in reality expects, critical analysis in a practical setting, while at the same time is aware of an indescribable sacred presence.

Henry describes this presence vividly in her article when describing her experience with a life-threatening situation, '*My earlier story told of an awareness of a presence, a warm presence, a comfort, in times of difficulty. I call that presence God, without trying to define anything.*'

Robertson acknowledges the enormity of attempting to explain the image of God when she writes, '*God is much bigger than I can ever contemplate.*' There are people who are critical of progressive Christianity because they believe in its rush to explain the stories of faith from a rational, logical perspective it has lost something of the 'enchantment' of faith. Some people within the progressive Christian movement raise this as a criticism, but this is not how it is perceived by *Rowe* who writes, '*The ecumenical dream of a church sensitive to the presence of God in and through all creation, sharing in the human search for peace and justice, respecting those of other faiths and valuing truth wherever it is found, continues within the progressive movement and for that I'm grateful.'*

In concluding this salient point, '*A sense of Awe*' I return to *Henry's* article for a summing up of this issue in her comment, '*There is still much about the sacred that is unknown and perhaps unknowable but this doesn't deny that a force outside ourselves exists.*'

8. The Clergy Influence

Our storytellers explain that there are both positive and negative aspects of the clergy influence in the progressive faith journey. There are those clergy who have used their position to deny people the right to express their questions and concerns. However, even the negative influence can sometimes encourage people to explore their understanding of faith. We discovered in our research for the book '*Why Weren't We Told?*' that some of the most successful 'grassroots' progressive groups had grown, developed, even flourished and continued their influence, in spite of concerted opposition from clergy.

Our contributors report, in a majority of cases, that clergy influence had been positive especially where the clergy were people with open minds and open hearts. These clergy were more likely to present doubts as a positive basis for exploring faith and encouraged people to ask questions without fear of ridicule.

Unfortunately one of our contributors *Nowland,* was concerned that she had been duped by clergy, when they did not share their knowledge of New Testament scholarship. This concern is echoed by *Oakley* whose article title explains her annoyance that clergy lacked 'ticker'. *Harper* and *Burns* also recount stories of clergy being less than sympathetic to their need for pastoral support in times of distress. Some of these clergy even responded with pious guilt laden responses. Perhaps the greatest concern in this area was the experience of *David Tacey* who was actively pursued by church leaders to ban him as a layperson from speaking on Church property. Tacey's concern is expressed in his claim that, '*What we are not yet aware of is the level of 'spiritual abuse' in the church, and the thuggish ways in which church hierarchy treats its intellectuals and thinkers.*'

Although Burns experienced a negative response from one clergy she was supported by others as she states, *'Providentially, around this time I met a retired minister who opened my mind and encouraged me to question, to think outside the box, and widen my reading.'* *Henry* is also grateful for the ability of clergy to provide appropriate reading resources which assisted her in her journey.

Often a positive response came almost out of the blue as *Garnett* writes, *'I will always be thankful for a chance conversation with Rev. Bob Griffiths that led me into a renewed experience of relationship with a Spirit within me, within everyone, and within all creation ... '.* *Harper* who had also experienced a negative response at a young age from a clergy was grateful for the support he received while attending St James Uniting Church, he writes, *'Rex gave me comfort that I was not alone and that St James was a progressive church that would welcome me as I was.'*

Both *Carter* and *Richard Smith* show appreciation for the creativity and guidance of their ministers and as *Carter* explains even the young and enthusiastic clergy can be inspiring. *Porter* reflects on the powerful liberating influence of her minister's *'well ordered mind'* and ability to speak, *'to a community of wayfarers traveling in hope and following the way of Jesus.'*

The Structure of the Book

We initially toyed with the idea of simply presenting the stories alphabetically by the author's name, but realised this would make it difficult for people to use in a study format. Hence we have grouped the stories into four categories. However it is important to stress that these are not necessarily totally homogeneous, but the individual stories in each group do have significant similarities.

In Part 1 of the book we have seven contributors and we have referred to this group as *Progressive Christianity: An Evolutionary Approach.* In the main these people grew up within a supportive and nurturing church environment and have come to an understanding of progressive Christianity through a developmental process some punctuated by 'light bulb' experiences. Others began to question their beliefs and seek new ways of understanding when they came into contact with the wider community, such as university and work. Each story provides us with a unique understanding of their journey in faith.

Part 2 we have titled *Progressive Christianity: Searching for Self.* These stories are exciting journeys that have much to do with who the people are and how they see themselves. In their journey to an understanding of themselves they have found help from a progressive approach to faith. There are six stories in this section and two of these people were seeking acknowledgement and acceptance in relation to their sexuality. For others it was coming to an understanding of 'who' I am and what I need to do to achieve wholeness of being; or how I can bring about change. Some of these people experienced rejection and some still are for having the courage to stand up for their beliefs. Seeking a supportive community was a key element in the journey of these people.

Part 3 we have called *Progressive Christianity: Seeking Integrity.* In this group we have the stories of seven people who are seeking to intellectually understand their reason for living. Their journey is an attempt to make sense of the relationship between their lived experience and their faith. They are people who have purposively and intentionally set out to rationally and logically explore what they believe. In some situations they have sought out systems and structures to assist them in making sense of their concerns.

Many of these people have also grown up within a faith community and for a majority they have been plagued with unanswered questions about life and about faith. Some have experienced this questioning from the time of childhood while others have arrived at this point later in life. It is interesting for the reader to explore why these people have remained within mainstream Christianity. We know that *Durham Smith* was absent from a Christian congregation for twenty-nine years. *Oakley* also mentions that for a period of her life she did not attend the formal worship of an institutional church and of course there are others in the wider group who no longer attend a Christian church.

We have named Part 4 as *Progressive Christianity: Embracing A Faith In Action.* These storytellers emphasise the importance of the practical application of faith, which for many people on the progressive Christian journey is an imperative. There is a strong connection between faith in action and intellectual integrity in fact this is quite apparent in *O'Reilly's* story. These writers will often refer to the 'God-in-Action' activity of living and sharing within community whether that is in a 'faith community' or not.

Discovering the immanent in the lives of people around you, whether they profess a faith or not and being prepared to name it as a God activity appears very much to be a Jesus activity.

The last chapter of the book is a reflection on the Conclusions and Implications of this adventure. We examine what we have learned from these quite remarkable stories and suggest how we can positively use the precious information we have been privileged to be given.

So our grateful thanks go to all our storytellers. Also we wish to acknowledge the creative assistance given to us by Hugh McGinlay and the staff at Mosaic Press. Without them this project would never have been completed.

John W. H. Smith
Rex A. E. Hunt
2013

Part One: Progressive Christianity- An Evolutionary Approach

The Human Jesus Helps Shape My Life As A Christian

Elizabeth Burns

Along with many of my generation, I grew up in a Christian home that espoused traditional understandings of the Bible. I believed implicitly what I was told or read, particularly from the minister. Church was a happy place where we moved through kids club and then youth club. Home, too, was a happy environment with few of the negatives often associated with Independents—the original Congregational denomination who often looked askance at merrymaking, and alcohol was considered a tool of the devil—which my mother in particular upheld.

As far as theological understanding went, I doubt whether I understood much more than Sunday school thinking, raised on a diet of 'Jesus loves me this I know', 'Jesus wants me for a sunbeam', etc. which hardly needed thinking about. I am ashamed to say I have very little recollection of the content of sermons or the theology behind them.

When I emigrated to Australia as a young parent, I brought with me the political and theological conservatism which had defined my family for several generations, and joined another conservative congregation. However, when my marriage broke up I was astounded by the attitudes of many within the congregation, and particularly of the minister. I did not experience compassion but a judgmental indictment that had echoes of puritan thinking of former times. I was not seeing the God I loved in their attitudes and felt alienated. Gradually I began to see there was another side to the faith that was such an important part of my life. I began to probe and question in an endeavour to find answers as to why institutional dogma no longer answered my questions.

For some time I did not attend church, but the minister of the Presbyterian Church, whom I knew, asked me to worship there, I felt a lifeline had been thrown to me. Theologically, he was years ahead of his fellow ministers (this was almost 40 years ago) and through his compassion and new thinking (to me), he brought me back into the church, albeit a different denomination. This was just before Union of the Uniting Church in Australia. I was now experiencing freedom to explore different thinking, which helped cement my new marriage.

My new husband had no church background and therefore no prejudices to overcome, but he was of a more scientific, logical mind, and the unquestioning belief many had in the Bible was unacceptable to him as indeed, it was now for me. I had to rethink what I understood in order to make it believable for both of us.

Unfortunately, my minister moved to a new placement, with a traditional theology minded minister replacing him. My soul languished for several years but I read all I could to continue my journey and trusted I would be able to expand my understanding of Jesus.

Providentially, around this time I met a retired minister who opened my mind and encouraged me to question, to think outside the box, and widen my reading. Terry himself was rethinking much of what he had spent his whole ministry teaching, and at the time of his death several years later was undertaking an MA in Comparative Religions at university. Terry was a historian, as well as a minister in the UCA. He connected with my interest in history, both religious and societal and in the traditions we inherited. I understood that reading the Bible literally was not an option for serving the church in the twentieth century as educated people could no longer accept myths as truth. Incidentally, Terry informed me several years before the event that I would one day become Moderator of the Western Australian Synod of the Uniting Church, which I did not credit, and made it his project to prepare me as best he could for the role!

At the turn of the century it was my privilege to be Moderator of the Uniting Church in Western Australia. During that time I was not only exposed to the diversity of faith aspirations within the life of the church but was part of a multi-cultural and multi-faith environment. In such a fertile melting pot there was no place for the dogmatic certainties that served only to divide and alienate.

I had long felt we had lost the real Jesus and become more Pauline in our expressions of faith and we needed to get back to who Jesus really was (is) and follow his call to be fully human, as he was.

At this time I met and heard Jack Spong for the first time and this affirmed what I had been searching for was indeed right for me. His strong belief in Jesus and how he lived his life encouraging equity and universal love, encouraged my journey to a fuller understanding of my role as a Christian.

One of the great joys for me was to watch the transformation in my husband's thinking. From believing there is no God to thinking there is something beyond us, was a bonus that reinforced my quest for new understandings of the Bible and of my faith and how I live my life. When he died, it was a huge trauma for the family but knowing his mind was open to the eternal love of a Mystery beyond us was a comfort.

The egalitarian nature of Jesus called to my heart and confirmed my belief that Jesus was truly human but filled with the Spirit of God to such a degree that he was able to show us God. I am disappointed the UCA does not feel it can update its *Basis of Union* and the creeds to reflect the scholarship of recent years that have opened up the scriptures to more historical insights. We have wonderful offerings of modern creeds and affirmations that give a more accurate understanding of the Jesus of history, not the Jesus the early church fathers projected and then protected.

Attending all the Common Dreams conferences and some 'Common Dreams on the Road' events, with the diversity of interpretation, debate, and appreciation, not only allowed me to come to a new faith understanding but also developed in me the desire to share it with others so they might have the opportunity to grow.

As a lay preacher I have been able to point the way to a more 'rational' understanding of Jesus, to remove the magic aspect of his acts and sayings. When people tell me I have made them think or they now feel able to question what they have always been told, makes the risky exercise worthwhile. Sharing one's excitement in discovering the Jesus of history rather than the manufactured Christ of the church is a great joy and perhaps lay people have more freedom to say it as it is than the ordained, who often think they have to follow the line of orthodoxy. Being a co-leader of a progressive discussion group in my home church has challenged, clarified, and cemented my conviction that Jesus the man is our standard of reference for all godly actions, thoughts and words.

I continue to find inspiration from many scholarly speakers who shine a light into the darkness of myth and dogma. My understanding is still scratching the surface but I now know that God lives not in a remote eyrie, master-minding the world, but each and every one of us can show expressions of God when we live 'after the style of Jesus' as painters of a particular school title their works. This is true whether Christian or other. I find the mystery beyond human comprehension to whom we give human expression, a challenge to become more like Jesus and be his hands and heart in the world today.

Listening to and reading the likes of Richard Dawkins and others, I have much in common with them but we part company when they have no understanding of a force beyond our humanness. While we might make our own version of 'God' depending on where we are in our understanding, for me that is not an interfering God who stage manages humanity, doling out praise or condemnation, but the 'ground of all being' as Tillich calls the God who resides among us. Who knows what the next few years will bring on my progressive journey?

From Childhood Belief To 'A Work in Progress'

Neville Davidson

For me, the Christian journey started with my pre-school attendance at the Heatherton Methodist Sunday School, followed by Bible Class membership and later, the role of Sunday School Teacher and Assistant Sunday School Secretary. In the meantime, I became a member of the Methodist Church of Australasia and attended Sunday worship services on a regular basis. By the time of my mid teens, I was taking a keen interest in theological studies, to such a degree that my then minister actively dissuaded me from taking steps to becoming a lay preacher, advising me instead, to concentrate my energies more on obtaining my Matriculation Certificate.

During the late 1950s and early 1960s—despite having attended a "Men for the Ministry" Day conducted at the Methodist Theological Hall, Queen's College, University of Melbourne in 1960—my approach to Christianity was immature, dogmatic and fundamentalist, evidenced by a literal interpretation of the Bible. I also had a tendency to argue with theological students conducting Sunday services from time to time at my church. On one occasion I was quite shocked when told by a work colleague—a Baptist minister's wife—that the creation stories were a myth.

This outlook was reinforced by my attendance at the 1959 Billy Graham Crusade in Melbourne, an interest in the work of the Billy Graham Evangelistic Association, and my regular Sunday evening attendances at a nearby conservative, fundamentalist, evangelical, exclusivist, missionary centered and non-aligned mainstream church. Within this environment, the Bible enjoyed not only great significance and authority, but was unquestionably, seen to be the key to the prophetic events of the much anticipated second coming of Jesus, the rapture and Armageddon.

The importance of the Bible was emphasised further by unsolicited advice that, in the event of my ever offering myself for candidature to the Methodist ministry, I should first seriously consider undertaking a course of study at Melbourne Bible Institute. Here, I would receive the vital grounding in the Scriptures considered necessary before entering Queen's College

Theological Hall. This was to counter the fact that, once there, my long held personal faith would almost certainly be not only undermined, but seriously threatened and destabilised—as was so commonly the case for people taking up theological studies in the various institutions.

During this time, I was also a committee member of the evangelical Youth for Christ Movement in Melbourne, as well as a participant at the Belgrave Heights Easter Conventions. My daily spiritual life was centered upon the teachings of the Schofield Reference Bible and a desire to faithfully practice John Wesley's doctrine of "Christian Perfection."

In July 1963, because of my work, I transferred to Wangaratta and upon arrival there, I joined the local Methodist Church, moving later to the Presbyterian Church, where I became an active member of the PFA. This included organising and conducting Sunday Evening Youth Services. In the meantime, I was steadily maturing in my spirituality and moving away from a fundamentalist approach to Christianity.

On returning to Melbourne in December 1967, I continued my active involvement with the Presbyterian and then the Uniting Churches at Vermont and Heathmont, ultimately qualifying as an accredited Lay Preacher in the Uniting Church in 1990. As a result of such studies, together with the completion of the Higher School Certificate subject, Biblical Studies—which, among other things, introduced me to the writings of a number of Old Testament and New Testament scholars—I moved toward a more liberal approach to the Bible and to Christianity.

In 1989, I began part-time academic studies for a Bachelor of Theology degree as a private student at the United Faculty of Theology, Melbourne, finally graduating in the year, 2000, having completed majors in biblical studies, theology and pastoral care.

During this period my theological outlook broadened and matured to such an extent, that I found great comfort in the knowledge that the Bible was a distinctly human, rather than a divine product; and also, in the evolutionary theory popularised by Teilhard de Chardin, that a state of perfection—as in the Garden of Eden—lies ahead of, rather than behind, us—as in the Fall of Adam and Eve. I no longer believed in the sinlessness of Jesus or that he died as a pre-determined sacrifice for our sins, or that he physically rose from the dead.

In 2001, following my retirement from full-time employment, I was able to confidently apply for, and subsequently occupy, the position of part-time Uniting Church Lay Minister at Monbulk.

In accepting the challenges that lay before me, I was confronted immediately by the realisation that, like earlier generations, we are products of our time. But do we always act, accordingly—so often, preferring the security and the comfort of the status quo in matters of faith and belief? At this point, I was fast finding the theologically progressive and controversial works of Bishop John Shelby Spong and his rational approach to religion, most stimulating and greatly refreshing in their appeal to my longstanding interest in theology.

I was also becoming increasingly aware of the pressing and challenging need for people to rediscover a life of faith for the twenty-first century; while similarly deeply perturbed by the number of "Christians in Exile." A number of people, some of whom were pillars of the church, were seeking twenty-first century answers to their questions of faith and belief, but were receiving sixteenth century answers instead. Their questions were not being answered by the institutional church and as a result they were walking away from the church, often after a lifetime of involvement.

In the meantime, I had discovered and become captivated by the wonderfully ground-breaking, theologically progressive, and illuminating book, *The Heart of Christianity,* by world-renowned Jesus scholar and author Marcus Borg. My journey into progressive Christianity had begun! However, it was not until after the conclusion of my appointment at Monbulk in 2006, and my subsequent freedom from congregational restraints, that I began to explore and immerse myself in progressive Christianity in earnest and to experience its liberating openness of thought.

Since that time too, I have been actively involved in the Heathmont Uniting Church Faith Explorers' Group and I have also become a member of the Progressive Christian Network of Victoria. I attended the Common Dreams 2 Conference in Melbourne in 2010.

As an accredited lay preacher in the Uniting Church, it is my practice always to conduct services and preach sermons in the light of this experience and exposure to progressive thought and practice. In particular, as products of our time, I am deeply aware of how important it is for us to reflect on the credibility of our inherited faith traditions, while at the same time, also critically questioning their inferred wisdom.

As an avid reader of material pertinent to progressive Christianity and as a member of the committee of Heathmont Uniting Church Faith Explorers' Group—whose task it is to co-ordinate the monthly studies for discussion—I have experienced and enjoyed an ongoing, liberating and richly satisfying exposure to subsequent publications of Spong and Borg. I have also gained a similar exposure to a range of books, lectures, sermons and articles written by a number of Australian and international progressive scholars, theologians, and clergy. These include: Karen Armstrong, John Bodycomb, Michael Barnes, David Clark, John Dominic Crossan, Lloyd Geering, Jim Gertmenian, Richard Holloway, Rex Hunt, Gregory Jenks, Ian Lawton, Francis Macnab, Margaret Mayman, Michael Morwood, Robin Meyers, Ched Myers, Lorraine Parkinson, Fred Plumer, Keith Rowe, Jerry Stinson, Diane Teichert, Jaco and Barbara ten Hove, Libby Tigner, Gretta Vosper and Val Webb.

Because of the popularity of the ongoing and wide ranging nature of the progressive materials studied by our group over the years, I am firmly of the view that all of us have found our readings and subsequent discussions to have been a rich source of greater truths for each one of us in our Christian journeys.

Reflecting on my traditional past, that tradition tended to place a greater degree of importance on:

- the world and reality viewed through biblical spectacles rather than looking at the Bible from the world outside it;
- a set of beliefs and creeds rather than on Christianity being a way of life characterized by love and concern for others;
- the church as being a rigid and authoritarian institution rather than as a fellowship of friends who inspire one another and give one another mutual support and encouragement in walking the Christian way;

- personal salvation rather than the pursuit of social justice and the establishment of the Kingdom of God here on earth;
- salvation and eternal life with its rewards for the virtuous and future punishment for the wicked even though apocalyptic speculation played no part in Jesus' teaching;
- Jesus as the Son of God, the divine, super human, Christ of faith rather than the historical, human itinerant sage, Jesus of Nazareth;
- a concept of a personal God who created humanity in his image, a supernatural being who created the world and continues to control it, an external agent who intervenes, directs, reacts, sends, listens, punishes, controls and rewards rather than "God" being a symbolic word, a "Being" who is everywhere, an energy at work throughout the universe, holding everything in existence;
- Jesus' atonement on the cross rather than his death being a political killing for his refusal to compromise;
- prayer focused on addressing an external deity rather than being about awareness, affirmation, gratitude and challenge.

Undoubtedly however, the single, most significant, but most difficult discovery in my progressive faith journey has been my perception of God, which has changed over the years. That journey has taken me from a childhood belief in an old man in the sky, to an anthropomorphic, male God, remote, but personal, an overseeing deity dwelling in heaven, omnipotent, omniscient, omnipresent, one who listens and reacts, to my current notion of God as a Spirit or force or energy who lives in us, and in whom we live and have our being.

Above all, I believe that God did not make humanity in his/her image, but instead, that humans have made God in their image. God is a symbolic word for Love, as claimed in the New Testament—a love that encompasses compassion, forgiveness and justice, a love that respects the dignity and worth of every person. Those who abide in love, abide in God.

Now, while this may be my current notion of God, there is one disclaimer. In the true spirit of progressive Christianity—and for that reason—my perception of God continues to remain, "a work in progress!"

But the impact of the progressive movement on my understanding of my faith does not end there.

First, the journey has reaffirmed my view of the Bible being a human response to God, metaphorical and sacramental in its function, rather than being a divine product with divine authority, whose function is primarily that of being the revealer of doctrines and morals.

Second, the journey has changed my understanding of faith to one of seeing the Christian life as one of a relationship and transformation. Being a Christian is not about meeting requirements for an afterlife and belief. Instead, the Christian life is transformation in this life through a relationship with God.

Third, the journey has changed the way I see the church's responsibility—and that of its clergy—to both its members and to the wider community.

On a personal note, I have found at Heathmont Uniting Church a distinct lack of overall progressive thinking, both in worship and the exposition of the Christian message. This, together with the ongoing use of the anachronistic Revised Common Lectionary I have found really upsetting and disheartening. Sadly, as a result, I have long since discontinued my habit of a lifetime, and ceased to attend Sunday worship.

I am concerned about the integrity of the clergy and theologians. As a private theological student, I soon became aware of the benefits of modern New Testament scholarship, only to find that the clergy in the parishes were failing—and continue to fail—to pass on the results of that scholarship to their congregations from the pulpits each week. Hence, the now familiar cry from many older church people, today, "Why weren't we told?"

Given the unprecedented advances in scientific and general knowledge over the last century, a global awareness unknown to people of biblical times and the advances of life as we know and experience it today, much of the so called Christian message not only lacks credibility for our time, but is also in urgent need of a thorough revision. I wholeheartedly agree with Dr Francis Macnab, who argues that a new faith for the twenty-first century—one incorporating the tenets of the emerging paradigm of Christianity I have outlined, and much more—is required. Tenets such as:

- A faith that does not require a person to leave his or her intelligence at the door of the church;
- A faith that sees the Bible simply as a collection of books whose authors were searching for the meaning of life;
- A faith that is not patriarchal, male-dominated, or authoritarian and that does not manipulate people by the use of fear, guilt and shame;
- A faith which affirms that we are not children living in fear of some big parent in the sky, but instead, adults, looking for ways to be healthy, fully alive human beings;
- A faith that emphasises the liberation of individuals, their worth, dignity, freedom and potential and the liberation of communities.

Hence, my commitment to actively encouraging the spread of progressive Christian thought and action.

In the meantime, I remain firmly convinced that the church should have made a far greater and more determined effort to resist the power play of conservative and fundamental Christianity in the 1960s, by taking more seriously, the scholarship available to it. If the church had embraced with radical and evangelical fervour, the challenging and liberating progressive scholarship of such writers as Bishop John A. T. Robinson, for example, then it would be enjoying greater credibility and acceptance today.

Why Do I Still '*belong*' In The Uniting Church?

Desley Garnett

I have been a regular participant in the life of the Uniting Church all of my life and my journey into thinking about Christianity in a more progressive way was slow, up till about 2006, with just small insights here and there along the way.

I was introduced to 'progressive Christianity' in a more organised way, by a group of people whom I guess I would have called acquaintances rather than friends. They are now very truly my friends, teachers, and mentors. Prior to this my view of the church was fairly traditional. Its mission was to spread the good news of the saving role of Jesus Christ so every person had a chance to accept Jesus as Saviour and so have eternal life, even though I had no idea what this eternal life was, and I was not very interested in it. Part of this mission was also to show compassion in an active way.

Then I was exposed to a new understanding of who this man Jesus was, and that his death was a result of the way he lived his life, rather than the way I live my life today as I had always been taught. This helped me make sense of some theological 'truths' that had not sat comfortably for me for many years. Now my understanding of the role of the church is more about letting the world know about this man whose life is an example of what a life lived fully for others can be like and about working towards social justice for all people.

So, now, for me, what is faith? Faith in the past for me was always about believing something that was not common to my experience in everyday life; it was subscribing to a set of truths that could not change and these truths defined whether I was Christian; it was believing in the unseen and unknown. Today I tend not to use the word faith because of these connotations. However, if I was asked to give an account of my faith today, I would probably express it (at this point in time, and it might change) as an experience of a Spirit within in my life that is convicting me to always treat others with respect and compassion, and seek to create a just world for everybody where there is no poverty. One of my examples is the Jesus of history whose life as recorded in the scriptures challenges me to a way of life in tune with this Spirit of Love.

This change of emphasis from Jesus the Son of God and Saviour to Jesus the great example has certainly changed the way I would give account of 'faith' to the enquirer. No longer do I feel the need to convert others to Christianity by urging them to acknowledge their sin and seek forgiveness from a God who requires this of each person (I was never good at doing that!). Now I give an account of faith that expresses good for all humanity, acknowledging there are different paths to understanding this Spirit I have in the past called 'God'.

This change has also altered my understanding of the purpose of attending church. I often ask myself 'why go to church every Sunday?' Is it habit? Is it because I do not have the courage to say 'I think I won't go today?' Is it because I have a strong sense of commitment to assist with music? Is it because this is the community of people for whom I have great affection? Is it because the community of the church has been an important part of my own experience and I want it to survive, even though the majority of the populace have no interest in the continuance of the institutional church.

My experience of being part of my local Christian community on a regular basis gives me an opportunity to express some of my understanding of my spiritual life and its expression in my actions through song, and hearing others' interpretations of scripture and its application to life. Many folk in my church community are fairly traditional in their Christian understanding, but I believe many are also searching for a different understanding and are willing to think outside of the usual truth boundaries. In this community, I most often feel comfortable to express my doubts and my new understandings. Were this not my experience I would certainly be either looking for another faith community or I would be a 'drop-out'.

I am thankful for new expressions of Christianity in song by many contemporary writers, as music has always been an important part of how I express of my faith. I am no longer comfortable singing the songs of traditional faith as I did so passionately for many years. Recently I attended an afternoon of Wesley hymns thinking I might re-live some memories with great rousing singing. I found the theology in those oh-so-familiar hymns just wrenched at my spirit, and I felt anything but uplifted.

My experience of attending what I used to call, with a passion, 'worship', and not just 'church', is now about community and engaging my intellect to grapple with the story behind the story of Jesus—what was he really saying to the people with whom he travelled and engaged in conversation? It is about taking time out of my regular day to meditate on my relationship with this Spirit.

I accept that we are all in different places in our life experiences and our spiritual journeys, but the fact the minister of our local church is also on a journey into looking at Christianity with fresh eyes is what keeps me within this community. If I were in a church that wanted to 'keep the faith within the tradition' then I would be questioning regular attendance at church.

What is different for me now is I am invited to think within the structure of the gathering together, not to just tune out my brain and listen to another person's ponderings. There are many expressions of Christianity in the old paradigm I find disturbing and confusing, especially in the words of many songs and prayers. These I can try to interpret in new ways so long as there is sufficient 'other' to engage my intellect and my spirit. But it does cause me to wonder sometimes.

I often ponder why it is my husband and I have such a strong commitment to our local church. Why have we not walked away, as many others have? Why have many of our friends who have also become part of the progressive movement, remained within the church? I can only attribute this to the very strong examples of commitment we had in our church youth groups, the 'godly' lives that influenced us. Though some of the teachings I accepted then have long ceased to be meaningful, the experiences of a relationship with a Spirit that inspired me to have compassion for all, can never be denied.

My experience of Christianity in the past was about personal holiness, compassion, and sharing the good news of salvation. It was about 'gentle Jesus, meek and mild' who was the Son of God. I heard little about the man Jesus who saw the injustices in his society and spoke out against them. This different way of looking at Jesus, using modern scholarship to try to understand the nuances of his teaching in relation to the time in which he lived, challenges me to think about my contribution to society and to the inequities and the injustices that pervade our world in our time. It challenges me to think about how would Jesus have responded to today's world.

I liken my current journey in the progressive movement of Christianity to the Israelite people leaving Egypt, crossing the Re(e)d Sea and then wandering in the desert. The Israelites were unhappy as slaves caught up in an oppressive system in Egypt, much as I felt I was a slave to a correct or 'right' set of beliefs. I had the opportunity to 'cross the Red Sea' when a friend invited me to go along to their group where many of the participants could not authentically say the creeds. Having 'crossed the Red Sea', I have found a freedom from doctrine, but the uncertainty of the desert experience sometimes sees me looking back to Egypt where I knew what to expect—sometimes the surety of the known is easier than the unknown. The intimacy with the omnipotent God I once knew is lost, and I seek a new intimacy with the immanent God—the Spirit within that inspires me to be the best I can be. That is more elusive for me and I find I am engaging with progressive Christianity more intellectually than spiritually.

This is the journey. I am wandering in the desert, and manna falls from time to time in new experiences and new understandings—just enough for the day, to remind me I am not alone on the journey. Still I sometimes long for the surety of Egypt when I see people so sure of their faith in a God who protects and saves. What I don't long for is the surety of belief that Jesus is the only way of salvation, and that he will come again to be the judge to decide where I will spend eternity. This I find to be a most judgmental attitude that makes me embarrassed to call myself Christian.

I am free! I am free! Not from my sin but from having to make myself believe things my mind cannot accept. This is why I want to share this good news—to become a 'missionary' for the progressive movement within Christianity.

Too many people have rejected any concept of a Spirit within, because they were bound by doctrine. Too many people go through life with a 'Sunday School faith' that is really inadequate for the twenty-first century. I want these people to know the freedom there is in not being sure, having questions and no answers, doubting and not feeling guilty. I no longer want to pretend that Christianity has all the answers. I want others to know the strength that comes from experiencing the Spirit within that urges me to be more compassionate, more understanding, more forgiving, less judgmental, living more fully into my human capacity.

When my eyes were opened to the concept of the Bible as story and metaphor, I was dismayed that four people within the group were retired or close-to-retired clergy. I asked the question 'how is it I have sat in the pew every Sunday and attended numerous Bible Study groups and I have not heard or known these things?' These men, just a little older than I, who had been part of the same SCM group at university, told me they had learnt this in theological college. I felt duped. I had spent forty years trying to believe the unbelievable, only to find the scholarship that was new to me had been known for forty years and more. There was no answer to 'why wasn't **I** told?'

However, I have come to understand that part of the answer was I was not ready to hear. Maybe my mind had not been freed sufficiently to be able to understand some of the sermons I had heard over those many years. I was not open to new and 'heretical' ways of thinking about the sacred. I had tried for many years to believe in answered prayer, but I had been taught God always said 'yes', 'no' or 'wait a while'—there was always an answer to prayer with these three options! Now I do not have to think about an external God who has a plan for my life that I have to discover and follow. I can feel grateful for the Spirit within that I have experienced who is part of my everyday ordinary life. I no longer have to try to think about what I feel guilty about; that I have to confess to 'God' who requires this confession to restore me into relationship with 'him'. I can come from a position of strength knowing I am on a journey of learning to live an authentic life using the historical Jesus (and others since then) as an example. I can have a faith that is intellectually satisfying even amid all the questions.

I will always be thankful for a chance conversation with Rev Bob Griffiths that led me into a renewed experience of relationship with a Spirit within me, within everyone, and within all creation, just waiting to be woken into the reality of authentic humanity.

God Does Not Create Parking Spots! Yet Magic Does Happen

Lorna Henry

Over the past two decades I have enjoyed reading and hearing about the new biblical scholarship, becoming vastly better informed about the Bible, especially the New Testament, and the life and teachings of Jesus. These have added vitally to my understanding of God.

First however, I must tell you about important early experiences, because they have formed my ongoing idea of God.

As a child, these experiences of God took place in a beautiful little bluestone Anglican church built in 1863, every window of stained glass; there was a brass lectern, a carved white stone pulpit and an ornate, high-Gothic style wooden altar up at the front. The Anglican liturgy at the time came to my ears through the poetry of the 1549 *Book of Common Prayer*, with its magnificent use of the English language. I was overwhelmed by a God of awesomeness, goodness and beauty.

We didn't talk about God at home or anywhere else. My family got on with quietly living out the great commandments; no boasting or blowing one's own trumpet, and no questions. We knew that all around us was a loving God, a helper and sustainer.

My view of God fitted into a hierarchy: that's how the world was for me in country Victoria. Children obeyed parents, parents deferred to the church hierarchy, admired Henry Bolte our local member, Bob Menzies as Prime Minister of Australia, over him the happy and glorious royal family with the lovely young princesses, then the young Queen, and over them and all of us, God. This was a simple, but blissful childhood. Lucky me!

The Bible entered my consciousness when at university I was introduced to the Evangelical Union, not necessarily out of conviction, but because of a friendly contact. Issues of personal salvation, a sound theology and doctrinal basis, and a much more prescriptive God entered my life. I don't remember being too upset about that. In general, it was all very serious.

After university, I continued going to church, but left aside any extensive thinking about God. First came a real job and a new social milieu, which was demanding, exciting and totally absorbing. I did have questions about church teachings, things that didn't 'add up', but I didn't know where to turn to find answers. Nobody else was concerned, and as they were not desperate questions, I did not pursue answers! It is fair to say that the Anglican Church I experienced was not a hive of biblical scholarship.

Marriage and motherhood brought a powerful dose of chaos into my life, something which I hadn't experienced before. It included a necessary change of denomination to Presbyterian, and some losses and hard times. Having put aside the demanding God of the evangelicals, I was now living again with my God of beauty and goodness, of song and poetry. Was this God up to the task of sustaining me through the rough times?

If God was active in my life, as I truly hoped, He/She had made an interesting move. I was now teaching Religion, not something I had planned, at a highly respected girls' school, and intelligent teenage girls ask a lot of intelligent questions. I was now being forced to think about and justify my faith in God. Fortunately help was at hand in a wonderful colleague in the religion department of the school. I wrestled with understanding what the Will of God means, whether God is all-powerful, all-knowing, everywhere-present? Is God an intervening God? What can I pray for? Basic questions were now demanding an answer.

A turning point in my understanding of God came in an article given to me by this colleague. The author was the Rev William Sloane Coffin, a peace activist in the USA in the sixties, and later Senior Minister of the Riverside Church, New York. He had suffered the loss of his young adult son, who had been killed in a road accident. Appalled by some of the meaningless condolences offered to him, such as 'It was God's will', the father wrote that he never believed it was God's will; the night of the accident was dark and the road slippery; his son was probably travelling too fast for these conditions. And when his son died, William Coffin wrote, 'I believe God's heart was the first to break.' That introduced me to a God deeply involved in our lives, full of sympathy, emotionally and mentally present, but not able to physically change what we set in motion or what happens to us.

I have held firm to this notion of God, and it was put to the test over the next few years, the period of the losses and the hard times. In 1989 my husband became desperately ill and died about a month later. Needing to be strong to support the children with their own fear, I was dependent on God for that strength. An amazing thing happened. I had never before had any experience of meditation, nor had I wanted it. However, I was several times led to go and sit perfectly symmetrically in a quiet place, hands on knees, eyes closed, and not think of anything. The position was quite specific. (This leading might have come from anywhere. I choose to think of it as coming from God.) There was no praying, nothing. But many times I reached a depth of peace in that place; I was enveloped by a surrounding sense of beauty and calm and—did I imagine this?—a sympathetic understanding presence. Not that all would be well; it wasn't. But things were 'all right' in a larger sense. I sensed that there is something good, powerful, and active which is much bigger than our pain and suffering. I had cause later to be very grateful for that teaching and gift. I remember thinking I had seen the difference between joy and happiness.

Some two years after my husband's death came another of the hard times when I was diagnosed with leukaemia and hospitalised immediately. What I didn't realise at that moment, as I entered the hospital, was that I would be there, unsure of my chances of survival, for most of the next twelve months. Here it was a matter of learning to deal with uncertainty.

I wasn't angry with God—such things and worse happen to people every day; I didn't bargain with God. And I surely wasn't in denial about what was happening! It was very real. What I discovered was the ability to see again that bigger picture, and it enabled me to get through each day, so long as I took it 'one day at a time'. 'I can do today' was an important statement. I think it was another gift. I knew God at that time as the 'something bigger', a sustaining strength, an energy for the mind (not for the body, unfortunately), and a warm presence. I don't remember praying much. When the body is very ill, the mind is compromised and doesn't function well. So thinking is limited, and offering a thought-filled prayer is not possible. I just knew God was on my side, that is, on the side of healing, and I relied on that.

During this illness I had an image of God. I leaned back into the good, the powerful sustaining 'arms', when no other arms were available. I needed to give God, this something bigger, a physical form. For a long time then, my mantra was 'Underneath are the everlasting arms'. That really helped—and it isn't important whether the arms are an objective reality. Anyone who has lain in a hospital bed for a long time, or waited with dreadful uncertainty for news of a loved one, will know the power of those imagined but real arms, a sustaining presence.

I survived to tell the tale, and I live in gratitude for all that this life brings.

Now released from this illness, and no longer in the workforce, I had time for a deeper exploration of matters of faith, the opportunity to pursue those questions about Jesus and the nature of God, the ones that had lain dormant for a long time. So began an acquaintance and friendship with Progressive Christianity.

Even in my teaching days, I had discovered a very positive statement of the Christian story through Matthew Fox's *Original Blessing*. When you teach teenagers, it is imperative to offer a positive message. I had never taught the 'we are all sinners in need of redemption' message, and I found an ally in Matthew Fox. He was good for me and good for the teenagers.

Through long and leisurely talks with friends, there had been mention of Bishop John Shelby Spong, whose ideas for an inclusive church were very appealing. It's time, he said, to welcome into the church and its sacraments, divorced people, those living together outside marriage, and all those whom the church currently deems unworthy of its sacraments and care. Spong brought to the public arena a fresh statement of Jesus' own inclusive living. Powerful, engaging thinking—with its necessary detractors, of course. Spong was much debated.

Then I came across a slim volume by Melbourne Catholic, Michael Morwood, entitled *Is Jesus God?* Its honesty astonished me, and he was a Catholic! At our parish church we organised a discussion group to talk about these ideas, and invited Michael to come and speak to us. We knew this had to be leading somewhere, but it was very hard to imagine how the church could cope with this thinking and still be the church. It was hard also to imagine how one's own faith could survive these challenges to its traditional basis. This was the beginning of something new, and as these things do, it felt exciting but a little scary to be rejecting things once regarded as sacred, especially the death of Jesus as atonement for our sins.

Thanks to the new minister at our church, John Smith, also co-editor of this book, our discussions continued along progressive lines, and a second book of major influence came into my hands. Marcus Borg's *The Heart of Christianity* drew together the heartfelt, traditional Christianity of the past, while proposing a coherent faith for the future. He 'reclaimed' much of the old language and reframed it into new concepts. (As an example, the notion of being 'born again', 'dying and rising', 'having a new heart'—in Chapter 6).

After Marcus Borg comes his friend and colleague, John Dominic Crossan: the man whose deep scholarship of the Bible and history is conveyed in a charming Irish accent. Individually and together, Marcus Borg and John Dominic Crossan recreate Jesus in his own world, with the fear of Roman occupation, beggars in the street, the crush and the tension of Jerusalem at Passover, and they enable readers to hear Jesus' teachings with a new understanding. These scholars have also enabled me to travel with Paul, and to see how the messages proclaimed by both Jesus and Paul have been differently interpreted (one can also say, misinterpreted) over the centuries.

Now I understand why Jesus died. That Jesus was ordained by God to die to save us from the consequences of our sins—that was not believable. That Jesus challenged the existing order of Roman/Jewish society by preaching justice, non-violence, care for outsiders and losers, and by implication a restructure of the whole social order—that was enough to mark him as a dangerous man, especially in a time of uprisings against the Roman occupation.

Thanks to these writers, and others, there is now an understanding of God that sustains us in the twenty-first century:

- God expressed through many different religious traditions
- God with a passion for justice and healing,
- God protesting against the wrongs and suffering of the world,
- God needing human hands, feet and voices to do the protesting, by non-violent means, even in a world given to violence as a means of creating order.

There is a new understanding of Jesus, the totally God-filled human being, who lived out this vision. His public life was devoted to bringing this vision to reality.

That is the public, social side of Jesus. However, there is another, private life of Jesus, which now interests me. This is his life of prayer and solitude.

In the Bible, these are the times when Jesus goes off, on his own, to pray.

- If we are to be followers of Jesus, how are we to emulate that?
- Where and how do we find the strength and inspiration to lead our lives, filled with God, as he did?
- How do we pray?
- How can we create a relationship with God that matches the intimacy and trust apparent in Jesus' own relationship with God?
- What is prayer and how are we to envisage God?

My earlier story told of an awareness of a presence, a warm presence, a comfort, in times of difficulty. I call that presence God, without trying to define anything. Can you pray to a warm presence? I believe so.

To pray is to open oneself to that presence, that energy, that inspiration; to pray for someone else is to envisage that person surrounded by love and the warm presence, by God. God is creative, good, nurturing, growth-producing energy. The life force. Energy for the good of all. If we get involved with that energy through prayer, therein lies our hope and strength.

The prevailing progressive Christian view (as it seems to me) is that God is not an interventionist God. Right, in the sense that God does not create parking spots. Yet magic does happen. Is God able to inspire, move within the human mind and send things in a new direction? This is at the level we might call 'spirit'. This is perhaps what Jesus was doing when he went off to pray. He was pulling aside to let God's inspiration move, direct, encourage, strengthen him.

The Christian life as a follower of Jesus is not obedience to a social or religious manifesto. True, it does call for a commitment to a way of life; it does ask for a renunciation of the self as centre of the universe; it requires effort to effect some change and offer solace in the face of the 'sin' of the world.

But we are not left alone. There is nurture and help for the task. This is the interaction with God, which makes life fulfilling and exciting. The writer of John's Gospel has Jesus proclaim: 'I have come that you might have life, and have it more fully' *(Jn. 10:10)*.

A Journey Away From Certainty

Pamela Raff

I married an Anglican priest.

This was in a decade when most lay people had no hesitation in accepting the doctrines and dogmas of the church. I was surrounded by people who assumed, no doubt quite rightly, that they knew what I believed, who probably had similar beliefs to mine and who, like me, did not question. Even those in the wider community who didn't practice a faith did not contest my beliefs. Only once do I remember having to defend my beliefs and that was when they were being strongly challenged by a work colleague—a firm atheist. At that time, though, I was so convinced about faith matters that I was immovable. No one could have convinced me that I was mistaken.

Over the years, decades, and even centuries, there has been an element of discontent among Christian theologians as they struggled with doctrines set in stone at the Council of Nicaea in 325CE. For much of this time there was no medium available for new ideas to be widely disseminated. Although that has changed, the concepts expressed in Process Theology, Liberation Theology, Feminist Theology and Progressive Christianity have left the vast majority of people in the pews relatively unscathed, largely because they have had little or no exposure to new ideas. Throughout much of my life, there seemed to be an implied understanding that church doctrines were accepted or else one wouldn't be at worship or at church meetings. My recent experience of church study/discussion groups is limited, but I find little evidence they are based around modern theological scholarship and, in fact, it seems to me that very little of this scholarship is purposefully presented to lay people. This bewilders me.

More recently, I belonged to a private discussion group where questions were welcomed and I was encouraged by the support and insights of others also searching for a faith that offered intellectual integrity rather than blind acceptance of out-dated doctrines. Although many of those who attended were affiliated with one or another Christian denomination, some regarded themselves as agnostics or atheists. I was eager for others in my parish to experience modern theological scholarship for themselves but I have found that there remains a general reluctance by many people to unsettle the status quo within the established church.

Meanwhile, in spite of, or maybe because of, this hesitancy to disturb long held religious practices and beliefs, attendance at church services has fallen considerably. Attempts have been made to rectify this. I remember occasions when we were encouraged to bring lapsed Anglicans or new people to church. I didn't succeed in this because I didn't try. I didn't try because I didn't know how I could convince others to come to church if they didn't have a strong enough faith to be there already. What I didn't realise at the time was I didn't believe it all myself. There was no sudden increase in church attendance so I obviously wasn't the only one who failed to contribute to achieving the goal.

I am disappointed that there doesn't seem to be a need among the laity to discuss the role of the church in the twenty-first century. It is hard to believe there can be widespread acceptance that the role of the church remains the same as it was last century or the century before. Yet, despite murmurings, that seems to be the accepted position. These 'murmurings' suggest the role of the church is not what it used to be and that the church is no longer the centre of city, town or rural life. The church and clergy are no longer revered by society in general as they once were. The church no longer fulfils everyone's spiritual, social and recreational needs. Fewer people are being married in a church and even fewer are being buried from a church. Some parents still bring their children for baptism either because of a personal belief or because baptism is still regarded by the family as important. More parents are having secular naming ceremonies for their children instead of Christian baptism ceremonies.

Despite changes in my own beliefs, I still attend church services regularly. This is not a sign of the strength of my faith but rather because of habit. Another reason is that I already feel isolated from mainstream thinking in the church and I do not wish to separate myself from a group of people who, I believe, try to live their lives as expressions of love and compassion. Lest there be any misunderstanding, let me say that I know many caring, positive and generous people who very rarely worship in any church yet whose company stimulates and inspires me.

I do earnestly wish, though, that our church services did not require I say and sing words that express beliefs I no longer share. Usually, I find the services very tiresome. I am often left with the thought that I am no longer a Christian nor do I have a place in the expression of this religion. It is an interesting experience to feel in my early 70s that most of my life has been spent adhering to something I now believe to be of little or no consequence. It is also an interesting exercise to try to separate myself from long-held beliefs and work out my current beliefs, if any.

Many people say they believe in God, but there have been many changes in religious thought, and God, religion and religious faith mean different things to different people. To get around this thorny problem, different words or phrases are sometimes used for "God", such as "Creator", "Supreme Being", "The Force", but I'm not convinced changing the word changes long-held ideas nor does it really achieve the aim, which is to remove confusion. God by any other name is just as mysterious and unknowable.

The language we use to say what we mean is restrictive, but it happens to be all that we have. We gather our language from the culture we belong to and, more narrowly, from the country, region, religious community, and family of which we are a part. In addition, the meaning we give to the words we use may be quite different from that of the people who hear what we say or read what we write. Despite all this, we usually expect to be understood and, amazingly, we most often are, or well enough understood that slight variations don't matter. A further complication is that much of our language belongs to a particular period of history.

In its purest form, the Christian faith revolves around the person of Jesus. The Jesus we hear about Sunday by Sunday is presented as having said and done exactly what is written in the Gospels. However, various scholars, both with and without religious convictions, have cast doubt on their accuracy. The Jesus Seminar scholars are known for their use of red, pink, grey and black beads to show the weight they each give to the sayings *(Funk et al. 1993)* and acts *(Funk et al. 1998)* of Jesus. Don Cupitt *(Cupitt 1972)* suggests that a close study of Jesus in the New Testament does not make him less vague or blurred, and offers the following different images.

i. How Jesus saw himself: an eschatological prophet proclaiming the imminent coming of the Kingdom of God and his own work as helping to usher in the kingdom. He did not claim divinity, to be the Christ, nor did he call himself the Son of Man.

ii. Jesus as interpreted by earliest Palestinian Christianity: began with his baptism; a prophet and servant of God; after death, vindicated by God, now waits in heaven while followers wait on earth until he returns as himself, the Christ, bringing to an end the present historical age.

iii. Jesus interpreted by the Greek-speaking Jews of the Diaspora: sent by God to be Son of David, Lord and Christ; heavenly reign followed; culminating in the parousia.

iv. Jesus as interpreted in the Greek world: the pre-existent one, became incarnate, defeated demonic powers, died, returned in glory to heaven.

Further interpretations of the historical figure of Jesus from the centuries between the first and the twenty-first do little to guarantee consensus or certainty. What is generally accepted about Jesus is that he was very charismatic, compassionate, devout in his faith, and capable of inspiring people to trust him. He was a Jew and a religious and social revolutionary for which he paid with his life. I believe that Jesus' life exemplified the kingdom of 'God' within.

Religion has not been a unifying element of human existence. It seems to me religion divides, and always has divided person from person and, in the name of religion, many people have been destroyed. Religious affiliations often keep us from discussing what it is in the human spirit that unites us, and from finding ways to use what binds us to bring about a world that is better for all.

I find it difficult to separate the human spirit from the God Spirit—and note my long held habit of using capitals. God the Spirit has always been in the background, or in the foreground depending on the occasion. We hear a great deal about the work of God's Spirit in the world and, more specifically, in the lives of people. We are told that Jesus said he would send the Spirit to be with his disciples (both then and forever) because, after the Ascension, he would no longer be with them. It seems God the Spirit has a very important role.

More and more, what bothers me about the Spirit, as I understand church teaching, is that the Spirit is outside of us (why else would we pray for the Spirit's guidance) and impinges upon us at certain times of our lives. This idea negates the concept of the Spirit within, and the possibility that we have within us the capacity and capability of making decisions and of knowing how to live our lives. I think that, most of the time, we rely on our own intelligence, intuition, whatever, and just get on with life. I am not sure why, when we strike a difficulty that we surmount, we often feel the need to attribute this to guidance by an outside Spirit. Isn't it possible that we have just been forced by circumstances to access the depths of ourselves—maybe, the God Spirit within or that wonderful human spirit that is usually only acknowledged in the lives of great adventurers? Of course, showing reliance on God the Spirit can be a very useful tactic. When anyone says s/he has been guided by the Spirit, that person has an unassailable position because, after all, who can argue with the God Spirit?

We are told that having the Spirit of God within is a sign of life even if the body is dead because of sin *(Rom. 8:9-10)*. In my experience, most Christians have a hearty respect for sin, experience great feelings of guilt, and don't know where they would be without their Saviour, Jesus. Sin, especially 'original sin', is a powerful concept because it cements in people a need to make things right with God, a need for redemption. It is a belief based on fear, not on love. Maybe that is why it has remained powerful. If I don't accept the doctrine of original sin, I do not believe there is a need for a god-mediator to redeem me from my sins. Of course we offend and wound people and, when we do, it is surely incumbent on us to ask forgiveness of the person. That is surely much more difficult an exercise than saying the confession during a church service and also more difficult than confession before a priest. It means fronting up to a person we have wronged and asking for forgiveness. That takes great courage on the part of the wrong-doer and great compassion on the part of the person wronged. Very few of us choose to put ourselves in a position of such vulnerability.

There are other times where we are made aware of our vulnerability. Events happen that catch us by surprise. Even if we are not personally affected, our sense of helplessness in the midst of many catastrophes can be overwhelming. The earth we inhabit and the wider universe are disinterested bystanders of our lives. Therefore, whatever happens on this earth that is the result of natural causes (cyclone, earthquake, volcanic eruption, flood, drought) is indiscriminate as to who or what is affected. This earth operates according to certain natural laws and is not mindful of the people, animals, or things that happen to be in the way and might be destroyed. In other words, it is not part of the earth or of the universe to care. So, where does that leave us? That's right—at the mercy of earth's natural forces.

Where God is in the midst of catastrophe is part of the mystery and opens up the concept of prayer. It is that feeling of helplessness that prompts humans to cry out to a being/force greater than themselves. However, this is where I see the human spirit (or the God Spirit within) at work. The positive, creative energy within each of us, can be extremely powerful and the intentional release of this energy is what I call 'prayer'. I have found as a result of this 'prayer', my attitude changes and I become more open to possibilities—whatever they may be. I suspect we too often neglect the power within us in our haste to call on some power outside of us. Can you imagine the power that might be released when a number of people join in collective prayer?

At this time of my life I find I no longer believe many of the accepted Christian church teachings. I guess I just don't see the need for them. If I am asked where I am on my spiritual journey, I don't have an answer. I find it unnecessary to divide my being into separate compartments. I think one has to have been immersed in the life of the church to be fully aware of what it means not to be so involved. What I need is a community of people whose lives show love and compassion and who can inspire me to be more fully human—as Bishop John Spong suggests: to live fully, love wastefully, and be all you can be *(Spong 2001)*. At present I am very comfortable with where I am even if I don't know exactly where that is!

Notes:

Cupitt, D. "One Jesus, Many Christs?" in Sykes, S. W. & Clayton, J. P. (ed) *Christ, Faith, and History*. Cambridge: Cambridge University Press, 1972.

Funk, R. W. & The Jesus Seminar. *The Acts of Jesus: The Search for the Authentic Deeds of Jesus*. New York: HarperSanFrancisco. 1998.

Funk, R. W., Hoover, R. W. & The Jesus Seminar. *The Five Gospels: The Search for the Authentic Words of Jesus*. New York: Macmillian Publishing Co., 1993.

Spong, J. S. *A New Christianity for a New World. Why Traditional Faith is Dying and how a New Faith is being Born*. New York: HarperSanFrancisco, 2001.

The Importance of Questions, Doubt and Exploration

Kathleen Rowe

My story begins over seventy years ago when I attended a small rural Methodist congregation with my parents and siblings. The church we attended had originally been a School. Anglican, Methodist and Presbyterian ministers took turns at taking the monthly service. After a period of time the Anglican and Presbyterian ministers stopped coming so Methodist lay preachers and occasionally the minister conducted the monthly services.

My parents who had a Presbyterian and Anglican back ground soon became faithful supporters of the small congregation. I heard my mother phoning people each month to remind them of the service. The church was one of many in a sprawling circuit so students from the Theological College in Auckland assisted. Sunday School was very hit and miss and it wasn't until I was old enough to go to well attended Easter camps that I had the opportunity to explore what it meant to be a Christian.

My Christian faith was relatively unformed when I headed off to Auckland to study to become a teacher but I joined up with the local Methodist church and enjoyed for the first time the sound of a pipe organ, a well trained choir and the beauty of some stunning stained glass windows. The preaching was well above the standard experienced in the church of my childhood.

My marriage to Keith (a theological student at the time) brought me in contact with a number of people who were wrestling with the 'big' questions and talking about how they would share their 'new 'discoveries with the congregations they would minister to. Some of my questions I kept to myself as I listened to the conversations. In a way I was lucky because I did not have too much 'stuff' to unlearn. Much of what I heard resonated with me and formed a good basis for further learning.

Over the years I have mostly had Keith as the preacher I have listened to. When you live with a person one has the opportunity to chat over ideas, insights and theories, and the dogmas and ideas presented by others.

Finally one has to do ones own believing and learn how to articulate it. I never heard Keith speak at length about what he didn't believe. Rather he built slowly on the knowledge-base that people had, introducing thoughts from the latest books he had read. There was always opportunity for people to question anything he said following the service but I think by and large people were happy to go away and do their own thinking and reading. I still shy away from preachers whose dogmatism denies me the opportunity to do my own thinking.

The Pentecostal movement hit the area where we lived in the late 60's complete with a large tent erected to cater for the curious. People came away speaking of healing, which had taken place following prayers and some learnt for the first time to speak in tongues. Friends who had previously appeared to reflect mainstream beliefs were swept up in their versions of the charismatic movement. Long term, some people seemed to benefit from the experience but it was clear that there was no room for people to use their intellect. Indeed critical thinking was discouraged and in the name of the spirit the mind was denied. It seemed to me, followers were quick to drop the discipline of Bible reading and relied more on 'how the spirit spoke to them' when they stood to preach.

Choosing to complete a degree later in life allowed me to choose papers on Feminist Theology, World Religions, Aboriginal Spirituality and Art History. Studying portions of the texts read by Muslims, Buddhists, and Hindus helped me to expand my concept of God and to become a more inclusive believer. No longer was I comfortable with the inherited understanding of the Bible passage from John 14: 6—'I am the way, and the truth, and the life. No one comes to the Father except through me' that was frequently trotted out to claim the superiority of the Christian religion. No longer could I listen to people denigrating other religions and speaking in an arrogant way about the Christian way of believing and its beliefs. I learnt to question what earlier Christian missionaries had done and what some are still committed to, in their attempt to have people convert to Christianity without allowing for the validity of truth within the beliefs they had inherited. I recognised all people have asked the big questions of who am I? Where did I come from? Why am I here? And is there life after death? Reading material about Aboriginal Spirituality and Maori beliefs added to my thinking and questioning.

Taking an Art History paper in my degree accentuated for me how artists who painted what they believed centuries earlier still have the ability to influence the thinking of people. Too many people have been stuck with the concept of a God 'up there' and a heaven 'up there' that they will go to after death if they are good, while 'sinners' will go to hell. Too many people accept this belief without question. Study of art across the centuries helped me appreciate how religious beliefs, like art forms, reflect differing cultural settings.

Many people upon retirement, or when their children have left home, find themselves free to explore different churches and settle for one that 'feeds' them spiritually and intellectually. Upon retirement Keith and I did the 'faithful' thing and attended the nearest church. We were not fed intellectually or spiritually and for the first time in my life I considered dropping out of attending formal worship. Before taking this drastic step we attended a service at the Community of Saint Luke in Remuera, Auckland, New Zealand, where the late David Clark was minister. One service was sufficient for me to know it was the church I wanted to attend regularly even though it meant travelling further. The printed liturgy inviting congregational responses, lay participation in intercessory pray and Bible readings, along with singing clearly enjoyed by all and thoughtful preaching, captured my attention and fed my deep spiritual needs. Conversation following the service often embracing in-depth discussion attracted me. It soon became clear we were with people who wanted to be engaged in actively pursuing their understanding of Christian believing. Many people in the congregation, I learnt, had left churches where they had worshipped for many years to settle for one where a more progressive theology was expressed. As I look back over the years it's as though the pool of faith and belief in which I live has been steadily expanded. Questions, doubt, exploration have become increasingly important to me.

During the 60s and 70s one significant expression of ecumenism in New Zealand was the search for a form of church union between Anglican, Methodist, Presbyterian, Congregational churches and Churches of Christ. In learning of each other's cherished traditions we learned to critique our own unexamined convictions. During these years New Zealand churches and the wider community were swept into a wider discussion of Christian belief as people responded to questions posed by Lloyd Geering, whose honest questioning of traditional belief fired us all up to do the same. The failure of the denominations to reach sufficient agreement for them to unite was disappointing. In the years since, people have crept back into their denominational comfort zones. The ecumenical dream of a church sensitive to the presence of God in and through all creation, sharing in the human search for peace and justice, respecting those of other faiths and valuing truth wherever it is found, continues within the progressive movement and for that I'm grateful. I'm often embarrassed by the image of Christianity portrayed in the media. The rise of fundamentalism has produced a judgmental form of Christian life that owes little to the way of Jesus. Sometimes I challenge those who express views about Christian belief or practice I disagree with, but generally I stay silent in recognition that I'm unlikely to free them from the rigid prisons in which they live and seem to need.

Over recent decades I've gained a lot from the work of the Jesus Seminar. Videos and books of Marcus Borg and John Dominic Crossan have helped me appreciate the historical setting of Jesus and also to appreciate afresh the contemporary challenge of the Jesus way in our time. I cannot understand why many clergy deny their congregations access to biblical and theological scholarship.

The heart of progressive Christianity is life in a community of people who in an atmosphere of care are on a journey together, exploring belief, learning to pray, contributing as best they can to the search for a just, peaceable, and inclusive human community.

I know that many have fallen away from the organised church in recent years. I am not among them and don't intend to join their ranks. I belong in a community of faith where friendship flourishes, compassion rules, both intellect and spirit is honoured, and where everyone is encouraged to do their own believing.

Being A Follower Of Jesus, Singing A New Song

George Stuart

I am told that when I was an infant, my mother, who was the musician for the local congregation, used to play the organ for services with me sitting on her knee! I have no idea how she could manage such a feat but that's the story I'm told. So I was born into the church and have been an active member for my seventy-seven years. My mother trained our large group of Sunday School children for anniversaries and concerts and I can remember they were great fun.

The days of my youth were heady days for young people of the church. Nearly all my youth activities revolved around the church; dances, sporting clubs (cricket, football (AFL), basketball, athletics), debating contests, talent quests, camps and conferences. At our local church, about twenty to thirty of us would go to different parishioner's homes after evening Sunday worship and have a sing song. 'And Can It Be' was a favourite and also 'How Great Thou Art'. I cannot sing those lyrics today!

I attended many PFA (Presbyterian Fellowship of Australia) Easter camps throughout Victoria and for about fifteen years, was a leader at many: Camp Father, Camp Chaplain, etc. I can remember one of the first such camps I attended I got into trouble for being late to bed one evening and the reason was I had been arguing with a Seventh Day Adventist, declaring he could not be a Christian if he did not believe that Jesus was God and not just the Son of God. My explanation was not readily accepted by the Camp Father!

PFA Summer Conferences were great learning experiences for me. These were held over the Christmas/New Year period. One particular such conference I remember was at Scotch College Melbourne, and our chief speaker was a New Zealander, Professor George A. F. Knight. The theme of the conference was 'Genesis and Modern Thought'. The Professor would give a lecture each evening and have a question time after it. Some of us decided to try to trip him up with what we thought was the unanswerable question. On that evening, one of us gamely got to his feet after the lecture and asked "What language did God use when He said 'Let there be light' and how loud did He speak?" We had him! He would be stumped and for the first time in the whole conference he would be at a loss for words. Not at all! He quickly jumped to his feet and said, "God spoke in the language of love and so softly that no-one knew there was a baby born in Bethlehem.' After a short stunned silence the hall erupted with clapping and a few cheers. That particular conference was a life changing experience for me.

After qualifying as an industrial chemist I changed my career path and became a full-time youth worker in the Christian Education department in the Presbyterian Church in Victoria. After gaining a Bachelor of Arts degree, majoring in Political Science and Philosophy, I completed my theological training at Ormond College in the University of Melbourne. After a few years in 'the ministry' at Whyalla, SA, and then in Newcastle NSW, I resigned but continued in 'full-time ministry' as a lay person, working at BHP as Personnel Superintendent, in charge of the Safety, Compensation, Administrative Services, Medical and Security departments as well as the 'Sheltered Workshops' where the company employed the long term injured workers. I managed and, with help of dedicated staff, created the first internal industry integrated rehabilitation program with medical, psychological, physiotherapy and occupational therapy support services as well as tailor-made employment.

This whole experience in full-time secular employment, about twenty years until retirement, had a profound effect on my understanding of the need for the Gospel to be understandable, sensible and above all relevant to ordinary people in their everyday lives. The message had to make sense to people where they were, and what they were experiencing in life. I also learnt first-hand, that church activities had to fit in with the primary commitment, that of employment.

I am so thankful for my history in the church and I feel there has been a continual growing process in my faith and theological awareness over the years. I would not class myself as an avid reader of theology but reading many books of theology and biblical studies has been the main stimulus for the 'spiritual' growth I have experienced in the past decade or two.

I think my exposure to the physical world through my study of physics and chemistry, and my many intellectual encounters during my studies in philosophy and political science have been significant fertilisers in the soil in which my theological growth and the development of my beliefs and faith have taken place.

This brings me to my more recent involvement with the 'progressive' theological movements within the church. It has brought with it a greater challenge to articulate my beliefs and has encouraged me to continue my journey within the church.

One of the main reasons why I am still active in the church is I fervently believe people can be trusted to think their own way through to an adult faith. This is one of the liberating emphases of 'progressive' Christianity. Gone are the days, for me, when the church can dictate what must be believed and what heresy is. This is nonsense. The emphasis on control by the church reveals a leadership trying desperately to hold onto past power and domination over people. There are people in groups I organise that often say it is great being able to speak one's mind on matters of faith and belief without the fear of being ridiculed or 'corrected'. Bible study and 'religious' discussions must be done in an atmosphere where diversity and difference is celebrated. I believe people can be given assistance through Bible study, reading 'good' theology together and open discussion where outcomes are not pre-determined. Where intellectual honesty prevails and where freedom is given for people to accept their doubts as launching pads along the way to a more relevant, sensible, and significant set of beliefs, can be an exciting and liberating experience. I have been witness to such.

One of my dear friends has said and keeps on saying, "God is our problem." Well, for me, 'Yes' and 'No'. The 'process' theological contributions, as I understand them, have been very helpful to me. God is not almighty, using force to bring about 'His' will, but is, and has always been, totally involved and inherent in all the cosmos and in particular, from our point of view, in all humanity, to prompt, to urge, to lure us into goodness, kindness, love and compassion. For me, God does not have a predetermined plan for salvation or anything else, but participates in everything and particularly, from our point of view, in all humanity, as we work through the vicissitudes of life to the unknowable future and to a better world for all. God is love and yearns for a reciprocation of that love expressed in our love for others. These insights from process theology, but not the emphases of 'process' theology alone, have been encouraging to me in my journey more recently.

I would add to the 'God' problem another major stumbling block within the church: the way the Bible is 'worshipped/idolized'. Modern biblical scholarship and much contemporary theological writing has confirmed for me, that our 'sacred book' needs to be put into its first century context with all the vast differences of its understanding of God, the world, and universe, the human body and psyche. Biblical scholarship has also confirmed in my mind that our sacred book is one of many detailed records of a community's search for 'the sacred'. This process is ongoing for all thinking human beings and, in this context, I personally believe that modern psychiatry, psychotherapy and neuro-science will influence Christian theology more, in the next ten to twenty years, than modern cosmology has in the last fifty years.

I no longer see the church's main task as proselytizing or evangelising but entering into dialogue with other faiths and those of no religious beliefs, learning from them and sharing with them our particular faith emphases, in a cooperative search for meaning in life, and an endeavour to enhance the well-being of all humanity. This is totally consistent with my understanding of the 'progressive' stance of accepting that all religious endeavour is our human search for the 'sacred'. This is why I am thrilled that my lyrics *More Than Tolerance* have been sung in churches in other English-speaking countries as well as in many places in Australia. I list them here for your possible use. Please feel free to use them as you wish. There is no copyright attached to these or any of my lyrics.

"More than Tolerance" *(Tune: Austria AHB 374(i), 577 and TiS 93, 772)*

A Christian Minister of the Word recently said: "I find interfaith relationships challenging, disturbing, enlarging and enriching! I am happy to be a Christian. That's my home religion/metaphor/socialisation. Jesus (the one I read about more than the one I hear about) makes a lot of sense to me. But, like you, I am happy to gain those insights which make sense to me out of other religious traditions."

Coming to a place of candour
Where beliefs and creeds confer;
We will not react with anger,
Nor tell others where they err.
Can we speak of faith and doctrine?
Can we listen—really hear?

As we meet can we imagine
That new insights may appear?

When we hear some different teaching,
When we try to understand,
Different faiths can be disturbing,
And can question where we stand;
We need not forsake devotion,
If it's God whom we adore;
But we can share inspiration;
We can question and explore.

We can pledge to be accepting;
Put behind us lack of trust;
We can practice understanding:
Shun rebuke that is unjust.
If we can affirm each other,
Be as friend and not as foe,
We can meet and share together;
Plant respect and let it grow.

This brings me to my lyric writing. I have been writing new lyrics to traditional church hymn tunes for about eight years now and have published many of them in the *Singing a New Song* series of hymnbooks. A fourth volume is on its way. What stimulated me into this project were the insights of modern biblical scholarship, particularly about the historical Jesus and the New Testament accounts of the gospel writers' encounters with this amazing man.

I began writing new lyrics to the much-loved Christmas carol melodies. In hindsight, this was probably not the best place to start. I can still remember one of my dear friends in the congregation at Toronto saying to me after a Christmas service I conducted in which I used three or four of my new lyrics: "Well George, you have gone too far this time!" I might add we are still the best of friends.

I find that the third paragraph in the *Canberra Affirmation*, written by a group of Canberra 'progressives'—and edited into its final edition by Rex Hunt, a co-editor of this book—back in November 2008, still encapsulates for me much of the basis for my continued lyric writing about Jesus. I share it now.

> We honour the one called Jesus, a first century Galilean Jewish sage, nurtured by his religious tradition. A visionary and wisdom teacher, he invited others through distinctive oral sayings and parables about integrity, justice, and inclusiveness, and an open table fellowship, to adopt and trust a re-imagined vision of the 'sacred', of one's neighbour, of life. As we too share in this vision, we affirm the significance of his life and teachings, while claiming to be 'followers of Jesus' *(Hunt & Smith 2013:142-148).*

Being very pastorally oriented in my contribution as a 'follower of Jesus', I sometimes find it difficult to relate to people who have a very different set of beliefs to me, in a way I think they would find most comforting. When I visit people in hospital or nursing homes, or elderly people with failing health and who are losing personal control of their lives, or people who face years of caring for a partner with Alzheimer's disease, or the aftermath of a stroke, I perceive they would like me to pray for healing or for God to intervene in some way to 'make things much better'.

I know some such people who have given up on the church and who have been somewhat incensed when, in worship services, they are told God cares for them, and if they ask they shall receive, if they seek they will find and if they knock it shall be opened. When 'things' don't happen, this seems to indirectly convey the idea they are the ones to blame for not asking, seeking or knocking in the right way. My very wise Rabbi teacher, Harold Kushner, suggests this borders on 'blaming the victim'.

When I encourage them to think of God as being in them, surrounding them, and that God is a suffering God who shares their grief or pain, it doesn't seem to compute. This is so different to what they have heard in their church life for years and years. They have been taught that God is almighty and in control. When I encourage them to think they are not alone, this sometimes does not seem to be enough for them. It appears they want the comfort of knowing that God is in fact in control and hopefully might come with power to improve their lot. Otherwise it seems that God doesn't care much. Hope seems to be taken from them if God can't **do** something!

It would be so easy for me to pray for God to **'come'** with a remedy for the situation, but I cannot do this anymore. In the past I think I might have done something very like it. But now that would be making light of their predicament and would be engendering, what is for me, a false and shallow hope. I can assure them that love sustains us all in all situations and it is other people who make this gift available to us. Without that we are all history. I continue to struggle with this aspect of my discipleship. I suppose I have summed up my beliefs in the words of a recent hymn I have written. It is not published yet but hopefully will be soon.

"God's Incarnation" *(Tune: 'Grafton' AHB 343(i), 422(ii) Not in TiS)*
"Every person incarnates the divine call, i.e. incarnates God, to some degree."
From 'Process Theology: A Basic Introduction' by C. Robert Mesle.

We can be God's incarnation
When we live in love and peace;
God's own kingdom is reflected
When all wars and conflicts cease;
With the promise
Of true justice

We may see God's reign increase.
We can be God's incarnation
When we care for all around;
God's own kingdom is reflected
When in kindness we are bound;
In our living
And our giving

God's own action can be found.
We can be God's incarnation
When we link with Galilee;
God's own kingdom is reflected
In our life and ministry,
When with Jesus
We find purpose
Bringing love to victory.

For me, one of the most unacceptable and now objectionable doctrines of the church is that of substitutionary sacrificial atonement— 'Jesus took my place and died, paid the price, for my sins'. This pictures God as an aloof judge, 'on his sapphire throne, awaits his own anointed son.' (See Hymn No. 348 in *Together in Song*). I have written new lyrics about this doctrine in the words of 'At-One-Ment'

"At-One-Ment" *(Tune: 'Horsley' AHB 266 and TiS 350)*
At-One-Ment is experienced by loving—I John 4:16.b "God is Love; he who dwells in love is dwelling in God and God in him."

God dwells in us whene'er we love;
With God, we are as one;
For when we love we dwell in God;
Renewal has begun.

When loving others I receive
Fulfilment and release
From tension and hostility;
I taste a sacred peace.

If I take heed of self-esteem,
Accept myself in grace,
In love, I then begin to see
God's image in my face.

Love is itself the sacred place
Where God and I can meet;
Love is the scene, love is the time
When life is so complete.

We dwell in God, God dwells in us;
With God, we are as one
When love is that which guides our path;
The victory has been won.

I am thrilled that John Dominic Crossan, particularly in his set of DVDs *The Challenge of Jesus*, has put this destructive doctrine in its place, pointing out it is not built on biblical teaching but on that of Anselm, an eleventh century Archbishop of Canterbury. This doctrine may have 'fitted' in well to his contemporary culture with its primacy of giving satisfaction in payment of one's dues, but claiming that this is also foundational in one's understanding of 'the divine-human' relationship, is a gross distortion of the message of Jesus.

So, for me, in the movement of 'progressive' Christianity, I have found many others who are searching, who have shaken off the shackles of church dogma, who are open and inclusive. In these people and their beliefs I find hope and encouragement. What keeps me in the church is the possibility of change, the need for people within it to challenge 'immovable' structures, and who are willing to question fixed dogma.

Given much of the baggage that comes today with the label 'Christian', if labels need to be used, I prefer to be called 'a follower of Jesus'.

Notes:

Hunt, R. A. E & Smith, J. W. H. *Why Weren't We Told? A Handbook on progressive Christianity*. Salem: Polebridge Press, 2013.

Part Two:
Progressive Christianity: Searching for Self

Bishop Spong and St James Gave Me Back My Faith
Aaron Harper

A Way Of Truth And Life
Fiona McDougal

Discovering What It Is To Be Fully Human
Frances Porter

Found: A Theology That Matched My Lived Experience
Lynne Robertson

Faith From The Edges
Betty Shore

The Light Of Faith In A Dark Time
David Tacey

Bishop Spong and St James Gave Me Back My Faith

Aaron Harper

There are, I believe, three major influences in my early life that have lent their silent, guiding hand towards me walking the progressive Christian path: I have always had a sense of 'God' or the sacred; I grew up knowing I was gay; my mother dying of breast cancer at the relatively young age of 47.

My parents, Graham and Ruth, provided a loving and supportive home, something my siblings and I will always be thankful for. We never went without. There were the usual growing pains, but nothing out of the ordinary. My parents were always devout, fundamentalist Christian believers, with a strong commitment to social justice.

I was raised attending Pentecostal churches, particularly the Assemblies of God in Tuggeranong, Canberra. In many ways, the church we attended was a 'Hillsong' want-to-be, with a large congregation (about 400), a dynamic expression of the arts—particularly music, dance and drama, a focus on youth, and a strong theological emphasis on faith, conversion, healing and prosperity.

I was the music director of a skilled group of musicians and was training to be a youth pastor (noting that the educational requirements to be a pastor in a Pentecostal Church are somewhat lower than many mainstream churches). In many ways, they were happy days. Playing in a large band of talented musicians was a continual joy. Many of the friends I made in those years are still friends today. And there is no doubt that I experienced 'God' and gained a limited understanding of the Bible.

And yet, the older, more educated, and hopefully wiser I grew, the more the theology of the church rankled against my experience of God as love, grace and acceptance. Deep spiritual questions could not be answered and conundrums could not be explained. Rather, the very fact you asked questions was attacked by those in authority as a lack of faith. I realised this to be their security system activating, as for them to self-reflect and admit errors in their belief system would have been to open questions about all aspects of their belief system, which was something that they were not willing to face.

To me, praise and worship had become a manipulative concert, which we were very professional at. We could lift the spirits of the congregation, or reduce people to weeping. And yet, the constant thought running through my head was why would a God who was all-sufficient want our praise? Wouldn't praise, in actuality, be an insult to an all-sufficient God as it presumed that 'he' needed or wanted our praise?

Prayer was another issue. It is tempting for me to look back at my days of evangelical faith in an external, all-powerful, interventionist God, and convince myself that faith was easier and simpler back then. But it just isn't true. One day each month, we would gather to pray for revival in Canberra. A day of fasting would proceed it. I perceived this as a type of blackmail – God I've starved myself for a day, so you must listen to and act upon my demands! We would then enter a period of praise. This seemed like a type of flattery, of getting into God's good books. It did not accord with my view of a God who washed people's feet, or the Christ who called us friends, brothers and sisters. We would then quote God's promises back at him, as if he might somehow have forgotten them. We then brought our requests to God, like as a helpless child might ask something of their parent, or a servant might request something of their master. Worship would then close the experience, which was another attempt at flattery, all in a vain hope that our wishes would be granted.

Most remained unanswered.

For many years, I went through the motions of prayer without it according with my experience of God. This deep unease came to head with the death of my mother in 1999. She had breast cancer which quickly spread to her liver. She died despite a church of over 400 people fasting and praying for her healing, sometimes twenty-four hours a day.

Of course, when belief systems fail, excuses begin. A few weeks before she died, the pastor called me around to his house and told me the only reason mum was not being healed had to be because there was sin in her life blocking that healing.

This made no sense to me. We were told God had promised healing. We were told that faith the size of a mustard seed could move mountains. We were told because of the sacrifice of Jesus, we were blameless in God's sight. And so, the questions began. With all the prayers and faith of the church, why wasn't God healing mum? If we were blameless in God's sight, how could sin then block God's healing? If the almighty God of the universe was unable to heal one of his children because of one small sin, how powerless is that God? In a very sad but ironic fact, that same pastor died a few years later at a young age of heart failure. It took me a while to forgive this pastor for what he said, but I now accept we all operate within our limited boundaries of understanding, skewed as they may be at times.

Interestingly, knowing I was gay was not such an issue to me. I knew I was attracted to men and had no sexual attraction to women, and that was that. I never fell into the trap of 'trying' to have a girlfriend. My view then was if God honestly thought homosexuality was wrong, it would be my secret and a cross I would bear. I didn't beat myself up over being sinful or less worthy of God. I just accepted that was the way I was (although the annual prayer that God would send rain to drain out the evil of the Gay and Lesbian Mardi Gras was somewhat disturbing. Funnily enough, the rain never came, but still the pastor never got the message!).

I will never forget the day I decided to leave the church. The pastor had stood up on a Sunday morning and announced that God has told him that a day was coming when there would be such revival, and the churches would have so much money, that the banks would be coming to the churches for a loan. From what I can tell, I was the only person in the whole congregation to confront the pastor about his somewhat ridiculous statement, which I saw as a significant failure of the Elders who were caught in the trap of what I call 'Pastor worship'. I told him I didn't believe God had told him that, that it was against the way of Jesus, and the church was at its most corrupt when it was its most wealthy in medieval times. The pastor stated that God had told him that it was to be so. I made the decision then and there that I could not remain in a church that could not remain true to the way of Jesus.

I left church for many years after that, although a sense of God never left me, nor my desire to learn.

The first major paradigm change for me came when I was reading a book by Phillip Yancey, a sometimes profound evangelical Christian writer, who suggested something along the lines that not every Psalm in the Bible could be said to be directly inspired by God, but that the Psalms as a whole show us that we can come to God as we are—loving, hating, joyful, sad, vengeful, forgiving.

The idea that not every sentence of the Bible was literally true, but that we should look for the overall principle, was revolutionary to me. It meant standing back, taking scripture in context, and looking beyond the words to the meaning behind the words.

The next turn in the road came when I purchased a book from a local bookstore by a man named Bishop John Shelby Spong with the provocative title *Why Christianity Must Change or Die*. I will never forget the roller-coaster of emotions I had while reading it the first time: celebration that I was not alone in my doubts about traditional Christianity; a sense of deep loss as the last remnants of that old faith system died; a feeling of emptiness at not knowing what would fill the gaping hole in my soul; anger at not being told about progressive Christianity earlier; confusion about what to actually think; and hope that I would fashion a new faith for myself based on honesty, integrity, love for myself and others.

I consumed Spong's books with savagery. They breathed life back into the dead bones of my faith. They helped me reconcile Christianity with my sexual orientation, to accept that being gay was part of my being, and that I would only live a full, loving and honest life by fully embracing who I was. I have now been with my partner, Ryan, for a joyful ten years.

One day in 2003, I heard that Spong was going to be speaking locally in Canberra at the Albert Hall. It was an event I would not miss.

I went and heard him speak and yet I cannot remember what he spoke on. What I do remember is a welling heart of thanks and love for this man who had given me my faith back. After delivering his address, there was an opportunity to meet Spong and have a book signed. I waited until everyone had almost left before I approached him. As I did I literally fell to my knees as years of emotional pressure was released. It was probably the closest I have been to a 'road to Damascus' experience. I thanked him for his books and told him how he had saved me and my faith in ways he may never understand (although I think he may have got some understanding from my almost confessional state!). By the end, I think we were both equally moved.

Organising that event was the minister of The Uniting Church of St James, Curtin, Canberra, Rex Hunt. Rex gave me comfort that I was not alone and that St James was a progressive church that would welcome me as I was. It took me a few months for gather the courage to return to church, but I realised in a short time that I had found my new spiritual home. Rex's liturgies and contemporary words spoke deeply to me and challenged me. People showed me love and acceptance. I was free, and even encouraged, to question and search.

I have now been at St James for what seems many years. I play piano fortnightly, have written new contemporary progressive Christian songs, regularly prepare liturgies and deliver contemporary words, and am on the Church Council. The two challenges I am particularly grappling with are: (i) how we as a church community might better reach out to un-churched seekers and church exiles to let them know there is a safe place for them to question, search and grow spiritually, and (ii) how the progressive Christian movement might better address the heart as well as the mind, without delving into the emotional excesses of Pentecostalism.

Gretta Vosper's book *With or Without God* has been an ongoing source of challenge and inspiration for me since reading it some eighteen months ago. In it Vosper suggests that because Christianity is a human construction, you and I can also be co-creators in a new Christian story. She states "we need to release words, statements, and concepts that reiterate dogma we no longer truly believe ourselves" and to "boldly, comfortably, and confidently write our own sacred wisdom again, this time gleaning from scripture all that is life enhancing, but none that is not, discovering new and not so new spiritual expressions that come to us from other traditions and ideologies, and stretching ourselves to seek new sources of inspiration".

In this spirit, I have been busy creating new forms of liturgy and writing new, contemporary styled songs that reflect this new Christian story. I am currently working on a meditative-styled liturgy that will focus on music, reflection and silence. In the second section of this story is an affirmative-styled liturgy I have recently written for St James which celebrates progressive Christianity and is based on 'The 8 Points' of Progressive Christianity (progressivechristianity.org/the-8-points) and The Canberra Affirmation, which can be found in Rex and John Smith's book *Why Weren't We Told?*.

The Liturgy

Preparing this liturgy was a great challenge for me. I was wanting to build on the chassis of Rex's liturgies for St James, but using a group of people who have been inspirations on my progressive walk, and build them into an affirmative style liturgy.

I'm trying to challenge my local congregation of St James to continually expand our thinking in regards to spirituality and how we live that out, and to broaden our horizons into new paths of 'worship'.

I'm also starting to shape some new songs in my imagination now, which is satisfying. It's been something I've battled with, mainly due to experiences in the Pentecostal Church. But I think some more modem style progressive Christian music is needed. (I think Scott Kearns is doing a tremendous job at this—love some of his songs!). Next year, as my next project, I'm hoping to record an album of those songs.

THE UNITING CHURCH OF ST JAMES, CURTIN, ACT

http://www.stjames.unitingchurch.org.au/

Theme: 'Freedom'

This Liturgy is inspired by the 8 Points of Progressive Christianity (progressivechristianity.org) and The Canberra Affirmation (Published in 'Why Weren't We Told'?)

30 June 2013

St James is a safe place for all people to worship regardless of race, creed, age, gender, cultural background or sexual orientation.

We Are A Community Coming Together That Is Inclusive Of All People

Entry into the Celebration

The gong is sounded three times

We come into this place
All **With thanksgiving in our hearts.**
We come into this place
With hearts of praise for all that is.
All **For this is God's day, it is our day, and we are glad** *(AHarper)*

Lighting of the Candle

The community candle is lit in silence.

All **We commit to St James being a safe place for all people to worship regardless of race, creed, age, gender, cultural background or sexual orientation.**

Hymn *People stand as they are able, to sing*
"**Gather The Spirit**" (Jim Scott)

Opening Prayer
In the depth of ourselves
We discover the source of love, the source of life
and the ground of being.
As a Church, we desire to express this,
Through living fully, loving wastefully, and being all we can be.
May living, loving and being, be a river flowing through us
Out into the world.
Bringing transformation for good.
Amen. *(AHarper, Inspired by John Shelby Spong)*

Welcome

Hymn *People stand as they are able, to sing*
"What Strange Land" (Shirley Erena Murray)

We Strive To Protect And Restore The Integrity Of The Earth And Its Inhabitants

As Christians, we are inspired to be the imitation of Jesus.
All **We will not retreat from the world, but will act within it**
To bring around the implementation of justice
For all of Earth's peoples,
For all its creatures,
And for the Earth itself *(AHarper, Inspired by Dietrich Bonhoeffer)*

This is a time to reflect on a social justice or environmental issue.
Today we will focus on the Uniting Church's Vision
for Recognition, Respect and Justice for Aboriginal Peoples.

We Strive For Peace And Justice Amongst All People

Peace begins with us.
All **We commit to peace:**
Peace with ourselves
And peace with our neighbours.

We pledge to strive for justice.
All **Our hope is that the peace and justice we know**
Will one day be known by all peoples of the world *(AHarper)*

You are invited to share peace with each other,
as a symbol of hope for peace and justice in the world.

The Way We Behave Towards Each Other Is The Fullest Expression Of What We Believe

Care Candle

We are people of all ages who enter this space
bringing our joys and concerns.
Joys and concerns shared.

Response

All **Awe inspiring mystery**
Beyond our limits of understanding
We release our joys and our concerns
Believing that in speaking them
It may not change the situation
It may not change others
But it will change us.

Where there is hurt, let us bring healing
All **Where despair reigns, let us create hope**
Where there is joy, we'll join in laughing
All **Love be our guide, on life's winding road** *(AHarper)*

And so we take this flame and light our special care candle.
The Care candle is lit

Wisdom From Diverse Sources Helps Us On Our Spiritual Journey

Today, we recognise there are many paths to the 'sacred'.

All **Within this diversity, we honour all those who like us seek the 'sacred', including progressive Christian thinkers, other religious traditions and the people who practice them,**
philosophers, artists and scientists *(Based on The Canberra Affirmation)*

Meditation

"Musing on God"
Jim Burklo

Music of Reflection

The Path And Teachings Of Jesus Lead Us To An Awareness And Experience Of The Sacred And The Oneness And Unity Of All Life

We honour the one called Jesus:

All **He invited others to share a re-imagined vision of the 'sacred',**
and to build a realm of grace, love, integrity,
justice, and inclusiveness.
He demonstrated an open table of fellowship to all.

We too share his vision

All **And affirm the significance of his life and teachings,**
And those writings inspired by his life and teachings
(Based on The Canberra Affirmation)

Reading

Galatians 5: 1, 13-25

Contemporary Word

We Find Grace In The Search For Understanding, Believing There Is More Value In Questioning Than In Absolutes

Affirmation

Women *We commit to be a community of faith that speaks a language that is open to intellectual exploration, spiritual quest, and new experiences of the divine.*

Men We will encourage critical thinking and engage in a conversation about the big things, issues that matter, such as values, meaning, and relationships.

All **We will do this with an open mind, passion, creativity, intellectual vigour, honesty, courage, respect and patience.**

(AHarper, Inspired by Gretta Vosper).

Hymn *People stand as they are able, to sing*
"**Colour and Fragrance**" (Norbert F Capek).
Tune: 'O Barvy Vune'

We Commit to a Path of Life-Long Learning, Compassion, and Selfless Love

Offerings

Our offerings for the celebration of life in this place and beyond, shall now be received.

Presentation *People stand as the gifts are presented*

All **May these offerings be used to extend God's realm of love and compassion, grace and inclusion, hope and forgiveness.**
Amen *(AHarper)*
People sit

Words of Mission and Blessing

The presence of God reaches beyond this place...
The candle is extinguished
As we depart, we will walk the transformative path of Jesus.

All **We dedicate ourselves to non-violent peacemaking and considered forgiveness, action for social justice, and stewardship of the earth and all life upon it.**

We will encourage humour, challenge, and acts of generosity.

All **For we are all connected.**
At our centre is a oneness:
we are one with the 'sacred',
one with ourselves, one with others,
and one with the universe *(Based on The Canberra Affirmation)*

Hymn *People stand as they are able, to sing*
"**We Are Many, We Are One**" (Colin Gibson)

Sharing in Community

'This week' at St James

Notices
Birthdays and anniversaries
Significant events
Journey candles

Fellowship

Morning tea is now served.
You are invited to share in the moment of fellowship.

A Way Of Truth And Life

Fiona McDougal

Sometimes, driving home after a busy night shift, windows wound down and radio blaring to stop me falling asleep behind the wheel, I catch the end of Radio New Zealand's "Hymns for Sunday Morning". I listen with a strange mix of nostalgia, negativity and acceptance, recognising the fact that I have been on a long journey. That journey has taken me from a trusting faith, through challenge, disillusionment and deconstruction, to a slow and ongoing process of healing, a place of surprising hope, energy, meaning and wholeness. The journey has been a geographical one also, from Aberdeen in Scotland to Wellington, the capital city of New Zealand.

Like many people in Aberdeen my family lived in a block of flats with a shared stair. Our flat was on the top floor. In the summer of the year I turned eleven, my Dad had his first heart attack and nearly died. I have a vivid memory of him making his way slowly up the stairs after being discharged from hospital, and reaching the top landing, where the walls were covered in pictures my sisters and I had drawn for him in his absence. That was the only time I ever saw dad shed a tear. In many ways that was the end of my childhood as I realised how close we had come to losing him, that nothing could make things the way they had been before, but also that he could have another heart attack and die at any time.

This illness resulted in some changes as my parents stopped smoking, chose healthier food and moved twenty-five miles inland to a farming village called Alford, seeking a less stressful lifestyle. There my father taught English and my mother Music at the local secondary school and bought a house for the first time in their lives. However despite these lifestyle changes, dad had two further heart attacks and sadly died when I was sixteen. It was a painful time and dad's death affected everyone in the family deeply. I wonder sometimes, though, if living close to someone whose health was so precarious was a factor behind my later decision to become a nurse.

In the next couple of years, both my sisters and I left home, moving into Aberdeen again, where we attended different educational institutions and shared a small flat. During one summer vacation I met a young man called Paul, to whom I became engaged. Just after my twin sister and I had our twenty-first birthday, she got married and a little later Paul and I parted company. This was not of my choosing but was probably influenced by the fact I had started working in a Rest Home in the summer and had decided in my last year at university to carry on working there during the weekends. I had somewhat unexpectedly discovered a caring side to my personality and enjoyed looking after elderly people and being part of a team.

I was heartbroken when Paul left and my feelings of loneliness and desolation were compounded by the fact I had in some sense also lost another "partner" at the same time, as my twin began a new life with her husband. I studied hard and carried on working at the Rest Home. As winter turned into spring I lost hope and could see no way forward. It was at this point that I had an inner experience of being deeply known and loved by God. It was something I found impossible to explain and had some difficulty reconciling with my experience of being in a local Presbyterian Church on a Sunday morning. It did however, mark a turning point, enabling me to reengage with my life, finish my degree and follow through on the plans I had made to start nursing training in London in 1984.

St Thomas' Hospital is in central London, on the south bank of the river Thames. My training was hospital based, with extended periods on the wards. I was idealistic and committed, finding in nursing a career that was physically demanding, intellectually stimulating and emotionally and spiritually challenging. My class mates and I also had a lot of fun, invading the Waldorf Hotel for breakfast after a week working night duty to eat our fill and drink champagne, or picking up free tickets to concerts and plays at the nearby Royal Festival Hall and National Theatre. However at the end of our training the class dispersed to various places round the UK and I returned to Scotland late in 1987, this time to Edinburgh. My twin sister had moved there with her family and mum had remarried and now lived in the Borders, twenty-five miles south of Edinburgh.

At this time I first experienced what it meant to be an active part of a church community. I became involved in the life of a broad-based local parish church in the south of the city, joining groups, helping with the Youth Club and singing in the choir. I felt my spirit blossom as I made friends, discussed ideas, shared feelings and participated in intellectually stimulating and lively worship.

After six years living in Edinburgh I applied for a Charge Nurse post in a hospital in Angus, moving there in early 1994. There were many things I enjoyed about working there, including collegial relationships with the other team leaders, but there were difficulties too. With little managerial training and a lack of support I found myself floundering. A change in nursing leadership exacerbated my difficulties. Exhausted, anxious and depressed I had a breakdown.

Going back to work a month later is one of the most courageous things I have ever done. However things went from bad to worse, as the bullying I had experienced at the hands of my manager escalated. Fortunately I had support from the Occupational Health doctor who eventually witnessed firsthand my manager's behaviour and recommended that I refuse to meet with her unless I had a union representative present. With assistance from my union a meeting with HR and the manager was held, and I was at last able to speak up. Things changed somewhat from that time on. I stayed in that organisation for another six months, but the damage had been done and in April 1998 I left to follow up a job offer from a New Zealand nursing agency.

A year earlier, unhappy in my work, and recalling a yearning to travel, I had applied to work for an agency supplying nurses for individuals and private and public hospitals in Wellington. I found it a pleasure to work in different places around Wellington. I shared a house with another nurse working for the same agency, bought an ancient, yellow Toyota Corona and threw myself into my new life.

A permanent job on the gynaecology ward at Wellington Public Hospital meant I could develop a more active social life. I worked night shifts for two years, leaving the evenings free to go to the tramping club, join a choir, take up flute playing again and go to a yoga class. At work, I gradually learnt to feel compassion for patients once more, working in a supportive team with a strong emphasis on woman focused care and some truly impressive nurses.

Somewhat tentatively, I also attended a city centre church. At the time of my breakdown, I had made a conscious decision not to discard my faith, which had sustained me in previous years. During that time though,

I had felt a lack of connection with God that only added to my distress. Nothing in my life or faith journey had prepared me for encountering a person who actually enjoyed inflicting pain or dealing with the feelings of worthlessness, shame, fear and anger I experienced. Now, as outwardly my life improved and became stable, I felt a growing restlessness and deadness at church. At the time I was unaware that this was linked to my experience of being bullied and left the church feeling that the whole thing was unreal.

There followed a period of some disorientation, loneliness and feeling lost, until one weekend in 2001 I read an article in a local free paper describing a group called Spirited Exchanges, which was for "people grappling with issues related to faith and church". I participated regularly in this group for a period of over two years, finding in it a safe environment to ask questions, let go of old ways of believing and find beginning answers to issues that had troubled me for a long time. Speaking to one of the leaders, Jenny McIntosh, led to me contacting a spiritual director and working through the issues that arose, and the difficulties I had encountered at work, moving towards a healthier and more authentic spirituality. I read voraciously, journalled furiously, joined a women's spirituality group and was drawn to silence, learning to meditate and starting to go to retreats. I felt I had spent all my life learning about external things and how to care for other people. Now I wanted to learn about the inner world and what was happening inside me and in my life. This was coupled with a fierce desire for what was real. It was an exciting, challenging, anxiety provoking and life-changing time.

I reengaged slowly with some church activities, sometimes going along to an informal contemplative service at St Andrew's on The Terrace church and joining the monthly "Living the Questions" discussion group there. It was a couple of years before I felt able to go to a Sunday morning service where my initial response was simply to notice the lack of "pinpricks"—the absence of sexist and power language. Gradually I was able to relax a little and appreciate the beautiful liturgy, thought-provoking reflections and most of all the open, inclusive invitation to communion. Reflecting on where I find myself now, three themes emerge: words and silence, work and faith, and community.

Words and Silence

For a time I had a deep suspicion of religious words. Gradually that changed. In Spiritual Direction I learnt to name my feelings and express what was deep inside me. Writing words down allowed me to access a wisdom inside myself I didn't know I possessed. Focusing for a time on values, such as generosity and courage, was freeing and empowering. Later as part of a group studying Marcus Borg's *The Heart of Christianity* I learnt of faith as relationship and way, rather than as adherence to a certain set of beliefs, revolutionary to me at the time. Now I study theology at an introductory level, engaging with the texts and savouring the richness of the words and stories and different methods of interpretation. I am learning also to use words creatively, choosing and writing words for liturgy, prayer and song and also in expressing caring for members of the church community to which I belong at St Andrew's on the Terrace.

Paradoxically, silence has also been part of my journey. As much as I love words, I realise their limitations in attempting to communicate spiritual realities. Yet words that come from within silence can have great depth to them, and the deep listening of silence can spill over into relationships with others. I recognise my own need to be immersed in silence regularly in order to sustain my outward life. For me this means creating space for silence in my daily life, sometimes going on a silent retreat and also participating in a regular monthly group meeting for meditation and *lectio divina*.

Work and Faith

Being a nurse is a fierce spiritual practice. Caring for people in crisis and working in that fraught place where limited resources meet unending need is very demanding. Constantly giving of yourself regardless of what is happening in your own life can be challenging. Daily, we do the impossible together. Despite all that, at times I find great joy and satisfaction in my work. People show much appreciation and it is still wonderful to see someone you have cared for walk out the door, or be alongside them as they come to terms with a different way of life, or as they journey towards death.

Nursing is part of who I am now, and I take that with me into my life in church. This takes the form of a basic mindset of compassion, some communication skills, and organisational and leadership skills. There are also skills and experiences from my church life I also carry back to my working life. However the main contribution of my life of faith to working life, is the alternative values embodied in the community and weekly liturgy at St Andrew's on The Terrace. Nowhere else do I hear so clearly and consistently the affirmation of peace, justice, and love. In a working world where the bottom line is often financial, and where targets, policies and protocols have priority, I feel strengthened, inspired and empowered by being part of that church community. My fear at work these days is not that I will experience some further psychological breakdown, but that slowly and imperceptibly, I will lose my capacity to care due to the overwhelming workload. Being part of the community at St Andrew's is one of the things that helps to prevent that happening.

Community

Becoming part of the community at St Andrew's on the Terrace was a gradual process for me. At first I felt too turbulent to relate to others easily. It took some time to get to know people and make friends. Becoming more involved meant moving beyond self-protective independence, suspicion and anger, and taking the risk of openness and trust. Glimmers of the sacred in the form of individual conversations, moments of connection in worship and shared meals drew me on. In particular being at St Andrew's for the series of services over Easter offered a way to integrate the psychological abuse I had endured at work within a larger story. Holding that painful period of my life alongside the story of Jesus' death, the losses of others in the community, and the pain of the world, on Good Friday was very healing. Finding a place to acknowledge the reality of evil, to honour and remember my own experience, but hear also a strong call to the struggle for justice in the face of oppression, was liberating and life giving.

At St Andrew's I have participated in many shared projects, creative endeavours and joyful celebrations. Learning to value people who are very different from me, negotiating times of conflict, working hard, doing the practical things that need to be done and being patient with myself are all part of what our life together means for me. Sometimes still, I need to withdraw a little to work out what is happening inside me, so I can reengage in a healthy way with the community I have grown to love. Looking around in church on a Sunday morning at St Andrew's you see some very ordinary people. It is surprising how truly extraordinary they are. Listening to the notices gives a small insight into the amazing range of activities in which people are involved in the wider community at local, national and international level.

Nowadays I live in a small, peach coloured house near the river, just beyond Upper Hutt. Frosty winter mornings remind me of the Scotland I left fifteen years ago. It's a 40-minute drive to Wellington. I choose to make the journey to church most Sundays and sometimes during the week for meetings, talks or just to catch up with friends. We are a regional church.

It was some time after I first came to St Andrew's on the Terrace, that I noticed a poster on the notice board. Its title was "We Are Progressive" and it outlined eight points about what it means to be a progressive Christian. None of it seemed very radical to me by then. I had experienced the reality of that term before I knew it had a name. More recently I read this definition on the Canadian Centre for Progressive Christianity website:

> Progressive isn't a place. It is a state of mind and the next step from wherever you find yourself entrenched. Whether in the church, in your workplace, or in your relationships, a progressive perspective is characterized by openness, passion, creativity, and a willingness to explore beyond wherever you are at the moment.

This is a way of truth and life for me.

Further Reading:

M Borg. *The Heart of Christianity.*
S Dowrick. *Forgiveness and Other Acts of Love.*
A Jamieson. *Chrysalis*
www.progressivechristianity.ca
www.progressivechristianity.org/the-8-points/
www.standrews.org.nz

Discovering What It Is To Be Fully Human

Frances Porter

"Nobody", said our Hawera Presbyterian minister to my mother, "sends their daughter to Victoria; Frances will lose her faith." This was in 1943, I was seventeen, Victoria was a constituent college of the University of New Zealand and considered dangerously ensnared in socialism.

'Faith', in our church was largely a conviction that God was on the side of the Allies plus judgement between Heaven and Hell and the imperative need for personal salvation. Sin loomed large. But, like Sunday-best clothes, these beliefs could be set-aside on Monday. Strangely enough, from my present point of view, no attention was paid by the church to the devastating effect of the 1930s slump which left many in Hawera out of work, out of house and out of food. My mother organised food relief but our church turned a blind eye. And yes, at Victoria I did lose the burdensome clutter of that faith and rejoiced in the heady exploration of freedom and the intellectual stimulus of scepticism.

While in Wellington I sometimes attended St Johns Presbyterian Church but resigned in impotent protest when a remit from the General Assembly suggesting that it might be possible for women to be elders was overwhelmingly defeated. Out of that large congregation only two—myself and a fellow student—voted in favour of women's potential in church leadership.

Looking back, after a lifetime in which love and happiness have shared space with failure and grief I have no regrets about that loss of faith. It was simply a step in a journey, now nearing its end, to discover what it is to be fully human.

oo0oo

Happenstance brought me to St Andrews on The Terrace. In 2004 my book group read Yann Martel's, *Life of Pi*. It is a gripping phantasy adventure novel but what caught my attention was Martell's subtext, or what I deduced from it. Religion is timeless; always human beings have probed mystery and told stories of their god or gods and of the faith that those stories have manifested. There is, for example, an Islamic story, a

Hindu story, the dream-time stories of Aborigines, and the Judeo-Christian story which we of the west have largely inherited. All these human stories contain within them an awareness of the transcendental in an attempt to explain the mystery of being. At the heart of many of the faith stories is compassion, as it is with Christianity—although when one religion seeks aggrandisement then, as history and the present day often show, the story can become vengeful and bloody.

Concurrent with reading *Life of Pi* I happened to see the tail end of a news item on TV about the debate over civil unions then taking place in parliament. Standing precariously on the wall outside parliament was a youngish woman passionately advocating the rights of same-sex couples to express their love for each other in civil union. The commentator called her Dr Margaret Mayman, Presbyterian minister of St Andrews on The Terrace. Although I heard only the end of her speech, it resonated with me. My son had died of HIV Aids in 1993 after being closeted from society because he was a homosexual. I use that word on purpose. In the 1960s and 70s homosexuality was treated as a criminal offence; it was not acknowledged by the friendlier term 'gay'. I had not really understood or defended David in his lifetime—was it possible to take up his cause now? Was it possible that the Presbyterian Church which I had eschewed nearly 60 years ago had moved on—progressed? But I lived a comfortable, elderly life which the challenge of a new thing threatened to disturb. And then, it seemed, the voice of the American poet, Mary Oliver, shouted in my ear: 'Be ignited—or begone'.

My first Sunday at St Andrew's was a constant series of surprises. I entered expecting the unobtrusive Sunday hush of individuals at prayer. In contrast St Andrews bustled; some people chatted, others set up tables for tea and coffee which followed the service, children played with toys in a corner and, at the beginning of the service, one of them lit the rainbow candle which proclaimed an open inclusive community. During the service we exchanged the peace with warmth, even gusto. Completely unused to this I wondered if it was a little unseemly. But there was no doubt I was in a community eager and willing to share. The 'announcements' in those former days had been always delivered by the minister and were all about in-house meetings. Here, they came from people in the pews and concerned larger causes outside the church doors which called for our engagement. The biggest surprise came with the hymns. They were not hymns as I had once known them in the *Presbyterian Church Hymnary* where the early verses announced trial and struggle in this world but the last verse promised glory in the next—'O Jesus I have promised... O Jesus thou hast promised'. The songs we sang at St Andrew's celebrated this world as our only home—its joy, its peril, our connectedness to it and our responsibility towards all life, to care beyond the confines of our own particular religious grouping. Margaret's sermon—well was it a sermon?—no mention of sin or of that angst-driven need for personal salvation, the two bugbears of my youth. Rather it was a reflection from a well-ordered mind, not to pilgrims journeying through trial and tribulation to a celestial city, but to a community of wayfarers travelling in hope and following the way of Jesus in the context of this world at this time. Communion followed. I was hesitant about that: I had no elder's admission card but the 'invitation' came in these terms:

> 'St Andrew's is an open community and all are invited to the table.
> Wherever you are on your faith's journey,
> wherever you have come from, and wherever you are going to,
> whatever you believe,
> whatever you do not believe
> you are welcome to participate in the communion.
> This sacred meal is for all people.'

I came. And I have continued to come so that St Andrew's on The Terrace with its enlivening progressive Christian community, in which age is not an inhibiting factor, has become my familiar place. It has also become a familiar place for many Wellingtonians who, with no church affiliation, come to enjoy the music in the weekly lunch-hour concerts or to listen and participate in lectures on current affairs, sometimes on the interplay between religion and society, often given by Lloyd Geering, our theologian in residence. The billboard outside announces 'this is our place. This is your place.'

However, religious faith carries the baggage of words and inherits the bondage of certainty. I have come to accept that my faith will always mean living with uncertainty; particularly over the mystery *we* name 'God'. Gone are the clear-cut creedal certainties of previous worshiping generations.

Science reveals an expanding universe in which the anthropomorphic god figure seems out of place and out of touch. Perhaps 'God' is better understood as creative energy. Yet ' Father' or 'Mother ' are the permeable human terms we still relate to, drawing from our experience, from our myths and from our imagination. 'Praxis not gnosis must be the fruit': the way we behave, particularly in striving for social justice and peace, is the fullest expression of what we believe. After fussing about in my mind I am content with that. 'Prayer', at an earlier time, also presented a difficulty. It was if we were expected to ask an 'up-there' God to intercede in our particular affairs for our particular betterment. I now see prayer as simply the breath of life—an exercise in being focused and deeply aware of human connectedness and of our willingness to actively respond.

As a progressive Christian church St Andrew's is out of step with its parent body, the Presbyterian Church of Aotearoa New Zealand. I find it very strange that in a world threatened by the increasing exploitation of the environment, by the increasing gap between rich and poor, by the constant menace of nuclear devastation, the church is so hung-up on the supposed menace of sexual diversity. A remit passed by the 2006 General Assembly bans gays and lesbians as well as those living in de facto relationships from having any future leadership role within the Presbyterian Church. (A 'lifeboat' clause admits those already ordained.) A 'Confession of Faith', proposed as a unifying creed for the church, was voted on in the 2010 General Assembly and confirmed in 2012. This creed is quite extraordinarily unbelievable. It seeks to straitjacket faith, which is of itself organic, within the Westminster Confession and catechisms of the sixteenth and seventeenth centuries. It has no connection with realities of life in this day. And, like the homophobic remit of 2006, it seeks to define who is IN and who is OUT. Sadly, fundamentalism is extending its grip but, just as sadly, many ministers, for fear of disturbing the 'faith of our Fathers ' held by people in the pews, fail to communicate the findings of current theologians regarding the historical Jesus. Of course this paralyzing fundamentalism emerging in the Presbyterian Church when it meets in General Assembly has an impact on the lively, open Christian faith community of St Andrew's. But that inclusive commitment is dear to us, even though it often resonates more clearly within a largely secular society than within the institutional church.

Both in the St Andrew's community and outside it I have frequently and fiercely attacked fundamentalism, particularly the proscriptive edict of the General Assembly banning gay leadership. But, in speaking last year to a meeting of the Wellington Presbytery, Dr Margaret Mayman who has over the years endured vituperative and hurtful comments because of her stand on the human fact of sexual diversity, suggested another, and I think a better way forward—"to stay in relation with one another [is] to make 'space' for one another's theological convictions. Making space, means moving over a little, and sharing what is yours with another".

Looking back over the many years of my absence from church I doubt if I ever really abandoned that faith journey. I certainly abandoned a creed that said 'no' to my questioning, was centred in the life of a 'world to come' and hamstrung my will to find and explore what was real in the world I lived in. The History Department of Victoria College encouraged this journey with its ethic of scepticism—that truth about the past is multi faceted.

As one of the St Andrew's community I am learning what it is to connect spirituality with uncertainty, and to accept that faith still questions as we seek to re-connect and engage with the larger human family by recognising that other faith stories are true for people of other cultures. What it is, to re-connect with the natural world and see in its rhythm of birth, death, decay and rebirth, something of the pattern of human life and death and the fructifying compost of history. What it is to be fully human in community, to know that one belongs to 'the family of things' and therefore the determination to be actively engaged in issues of peace, social justice and the welfare of the environment. What it is to be open to love.

Found: A Theology That Matched My Lived Experience

Lynne Robertson

My earliest memories of God, both knowledge about God and awareness of God's presence, are linked with the reading of the Bible. My grandmother gave me a white leather zip-up Bible (King James Version of course!) and I vaguely remember her saying I could carry it up the aisle on my wedding day. As I must have been all of eight years old that seemed like ages away! But I was a bookworm and interested in the contents of this strange white book. So of course I started at the beginning.

The majesty and grandeur of the first three chapters of Genesis gripped me in a way I will never forget. I knew it was true—not in a scientific sense—I was never very interested in that, but what it said about God and creation and human beings and me! This transcendent, majestic "other" God somehow became strangely real and present.

Concurrently with this experience I was like most children of the 50's sent to Sunday school. It was a conservative evangelical church full of teaching about sin, redemption, salvation, justification, atonement and sanctification. The teaching felt harsh and seemed to bear no resemblance to the sense of connection with "the other' that I felt reading my little white Bible. The teaching however was somehow tempered by my lived experience—the minister was a warm, loving, funny man who took an interest in me and my family and I loved the people there and they loved me. As I grew into teenage and young adult years I enjoyed the active young adult group. In many senses the church was my life. I also often went to big rallies like Youth for Christ and Belgrave Heights conventions and from time to time responded to altar calls to "give my life to Jesus" or "re commit". Sometimes these were based on fear or emotional manipulation—all were an attempt on my part however to draw closer to God. But I often felt I never quite made it. There was a voice that said I was never good enough or pious enough or Christian enough.

When I left school I went to Melbourne University and completed an Arts degree and then to RMIT to study librarianship—I had a wonderful job working in the LaTrobe Library. Then one day at church, a representative from Wycliffe Bible Translators, an organisation that aims to translate the Bible into every language and dialect in the world, came to the church and talked about the needs in various parts—and they had a need for a librarian to replace someone on maternity leave in Papua new Guinea! I really felt this was God's leading but it was such a huge step. I was a shy, overweight city girl, never lived away from home before and here I was traipsing off to the wilds of PNG, flying in tiny little planes and living with a whole lot of people I didn't know. I look back on this time now and see it was really my rather dramatic way of leaving home. But there was another voice at the time: "Wow if I go all the way to New Guinea then surely I'll have to be a good enough Christian, won't I? When I returned it seemed to be expected I would study theology. Due to my background I didn't even know of the existence of the Theological Hall, as it was then called. I only knew of the Melbourne Bible Institute—that's where the "real Christians" went. Surely if I went to MBI I'd be OK wouldn't I? God would accept me? Wouldn't He?"

I had three years at Bible College completing a theology degree and there were some good times and great friends. The teaching I received was very black and white—black was black and white was white and there were no shades of grey in the middle. The teaching was about giving the answers, not engaging the questions. The God I learned about was quite a demanding God. We as evangelical Christians had all the answers and it was our job to set everyone else straight! I learned of a God who asked you to give up things. Every week we would have this thing called 'missionary seminar' where missionaries would come and talk to us and they'd nearly always start by saying something like: "Well I said to God, I'll go anywhere God, as long as you don't send me to... the pygmies or the Eskimos or the Zulus or whatever—name your horror place—and where did God send me… to the pygmies! (or the Eskimos or the Zulus!) So God became for me someone who demanded a lot and made us do what we least wanted to do. I came away with a whole lot of so-called correct doctrine, but not a whole lot that was really nurturing to my faith.

After Bible College while many of my friends were going off to "fulltime Christian ministry" with the pygmies or the Zulus, I couldn't wait to get away and back to the secular world. I went back to librarianship, made new friends and began a new life. During that time I experienced the breakdown of a very close friendship, a friendship that meant a great deal to me. The very scary thing about this was that this friendship was with another woman. Overlaid on the "normal" pain of close attachments which end, was a terrible secret guilt... the relationship wasn't overtly sexual but I came out of it feeling very, very hurt, and very lost. Most of my friends couldn't understand why I was so upset about the break-up of a relationship with a friend. "What's the big deal, you have other friends," I was told. The black and white answers of my Bible College days: "Just trust God and it will all be OK" or "It just wasn't God's will for you", or "homosexuality is a sin—God rescued you from it by ending this relationship" or "just pray a bit harder and have more faith". None of these helped one little bit. I felt God had abandoned me. I was in a very, very dark place that lasted several years.

But I was cared for in that dark space. I had separated myself from a faith community for a while but God had not separated from me. A minister, a chaplain, and a couple of dear Christian friends, accepted me as I was in all my anger and pain; didn't ask too many questions, didn't try to "fix it", but simply cared for me in the midst of my sadness. They showed me a God who didn't always take away and demand, but was simply there, loving unconditionally.

Strangely, while I was still in this dark space people started confiding in me. I was a librarian on the reference desk at RMIT, but I found that as I became more in touch with my own feelings I was also tuned more in to where others were at, and found that many of the students started talking to me about what mattered to them. I enjoyed that role. I felt at home, comfortable in it. So I did some post graduate counseling training, which I really enjoyed. During that time I met some Christian gay couples who seemed happy and didn't have horns and a tail. I began to wonder... Meanwhile, slowly, I was healing from the hurt of the previous years and was drawn back into a supportive faith community.

A friend of mine who was a school chaplain suggested I was well qualified for that role and that I would be good at it. I applied and was accepted. I spent 20 years in school chaplaincy and school chaplaincy management. I enjoyed the cut and thrust of working with teenagers and I tried to love and accept all of them, as they were. My office was always full, and still 20 years later I keep in touch with students and staff from those days. I made many friends—some of whom were gay couples. I didn't view them as sinners, and they didn't see themselves this way either. I almost unconsciously began to question all those old evangelical certainties.

This work however was emotionally exhausting. During that time I often felt depleted, drained, and that I had nothing more to give. But at other times, just often enough, I had direct life changing experiences of God. One was at a chaplains' conference where I had some leadership responsibilities. I can only describe it as a moment of grace. It wasn't expected or even sought after, and it's hard to find words to describe. I can only say as a result of this experience and of the subsequent opening of myself to this God, I no longer saw God as one who had to be appeased, or that I had to be good enough or Christian enough to please, nor as one who "takes away", but one who gives and gives and gives.

During this time I fell in love with another woman. This time my love was reciprocated, and the relationship developed quickly. Finally I could no longer pretend or circle around the issue. The pure joy of my love for this woman and the happiness the relationship brought me collided with what I thought were the teachings of the church, as I knew it on this subject. This time I knew that, no matter what, I would not give up a relationship which brought me so much life. This time I knew, no matter what, I would live my truth. Fortunately by this time I was part of the Uniting Church that was courageously exploring sexuality, and I discovered that not all Christians had the same views as my Bible College lecturers, and that while some of my friends struggled, none of them condemned my new relationship.

A dear friend suggested I read Marcus Borg's *The Heart of Christianity* which I devoured, feeling such relief that here was a theology that matched my lived experience. Later, my local congregation undertook the Living the Questions series. For me with my evangelical background I was blown away by what I learned. But it was not without pain. Although by this stage I had begun to read books on progressive Christianity I remember thinking "Why is everyone taking this so calmly, this is HUGE!" As a leading evangelical Tim Keller wrote recently

> You're asking me to read my Bible differently than my tradition has prescribed, and so I can't go there. If I do, my faith is kicked out the door... it really does come down to a disassembling of the traditional way of reading the Scriptures; not only on the gay issue but on all issues.

For me this has happened gradually, gently, privately, but somehow also with lots of support. I am now part of a progressive Christian network group and feel most comfortable and 'at home' with a more progressive expression of faith.

So where does all this leave me? How do I understand my past experience in the light of a progressive understanding of Christianity? Five key issues spring instantly to mind—of course there will always be many more.

My understanding of God...

My lived experience and my taking hold of progressive thought have always gone hand in hand. Both have impacted on how I see God. As I reflect on my life and the experiences of God that I have had, I see that God is much bigger than I can ever contemplate. I see God in people—in the good people of the evangelical church in which I was nurtured; in those who even though they couldn't match their evangelical understandings with my same sex relationship, loved and cared for me when I was hurting. In friends now with whom I can share wine and food and laughter; in all those, whether they would name a faith or not, who are working for goodness or justice; in the love of my partner of 25 years. I see a God who was and is big enough and safe enough to be real with, and as I am real, I can slowly change and grow. I am not so much interested in "correct" doctrines and creeds now, but in deepening my relationship with this God whom I experience everywhere. I am grateful for those special glimpses of God which cannot be manipulated or explained but are nevertheless very real. The eight-year-old reading the white Bible and the exhausted chaplaincy manager, both met God in a very real way. I welcome these moments and try to be open to them and find they mostly come at unexpected times and in unexpected places.

My understanding of Jesus...

Words like sin, salvation, sanctification and justification don't mean much to me any more. I understand Jesus now as a unique man, a man I want to follow. A man who teaches me about God and God's purposes; a man who reveals God in a particular and unique way; a man who paid the ultimate price for love and justice. I am relieved I need no longer adhere to the 'substitutionary atonement' theory and the mental gymnastics of aligning that to an understanding of a loving God, and that I can walk the Easter journey with more integrity with this new understanding.

My understanding of mission...

While this has been a very personal and individual account of my faith journey and it is helpful to share our stories, our mission is bigger than the individual. Issues of justice, of equality, of food for those who are hungry, special care for those who are vulnerable, a welcome for the marginalised, are core to the gospel. As we read in Luke 4: "He has sent me to proclaim freedom for the prisoners, and recovery of sight for the blind, to set the oppressed free, to proclaim the year of the Lord's favour". While I think there has now been some change, my evangelical friends used to see the core of the faith as being individual salvation and our mission as conversion of individuals by "accepting Jesus Christ as Saviour and Lord". Sometimes most of the rest was dismissed as "social gospel". A progressive perspective has shown me the pursuit of these things was Jesus' core mission and as his followers they are our core mission also.

My understanding of participation in the life of the church...

How tricky this is. Attendance at worship, and active participation in the life of the church is often seen as a measure of how faithful one is. I have been fortunate that in most of the churches I have been involved in, even when I have disagreed with the preaching, I have found something in a hymn or a prayer, or even a children's talk, to nurture and sustain me. Not so the endless meetings, committees, activities, 'same old same old' studies, doing things because we've always done them this way. I no longer put my hand up for anything that bores me, or exhausts me, or I see no point to. I live with the residual guilt around this, and choose to involve myself in activities that recharge my spiritual batteries, or are directly in line with my understanding of mission.

My understanding of pastoral care...

As I reflect on the journey so far I note that it has been the love and care of others that has been the most important factor, both in getting through the tough times and in helping me feel safe enough to 'shift' in my understandings of the faith. The intellectual changes—the changes in beliefs and understanding came much later, and were accepted because they were in line with my lived experience. I had support and some fellow travelers. For some however, this journey to a new understanding of Scripture and indeed of the core of the faith is very scary. Old certainties are shaken up; the very planks on which one has built one's life become wobbly. For many it's just too hard and they stay in their so-called 'certainties' because to move means they lose too much. I believe it is extremely important that people be cared for in this questioning transition time—that the feelings associated with this journey be acknowledged and people be provided with support as they wander and wonder. Some 'progressive' statements can sometimes be as fundamentalist as: "This is the only way to understand the world" (or the faith or the Bible) as evangelical Christian fundamentalism, and are not helpful to journeyers and seekers. As the progressive movement grows, its pastoral care ministry needs to grow in line with its intellectual endeavour. People will not be argued into a new way of thinking. They will come to that themselves when they feel safe enough.

So at this point I am grateful for the journey and for God's presence in all of it. I am grateful for friends who have walked the journey with me and for new insights from the progressive Christian movement that helped me to embrace a more adult faith—one that is more congruent with my lived experience. I look forward, mostly without fear, to more new insights as I seek to deepen my relationship with God.

Notes:
Keller quote from www.pathos.com/blogs

Faith From The Edges

Betty Shore

When I speak of faith, I'm talking about what I believe in, as in what I see worth giving my time and energy for, what I look to for hope, and what I trust to live by. It's about what I believe matters; how I see to care for it—what nurtures, what puts at risk, what strengthens and makes possible; where I look for hope; and whom I trust to search with and journey through life.

In this sense, I think there are no non-faith people. We have faith in different things, and sometimes we are not faithful to what we profess, but faith is whatever guides our living—what we work for, what we trust.

My personal faith has been discerned using a version of what John Wesley suggested we use in finding our beliefs. I learned this as a young Methodist:

- my faith community's common legacy—Bible, church history and current church experience, scholarly rigour;
- my personal experience including study and contributions from the wider world, as made sense of through the lens of my self and my several communities.

I choose what I personally believe, trust, and endeavour to live by. I believe that is my responsibility, and although I am fallible, that is the reality I live with.

In my personal journey, I am very thankful to my parents and to the wider church in which I grew up during the 1940s and 50s. There was strong commitment to searching honestly for the best they could find, and offering this in practice to children and youth as well as adults—those among them, and into wider communities and the world. There was input in the 1930s and 1950s from the Iona Community in Scotland, from biblical scholars making new translations and finding the Dead Sea scrolls, and from the Social Gospel theologians that reach through the 1900s to the current Sojourners. There was a strong movement for international peace during WWII supported by Methodists and Quakers around me in the United States.

While I have moved on in some particular ways, those foundations were very helpful to me and I would say my beliefs remain consistent with that early start. The greatest struggles I have had in terms of defining my personal faith have been with the congregations I came to when I found myself in a different country with different church history, even though the denominational names sounded the same. That is not to say there were no kindred spirits here in New Zealand, only that I found it very difficult to connect with them. I am thankful for the individuals I have found along the way in congregations I have travelled through. Although I tried to sift out what I accepted from the congregations I attended here, I found a lot of attitudes and what I consider fallacies, crept in. Clergy preaching from the pulpit and hymns sung strongly, can carry very powerful messages that reach beneath what we consciously sift out, and could cloud our continuing ability to do so.

I looked in this new land for a congregation that would be a caring community for my children and myself, as we sought to find our way in this place, so unexpectedly strange to us. I think the churches meant a great deal to the people in them, but we were not at home among them, and so after a few years we would move on. Eventually I was the only one of my family attending. There had been little offered for children or youth, so it depended on me to carry on with more resources than I had.

Then the loss of a family member by suicide shattered my world and caused me to stop and take the time to sift out what I could believe in and trust, and what would guide my living. I felt that much of what was included in congregational worship, was not what I could continue to participate in. I had to be honest in church if nowhere else. I did not think it would be helpful to stand up in the service and challenge the sermon, prayers, or certainly the hymns so I decided to take a step back.

I was able to remain for a little while, by standing with the people who were unable to kneel during communion, so I stood to receive rather than kneeling. I really needed to stand up not kneel at clergy feet any more. For a while I would quietly change the words of hymns to what I could sing with honesty, but in the end, I found the very relationships in my congregation unhealthy—the power plays were very undermining and draining and seemed contrary to the Gospel, rather than enabling faithful living. I left.

In retrospect, the relationships in an earlier congregation had entrenched the unhealthy relationships in my marriage and family life. I had gone to church hoping for a community in which I could find ways for healthier relationships. Sadly, I simply found more domination and submission couched in biblical terms. This was not a fundamentalist church it was mainline Protestant. I had also gone wanting a better understanding of faithful living in terms of how I invested my time and talents, but found I was simply more exhausted by the jobs that needed doing. There seemed little care for people, only a concern for getting the jobs done.

The notion that suffering is somehow noble in itself was preached, when indeed there was justification to challenge and stop the suffering caused by destructive relationships among that church council, and similarly in my home. The notion of being peaceful Christians and being accommodating without challenging was supporting very unhealthy power plays in that congregation. I believe it was a betrayal of the gospel that had tragic consequences in the lives of several parishioners. Some readers may not have experienced such things in their congregations, so my statements may seem harsh, but for those who have, I think it will be all too familiar. Such statements are about beliefs and how we live them, about theology and gospel understanding, and about faithful living in our time and place.

I did attend some other congregations, but personally I did not find groups who wanted to really think about their beliefs and how to live faithful to the gospel in our time and place. Nor did they seem open to other understandings, such as offered by Marcus Borg and others before him. Likewise, neither did congregations seem ready to engage in the social issues around them, nor take an interest in befriending a travelling soul. To be fair, I found a few congregations that might have offered more, but were too far away for me to continue with. Access is part of the reality for participation.

So I travelled alone until I found a small faith community that gathers for pot-luck meals with children every other Sunday evening, and on alternate weeks gathers later for study, discussion, and reflection. We also plan regular family gatherings that nurture children and adults, and members share in various projects and concerns in our community—play centre, play group for immigrants, schools, housing, addressing poverty. There is also on-going care for members as life's events arise.

That is what I understand faithful living and faithful community to be.

So that has been my journey. I have identified some of my beliefs, keeping these open to change. I am thankful for various internet discussions, so I offer my personal beliefs below. Perhaps they will open some possibilities for others.

- I believe in Good. I believe it exists and I look to the source and spirit of Good—that which provides for and sustains us. I understand Good to be honesty and kindness, compassion and healing, wholeness and healthy relationships for the care of all our precious Earth-home, and all creatures within it, including all people as extended family. I don't know just what spirit is, but for me there is something of Good beyond individual acts or concepts. There's some essence of Good that I look to and trust. Perhaps it is an aspect of God, but for me this spirit of Good makes sense.
- I believe that Creation evolves and includes forces for growing and also for dying. There are principles and there is chance. I understand its purpose simply to be that it evolves and grows to be what it is—components in it growing and thriving in their turn. That does not mean I believe it has no further purpose, only that this is as far as I personally have come to believe. For those who ask, "then what is the purpose or meaning in life or living?" I simply say that we can find meaning for living in what we see has worth: nurturing relationships among people, and for our Earth-home; parents and children and what a miracle that can be; and whatever inspires awe in us or calls up our greatest care.
- I do not personally look for Hope in an all-powerful God who steers all for some great purpose. I do not say there is no God, only that is not where I look for hope nor what I navigate by. The existence of so much in the natural world and in the human world that seem contrary to such a God leaves me looking elsewhere for hope and guidance. For that matter, I do not look to Might as deserving my respect in and of itself, so I would not worship All-mighty, even if worship were something I did.

- I do not worship in the sense of bowing down nor surrendering all. For me, to worship rightly is to practice Good—honesty and compassion and humility which are, I believe, part of caring for God's planet and people. Also, to care for this sacred self which has been entrusted to me, and to care for family, a sacred trust. It seems to me that sometimes in life, there is space to pick up from mistakes as we learn, but at other times, damage may be irreversible and the consequences fail whatever the intent. We are human so we make mistakes and sometimes we cannot know consequences ahead. We cannot expect that God will take care of everything. Responsibility rests with us to share in communities our concerns and our understanding, and to work together for healing. We are all connected and the smallest voice merits a hearing.
- I believe in Grace and Forgiveness. True repentance means looking honestly at what I have done and the genuine consequences, and how I will turn around. Forgiveness can be a difficult thing for me and for others. Grace rests with the Sacred Spirit of Healing and gives reassurance of sustenance and renewal as life continues.
- I find Growth and Renewal in study, discussion, reflection, music, art, time alone, time in gathered community, time in the natural world, shared meals, shared experience.
- I understand the Bible to be a library of the writings of sages in our Judeo-Christian heritage. In a sense I still see them as I was taught as a child—God reaching to people and people reaching to God. They are written through the lens of human experience and reflect the profound searching of people through these centuries. They include poetry, history, and the stories through which our sages endeavoured to tell something of the reality they found about what mattered in life, how to care for living, and where to look for hope.

For me, what I find in the Bible is summed up in three passages: The Psalmist's declaration (*Ps 24:1-2*), which I understand to mean that the Earth and the fullness thereof, are sacred—the land and all who dwell therein. This comes from Creation and is not what we have made. Next are the Prophets who declared what was required ultimately was not material sacrifices, nor rituals, but justice, compassion, walking humbly with Creator (*Micah 6:8*).

This message in different forms runs through the Jewish scriptures—care for the widows and orphans and refugees, jubilee from debts incurred. This message is expanded in the other books.

Then Jesus came and lived honesty, justice and compassion among us—fulfilling the ancient prophesy to heal the wounded, give sight to the blind, set at liberty the imprisoned, and declare that the time and place of Shalom are now and here (*Lk. 4:18-19*). He challenged oppression in all its forms—religious, political, social, economic. He named it, and practiced a different way of living. The people whose oppressive power was threatened thought to stop him by crucifying him, expecting that the example of his death would deter others and that his 'way' would be stopped. But what he lived and gave remained alive and powerful and continues among us to this day.

- The Church for me growing up was a place for learning and caring, for asking questions and searching, for working together, for practicing among us and in our wider communities and the world, healing care, challenging oppression, and bringing about a just and fair society with dignity accorded to all members, as Jesus taught and lived.

I know in many times and places that has not been what the Church did or does, but it was for me, and that is what I still search for. In this journey through life, I remember my various great grand parents travelling across the plains from the valley of the great Mississippi River, through the deserts and finally the pass in the Sierra Nevada Mountains and into California, stopping to settle before that last stretch. In the daytime the wagon trains stretched out slowly, and the young walked, lightening the load of the wagons. At night the wagons circled around and in the centre the meals were cooked, songs were sung that renewed vision and courage and the young were rocked to sleep. The scouts would then share their findings of the day, and the plans were laid for how to proceed and care for the members of the group.

I look for the wagon train in my time and place. I am thankful for a small Sunday evening group that offers a faith home for me, but still I look for the wider fellowship—the gathered wider congregation, so I find a network here, a network there, but I miss the wider gathering. Sometimes the congregations I have travelled with have became so ill that I left them and travelled alone.

Others hold to past beliefs lest questioning should leave them more at sea, rather than seeing what else there might be. Others say the healing words and welcome visitors, but do not challenge the political and economic systems that oppress among us, nor reach out to the wider community. I have been disappointed that despite my searching I did not find a congregation for my children growing up. The church for them was a busy place at best, with little time for children or youth, and at worst an institution that told them what to think and do. It was another place of repression in a society desperate for honesty and compassion, healing and care.

In our times and places, we are called to challenge and to bring about change. To do so, we need the gathered wisdom of searching community. By now, I look for this wherever I can find it—my small house group, the progressive network, the Green Party Aotearoa, Christian World Service, my local neighbourhood primary school—the central government has just declared will close due to their agenda of privatization. Do I need these communities to hold Jesus central? I don't need that for all, but I need that for some, because with some that can be our common groundedness. It's central for me, and I need to find others on this path. I find the challenges daunting at times and I need to invest my resources thoughtfully. For that, I value the vision and encouragement of community.

- As for Prayer, I don't know what all it can be but I learned to practice it, and at least it helps me focus and be open to the Spirit of Good. For some people, and sometimes for me, it may do more, but this is enough for me to continue.
- I think Evil is the distortion of people's drive to survive because sometimes in growing up the Spirit of Good wasn't nurtured, or it was stunted by oppressive systems—oppressive systems that went unchallenged by honesty and compassion resulting in an increased toxic illness. Maybe that sounds simplistic. It's what I can articulate here, after a lifetime of pondering and this understanding is what guides my work.

So I pray we may find and share ways to challenge oppression and transform the world in which we live by bringing about here and now the time of Shalom—care for sacred creation, and for all people, for we are extended family.

The Light Of Faith In A Dark Time

David Tacey

"We wander between two worlds, one dead, the other powerless to be born"
(Matthew Arnold)

I was not exposed to 'progressive religious thought' as a church member who was suddenly confronted with an alternative way of seeing things. Rather, I was progressive, critical and enquiring from the beginning of my thinking life. I had an intensely religious and very conventional upbringing, but even as a child I asked questions about the faith and was beset by heretical thoughts. However, one thing I never questioned was the reality of God. I was always sure that God existed and it was simply a matter of attuning myself to this abiding presence. Even throughout my academic and intellectual training, this remained a constant. I lost touch with church communities as a university student, and as a postgraduate engaged in advanced study, but always felt myself to exist within the 'outer reaches' of the church. As much as my educated mind wanted to rebel against the church and its institutional life, I could not expunge my childhood sense that I was called to be a witness to faith.

Although I felt the abiding presence of God in my life, I was never happy with the conventional images of God. I doubted the validity of the images which I saw on church walls, in church paintings and books, in pamphlets and newsletters. I felt embarrassed whenever I beheld visual images of God. To me, such images were blasphemous, and contradicted the second commandment: 'You shall not make for yourself a graven image, or any likeness of anything that is in heaven above.' I objected to the assumption that God was a 'father' and masculine—an obvious projection of a patriarchal society. I understood the need for humans to create images of God, as we need to bring the reality of God before our awareness. But the cost of this could not be underestimated: we risk making something infinite seem finite and man-made. We risk critical minds looking at our religious images and saying: these are idols, empty images, bearing no relation whatsoever to ultimate reality. Or as the philosopher Feuerbach put it: the Bible says God made man in his own image, but I say man-made God in his own image.

Was Ludwig Feuerbach a destructive atheist, as is often claimed? Or was he, rather, one of the first of the progressive Christians, breaking our attachment to man-made images so we could see their vanity and negative effect on the infinity of God, which is beyond comprehension? Here I like the Jewish and Islamic insistence that images of God are dangerous and the impulse to make graven images should be curtailed. But in my own Catholic tradition, it was as if this second commandment got buried or lost a long time ago, as we freely engaged in the art of making images of God. We thought that brought God closer to us, but actually in recent times the whole process has backfired. One of the reasons why modernity has argued that 'God is dead' *(Nietzsche)*, is that we have murdered God with our images. We made God too known, familiar and human. The anthropomorphic impulse, by which we make the non-human appear human, has had a detrimental impact in the West, and now, if we want God to live again, we have to strip God of all our human attributes, including 'his' supposed masculinity. We need a moratorium on all images that were apparently useful in the past, but today are merely a dead weight of baggage which serves to destroy any fresh or new apprehension of the living God.

In his book, *The Heart of Christianity*, Marcus Borg writes that progressive Christianity needs to give Jesus a demotion. I know it hurts believers to hear this, but it is one of the most important points that I have taken from progressive religious thought. But long before I dipped into progressive thought, I felt the same way about Jesus. This was one of the heretical thoughts that afflicted me since childhood. I was never prepared to see Jesus as God. The church preached this with vigour, but I could never swallow it. I remained silent in church when we were asked to recite the creeds as if we meant it. I could never believe in what seemed to be a preposterous idea. Indeed, this notion was linked to the Christian emphasis on making God familiar, known, domesticated. To me, God could be befriended without making him known through graven images, or without making him a literal man who walked the earth. I felt sorry for Jesus that he had been lumped with such a terrible burden, foisted upon him by generations of people who wanted to bring God down to earth and assume human form. At the bottom of the divinisation of Jesus was the fallacy of anthropomorphism, at work again in its destructive devices.

Here again I felt at home with Jewish and Islamic perceptions of Jesus as a holy man, a prophet of God, but I was happier to understand him in terms of his preferred epithet, 'Son of Man'. Jesus for me was a symbol of what we must all aspire to: an intimate and personal relationship with God. He blazed the way for us in that direction, but we messed everything up by confusing him with God. The Trinity made things worse, by solidifying this error and writing it into dogma. Michael Morwood's book, *Was Jesus God*, helped me to come to terms with this heretical view of mine, even though when I first read Michael's book I was disapproving of it, as it coincided with my own attempt to return to the Catholic church, and thus provided an impediment in my way. But the stumbling block or scandal of this idea was integrated by me into a more mature understanding of faith. My faith journey has been in fits and starts, certainly not a straight line from naïveté to enlightenment. I have had to readjust my thinking on a range of issues at every point along the journey. But I feel that much of my journey has been a groping in the dark, in a thick fog of uncertainty, especially since the Catholic tradition is afraid of change and sees every 'progressive' thought as a heresy.

It is a telling indictment on the church that every progressive Catholic who has influenced my journey, such as John Dominic Crossan, John O'Donohue, Karen Armstrong, Michael Morwood, Paul Collins, and others, had to step down from their respective orders as priests or nuns in order to express their true thoughts and come to terms with the new faith that was emerging within them. Of the other Catholic thinkers who have influenced me, such as Bede Griffiths, Joan Chittister, Thomas Berry or Thomas Merton, these have sought refuge in contemplative orders and monasteries, but even there, the dead hand of Rome has reached into their lives and tried to prevent them from realising their distinctive and personal journeys. I have come to see the Roman church as a real impediment on 'the way', and I hope and pray that it collapses as soon as possible, which is a possibility that is within sight at this stage in the twenty-first century. I think of the church now in the same way that Jesus thought of the synagogue in his time: as a corrupt institution that has lost touch with the spirit, that began as an inspired community, but over centuries of authoritarian rule and dreary cerebral administration, has lost its connection to the living God.

My view is that the church will implode, and we will have to start again, in the same way that the early church did, with small communities of the faithful, expressing their spiritual lives with intuition, hope and trust in the living spirit. In this regard my heretical thoughts resemble those of my Protestant brothers and sisters, who similarly see Rome as a dead hand of authoritarian rule. There are many Catholics who have the same Protestant aspirations that I have, and who see that the hierarchy has passed its use-by date, and now needs to be consigned to history. Unlike me, these Catholics do not have a public voice or a platform to deliver this point of view. Indeed, they are silenced and gagged as much as possible, but I have never had the respect for Rome that I am supposed to have. My respect is mainly for God, and for serving God in the best possible way that I can. Having said that, I remain respectful of the Catholic mass and its sacramental understanding. I adore its symbolic apprehension of the spirit, even if it tends to take this symbolism literally and thus to take it into the arena of idolatry. But as I sit through the mass, I tend to reinterpret much that is presented to me, seeing the images and sacraments as windows to the sacred, if not as literal bearers of sacred life, as many believing Catholics see them.

I am unlikely to go over to the Protestant side, tempted though I have been from time to time. But I feel the ongoing nourishment of what could be called Catholic substance, and especially of its remarkable mystical tradition, to which I feel closely aligned. I like Protestant principle, and its advocacy of ongoing critique of the Christian tradition, but Catholic substance is too attractive to abandon. It is unfortunate that the deepest sources of Catholic tradition, namely, the mystical insights of Teresa of Avila, John of the Cross, Joachim of Fiore, or Meister Eckhart, are buried and lost beneath the burden of Catholic prejudice and institutional thinking. It seems remarkably ironic that the very things that people are wanting today, the living waters of the spirit, are to be found in abundant supply in Catholic mysticism, but this sub-tradition is ignored or rendered heretical by the mainstream tradition.

In closing this short personal anecdote about my spiritual journey, I would like to speak about my own 'treatment' at the hands of Catholic orthodoxy. In the 1990s, I published a book that became a national bestseller, *Edge of the Sacred*. This book launched me into the public spotlight, and for a number of years I was in demand for talks, speaking engagements, keynote addresses, book launches, and so on. During this period the Catholic hierarchy began to take an interest in me and my ideas. In 1999, I delivered a talk on the future of faith at the University of Melbourne, and the then Archbishop of Melbourne, George Pell was in attendance. I noticed him taking voluminous notes, but was not aware that he was jotting down all the points that he disagreed with in my talk. I was expressing interest and enthusiasm for the diversity of religious views in Australia, and had noted the increase of interest in Buddhism, and the relatively recent interest in Aboriginal religions.

Just prior to that event, I had been invited to keynote a gathering of Catholic clergy by the minister of priests in the Melbourne archdiocese, Fr Brian Cosgriff. My talk was scheduled for December 1999, and I had already been working on the draft version when late one morning Fr Brian came to my house to deliver a message of 'disinvitation'. Fr Brian was as astonished as I was, but felt obliged to personally deliver the news that Archbishop Pell had forbidden me to speak at the congress of clergy. 'Was there some reason for the disinvitation?' I enquired. Brian said: 'I have been told you have publicly stated your support for other religions and have said positive things about Buddhism and Hinduism'. I said yes, but that is entirely within the spirit of the Second Vatican Council and its recognition of the presence of God in other traditions. I was told that Pell was not a supporter of Vatican II and anyone advocating its aims and ideals could be reprimanded. This was shocking news, as at the time of the Council, it was regarded by Bishops and Cardinals as a 'movement of the Holy Spirit'. Pell later described it as a failed marketing exercise, which had not put bums on church seats.

I had tried to keep my 'banning' quiet, but the story had been leaked to *The Age* newspaper, which had run a 'Page 3' sensationalist story called "Archbishop Bans University Academics From Speaking To Clergy". Along with myself, Professor Max Charlesworth had been invited, and then disinvited, to the same congress. I went to Max to discuss the problem but he regarded it with wry amusement and had not given it the significance I had. He was older than me and seemed more cynical about the church and its machinations. I had hoped that not many would read *The Age* article, especially my secular university colleagues, who might bait me by saying: 'So what are you going to do about your religious faith now?' But word gets around about such disagreements. The media seems eager to pounce on evidence of disquiet and controversy within the church, and this was one of those occasions.

As time moved on, I became aware of a vast number of Catholics, both in Australia and abroad, who had received the same treatment. Wonderful speakers and leaders such as Richard Rohr, Joan Chittister, John O'Donohue and others were similarly banned from speaking on church property, and in order to hear such speakers I usually had to attend Uniting Church halls. We are learning a lot about clerical sexual abuse in this year of the Royal Commission. What we are not yet aware of is the level of 'spiritual abuse' in the church, and the thuggish ways in which church hierarchy treats its intellectuals and thinkers.

Despite the official ban, I continued with my efforts in the church, although whenever an invitation was presented to the archdiocesan office, it was vetoed by Pell and his associates. Some of these invitations seemed to slip through the net and avoid being annulled. One such occasion was in 2002, when I was invited to present a keynote address to a 'Teams of Our Lady' conference at Whitefriars College, Donvale. I found a car park in the wooded grounds, and as I gathered my notes from the back seat, the former Archbishop of Melbourne, Frank Little, pulled into the parking spot beside me. We found ourselves walking together, side by side to the hall. I knew who he was, but he did not know me. I asked Sir Frank if he was giving a talk, and he said 'No, I have come to hear David Tacey. I want to hear what he has to say, as my brother George has been complaining about him and I want to see what the complaint is about'. He turned to me and asked if I were a priest. I said, 'No, I am David Tacey, the speaker for today'. He apologised for not recognising me and said I looked like a Catholic priest and could be mistaken for one. Naturally I was curious about what had been said, and so I enquired: 'What has George been saying about me?' He said he had been told I was a trouble-maker who was engaged in original thinking and creative thought. I managed to hold myself back from saying, 'Oh, we can't have that, can we, original thinking and creativity in the church?' Instead, I remained silent for a while, and stayed pensive.

Eventually I plucked up the courage to say: 'Sir Frank, would you please do me a favour? Listen to what I have to say, and tell me at the end what you think the problem is with my work'. He said yes he would, but he hastened to add he would never want to 'betray or contradict the views of my brother bishop'. I reassured him that I did not want him to contradict his brother, but to give me some insight into what he thinks the problem is about. At the end of my talk, Sir Frank made his way toward me at the edge of the stage: 'You have a prophetic voice', he said, 'and you know what we do with prophets don't you?' There was a kind twinkle in his eye as he said this, and he was trying to be warm and reassuring. But I was left in a quandary, which lasted for some days; in fact, some years and even today. I thanked him for his response, but realised it was double-edged. In the nicest possible way, he was condoning the practice of mistreating those who dare to speak with a prophetic voice. I wanted to say, but did not say, 'Why don't we stop doing it then?'

I am not sure about the suggestion that I speak with a prophetic voice. For a bishop to say this is to be damned with faint praise and forgotten. The church does not have to listen to a prophetic voice, even though it may accept that the prophetic voice is in its own territory and talking about the same things. I would like to be closer to formal religion than I am, but it hasn't turned out that way. When Pell left Melbourne to become Archbishop of Sydney, I received a surprising letter from the incoming Archbishop of Melbourne, Denis Hart. He said just because Pell has left town, I should not imagine that the previous restrictions have been lifted. He wrote that it was one thing for me to deliver lectures in the name of the university, but quite another to speak for or on behalf of the church. I was to henceforth make it clear during my public talks that I was speaking for myself only and not for the church. Moreover, the archdiocese would keep a close watch on my activities, and monitor invitations to speak to Catholic schools, hospitals, conferences and seminaries in the future. The church, he said, reserved the right to refuse a public voice to anyone who ventured to proclaim personal points of view that were not in accord with the church's official interests and directions.

Naturally all this has soured my relationship with the church, but I still enjoy attending the Sunday mass, as a humble citizen in need of spiritual nourishment, but no longer as a public figure in the life of the church. The candlelight of faith flickers and is almost blown out in a dark time. But fortunately, the grace and generosity of God is far greater than the malice and prejudice of man-made religious institutions.

Notes:

Arnold, M. 'Stanzas from the Grands Chartreuse' (1855), in Humphrey Milford (ed) *The Poetical Words of Matthew Arnold*. London: Oxford University Press, 1945, Page: 224.

Part Three: Progressive Christianity: Seeking Integrity

It Changed My Life: My 'progressive' Christian Journey

Richard Carter

I came to Progressive Christianity relatively late. Although I didn't become conscious of the term "Progressive Christianity" until quite a while later, my interest in it was sparked in 1994 when I picked up a copy of Bishop John Shelby Spong's *Resurrection: Myth or Reality?* while idly browsing in a Perth bookshop. My personal Christian theology at that time was pretty traditional, largely unexamined and, I now realise, not very well informed. While I had difficulty in reconciling biblical accounts of miracles, a physical resurrection of the crucified Jesus and so on with the scientific and physical realities I dealt with in my experiences of life, and particularly in my work as a mining industrialist, I was nevertheless able to put this uneasiness aside as just something that I didn't understand and which was probably inexplicable anyway.

Spong's book therefore came as a bit of a shock to me. First of all, I was made aware that my understanding of what the gospel accounts and other New Testament writings represented was woefully off course. Secondly, I was confronted with the concept that the importance of the resurrection for Christians did not require Jesus' body to have been physically resuscitated. The thought that Jesus might not have died as a predestined sacrifice to save us from our sins I found surprising, but not shocking, although Spong did not really explain in this particular book actually why it was Jesus came to be crucified. Notwithstanding these revelations I did little more immediately with my new insights other than to exhibit increased scepticism to theological claims that called for the suspension of normal judgment and belief. I continued to participate as usual in the life of the traditional suburban Perth Uniting Church congregation where my wife and I were members.

My failure to rise to the occasion and examine these insights in greater depth can be explained, at least to my satisfaction, by the fact that my professional life and the heavy travel load associated with it consumed the whole of my time and I had no opportunity for further exploration of what I knew were important questions.

After returning to live in Melbourne in 1996 we reconnected with Ewing Memorial Uniting Church, East Malvern. This was the congregation we had been connected with during a prior time of living in Melbourne and while it too was a fairly traditional congregation, the members were well educated and theologically well grounded. A good few of them had liberal leanings and a willingness to explore new paths. In 1999 the Uniting Church altered its system of congregational governance by combining its Elders' Council (responsible for spiritual leadership) and Parish Council (responsible for the congregation's administration) into a single Church Council and I became chairperson of this new body at Ewing. By this time I had also made a career change from full time executive to independent company director, which gave me considerably more free personal time.

Shortly before I rejoined Ewing, Rev Greg Crowe had been called to be its minister. Greg was quite youthful, enthusiastic and an agent for change– he still is for that matter. In time, he started to raise issues relating to the challenges of the future church. On my becoming leader of the Church Council Greg and I began a close working relationship and, particularly on Greg's initiative, the Council was encouraged to study non-traditional ways of "being church". At first this discussion tended to focus on what should be done to keep the congregation viable and to help it adjust to the changed Australian culture, where the greater part of the community did not see participation in regular church based activity as an essential or desirable part of normal life.

A resource we used at this time was Loren B. Meade's slim book *The Once and Future Church: Reinventing the Congregation for a New Mission Frontier* and, while not specifically 'progressive', it did make the point persuasively that the future "....requires moving ahead into a new paradigm of mission, rebuilding and reinventing the church as we go". Inevitably, this led to an examination of the core beliefs of orthodox or traditional Christianity.

About the turn of this century the number of new books being published on progressive Christian subjects started to increase noticeably. Most of these were by established and new international authors but Australian titles were pretty sparse on the ground. An exception to this rule was

Michael Morwood's *Is Jesus God?* which appeared in 2001. You may recall that Morwood is a former Roman Catholic priest who resigned from the priesthood after being proscribed by the then Archbishop of Melbourne who found Morwood's 1997 book *Tomorrow's Catholics* to be substantially "in error".

We invited Michael to Ewing to speak to us on a couple of occasions in 2002. Each time he drew a significant audience who found his teaching very persuasive, particularly his proposals that Christianity needs to move from an understanding of Jesus as "... an incarnate god-figure on whom our access to eternal life with God depends" to one where "... the 'good news' would be universally 'better news' if it were linked to Jesus' preaching about the 'reign of God' in our midst and the experience of the sacred in decent, everyday human actions" and that God had to be understood as being constantly with and in us and not an "elsewhere God" abiding in some remote place called "Heaven". I think this marked the time when Ewing started systematically to take up the progressive path and also when I personally began to devote myself to examining these progressive concepts in greater depth and began to read the new literature more avidly.

At this point Greg Crowe was influenced by the Uniting Church to transfer to a placement as a chaplain to the Melbourne Juvenile Justice Centre and Ewing then had to find another minister. The Church Council was determined that the exploration of the progressive way should continue and specified that the incoming minister should be a person with progressive characteristics. So it was that Rev John Smith came to Ewing in 2003 and under his ministry the theology and liturgies of the congregation began to reflect the progressive understandings that were developing.

Lorna Henry, a good friend and a lay leader in the Ewing community, took what I now recognise as a significant step early in 2005 when she hosted a small gathering in her home to discuss a progressive subject. There were only six of us present at that first meeting but it has since grown to the point where over thirty people are connected to the group, now named "Something For The Spirit", and attendances of twenty or more at its gatherings are not unusual. The meetings, which are like a social gathering, are still held in Lorna's home which is a deliberate move to remove the inhibitions and formality that might occur if they were held in traditional church spaces. The discussion is stimulated by a pre-agreed topic but it is unconstrained and those present feel safe to put forward views that they might not otherwise express. A diverse group of individuals attend—some are from Ewing, others from other churches nearby and some have no church connection at all. For me, and I think for others too, it is one of the most stimulating and interesting experiences I have ever had in my spiritual development, and I rather suspect that something like this type of activity may well be the form of the church of the future.

Another significant step for me occurred later in 2005 when John Smith and I together with our wives attended the Fall Meeting of the Westar Institute in Santa Rosa, California. We were impressed by the vigour and depth of the progressive Christian movement we observed in the United States. We lamented that our part of Australia lacked any organisation dedicated to encouraging individuals or groups of progressive Christians to join or work together to study, discuss and research progressive Christian thought and practice. We wondered whether there would be enough interest among like-minded people to justify founding an organisation to facilitate these activities. Other friends were recruited to help test the degree of enthusiasm for the concept and a public meeting was held in December 2005 which was attended by a handful of people representing discussion and study groups with progressive interests. This gathering strongly endorsed an initiative to set up an association to facilitate and promote interaction between progressive Christians. An interim committee was appointed to establish the new body and after a series of constructive planning meetings The Progressive Christian Network of Victoria Inc (PCNV) was launched in June, 2006 before an audience of 145 interested people, and I became its first President.

Five years on, the PCNV is one of the more successful Australian regional organisations promoting and facilitating the development of progressive Christianity. It is strictly non-denominational and it reaches out to other faith traditions in a spirit of ecumenism. Typically, it stages nine or ten events each year. These may be formal lectures, panel discussions, workshops and so on, and many of these provide for audience participation in some way. The leaders normally are local or other Australian progressive figures. Over the short life of the PCNV about forty of these events have been held and they are generally well supported (an audience of 100 – 125 is typical). On occasions, visits by eminent international authorities have been promoted and these events are often more elaborate affairs than the usual offerings and have attracted audiences of several hundreds.

My work with the PCNV has been personally very rewarding. Through it I have been privileged to meet many of the leading progressive thinkers and writers in Australia and New Zealand and also some of the renowned contemporary international scholars and authors. This contact has expanded my thinking and accelerated my spiritual development to a degree that would have been unlikely without it. I am excited about what the future might bring.

I have found my journey along the progressive path to be intensely liberating. Putting aside the notion that being Christian was principally about my personal salvation which was made possible by the substitutionary sacrifice of God's only son for the forgiveness of my sins was a relief - particularly as I had, perhaps deludedly, never felt particularly sinful and had never been persuaded that humans were inherently sinful because of the misdeeds of Adam and Eve. Being able to see that the real purpose to Jesus' life was the proclamation of God's reign on Earth—that it is possible for humans to create a just world where everyone has sufficient, love prevails and there is freedom from violence, war and oppression—suddenly made brilliant sense. The fact that Jesus was martyred by the authorities of the day for his audacity in promulgating this radically different way of ordering society, that his followers came to realise that Jesus still "lived" among them and that his "appearances" to some of them, whatever form these might have taken, showed he was vindicated by God, all made perfectly good sense to me. From this it seems self-evident to me that those of us who call ourselves Christian are also called to work individually and collectively to bring about Jesus' vision for a just world, even though the situation we face today is hugely different from that in Palestine 2,000 years ago.

Probably the most difficult thing for me to come to terms with as my understanding has developed is the change I have been required to make in the image I have of God. I suspect that many others have had a similar experience. Twenty years ago I still clung to a concept of God as a remote power which could sometimes willfully intervene physically in the world—an "elsewhere God" to use Michael Morwood's term—even if I'd given up on the notion of God being a supernatural anthropomorphic being beyond the sky. The change to a position where I sense God to be intimately with and in us and all things throughout our universe and all the other universes, if they exist, has been a real challenge and I'm not sure that I've quite got there yet. I am also still struggling to grasp why we can say with any conviction other than pious hope that "God is love". Perhaps I will just have to settle with the fact that God is beyond understanding and forever ineffable.

I am quite convinced that progressive Christianity offers Christians a way for the church of the future. A way that is true to the original message of Jesus is critically relevant to the way the world is organised and the way we live, and that does not require us to suspend our knowledge of physical and scientific reality.

How My Mind Has Changed

Sue Emeleus

I did not grow up in a religious family. But my brother and I went to Sunday School with a number of other children in our block, and that gave my parents some space on a Sunday morning.

Mine was a fairly dysfunctional family and one night, when I was ten years old, after I had gone to bed, I heard a fight occurring in the kitchen. When it became physical, I was scared and began to pray. I prayed something like, 'God, they tell us at Sunday School that we should pray, so if you are there, could you please stop that fight."

I don't remember what happened in the kitchen, but I do remember sensing a very near presence in the room and I don't think I have doubted the existence of God since then. Those experiences happened in Kensington, NSW. I had lots of school friends there and in the OC class at Woollahra where I went in fifth class.

Interestingly, my closest friend at Woollahra was Jewish, and in 2006 I met up with her in Tel Aviv and we shared our stories for an afternoon. When my family moved to an outer western suburb, I began going to the Anglican Church I found when I took my bike off the delivery van. That church became my spiritual home for the next fifteen years. In sixth class, the Anglican priest and his wife had a small group of children who read the Bible together each morning before school and the couple took it in turns of taking us through the set passage and explaining it to us.

At high school many of us joined the Inter School Christian Fellowship (ISCF) and we met once a week at lunchtime, again to listen to someone talking about the Bible. During my last year at school, I heard an African Bishop from Kenya addressing a meeting in the Sydney Town Hall, pleading for people to come and work in East Africa. While I was still a student at university, I began studying theology by correspondence courses, in case I should one day need such training. Applying to a missionary society after several years of science teaching, I was directed to spend a year in the Anglican theological college in Sydney. While I loved the study I was puzzled by the habit of the lecturers to go through reading lists and point out which books were 'sound'. I wondered what was wrong with the others, and began my more liberal journey in 1967 when I spent a second year in missionary training in Melbourne. Lecturers at Ridley College seemed a little more open to other ideas and I enjoyed reading some of the books from the 'unsound' list.

During my four years in East Africa, where I met my husband, a physicist from Northern Ireland, and our ten years in Papua New Guinea, I continued to study theology by correspondence, gaining my first theology degree in 1979. Still quite conservative theology, it was what I studied to keep sane during the years of having four children and doing some occasional physics teaching. Returning to Australia in 1982, I found a number of likeminded colleagues in the school where I taught science and Christian studies. Like me, they were dissatisfied with the exclusive and conservative theology of their upbringing and enjoyed exploring new ways of thinking.

It was during my years at that school that I joined *Eremos*, a group with its roots in Christianity, but exploring the faith more widely. Through the *Eremos* bookshop I came across my first feminist theology books, and it has been these that have sustained me for twenty-five years. In particular, the Process theologians such as Carol Christ and Charles Birch, as well as the writings of Mary Grey, Rosemary Radford Ruether, Carter Hayward, Catherine Keller and Diarmuid O'Murchu (all of whom I met at feminist theology conferences convened by Lisa Isherwood in Winchester, UK, in the first decade of this century) set me on the path of thinking that I have found in the progressive networks such as the Centre for Progressive Religious Thought (CPRT), the Movement for the Ordination of Women (MOW) and Women and the Australian Church (Catholic) (WATAC) in Sydney, in the last few years. Feminist theologians seemed almost to take for granted the findings of the Jesus Seminar, accepting their conclusions about the pre-Easter Jesus, but building on those to seek an understanding of God compatible with the new learning coming from many different areas of new knowledge.

In the 1990s, I began a friendship with Carolyn O'Siek, whose book *Beyond Anger* was pivotal for me. When she visited Australia I was privileged to attend a number of her seminars. She wrote, not for those who had become angry and walked away from the church, but for those who had become angry and stayed to try to change things within the church. I think we were angry about the resistance to inclusive language and to gifted women in leadership as well as the insistence on the scriptures being God-written. Professor O'Siek is both an archaeologist and a New Testament scholar. The two weeks in Israel with her and her theology students from Chicago in 2006 were life changing for me, and the Australian friend who came with me. The 'Jesus Seminar' conclusions were discussed by those leading reflections and meditations at each place we visited in the Holy Land.

In 1995, I left teaching to take up a position as Anglican Chaplain at the Children's Hospital, less because I thought—as I might have when I went to Africa, that my particular Christian message had to be preached to people because it was the only way to God—but more because I saw a ministry to sick children and their families as a way of living out my faith in a compassionate and caring God. It also seemed a natural step to seek ordination and to be ordained a deacon in 1996.

While women cannot be priests in the Anglican Diocese of Sydney, I was always given many opportunities to speak of my different understanding of God and of recent biblical scholarship, and since my ordination have worked in churches where this different understanding was welcomed and discussed. Indeed, my present church is the one where *Eremos* began as a group of people exploring their faith more widely. In my doctoral thesis—"The Dignity of Waiting: A Theology for Resources for Those who Accompany the Terminally Ill"—I speak of the journeying and connecting God who absorbs all that happens and is changed in the process. This has replaced, for me, the image of the avenging, punishing God who was part of the culture of Western Civilization since stories from the Bible and other faith traditions began to be written and circulated. My membership of the Women's Interfaith Network for the last ten years has enabled me to meet women from many other faiths who have been on a similar journey.

Viewing God as the Energy of Connection, I have come to believe that the stories Jesus told were of such a God. I believe that we are all co-creators with God and the writings of scholars such as Dom Crossan, Marcus Borg, Brandon Scott and Lloyd Geering have confirmed me in an understanding of the human Jesus who was tuned in to such a God. Feminist, Process and Jesus Seminar theologians, including the writings of Australian progressives such as Val Webb and Lorraine Parkinson, have contributed to my enjoyment of groups such as the Centre for Progressive Religious Thought, Sydney, where other members seem to be on a similar journey to mine.

Some of them have lost any sense of a God who is present, but I think I find an ever-deepening experience of the work of God's Spirit by joining with them in discussion. I do not think there will be a significant change in the teachings of conservative churches in the short term, but I am privileged to be in a church where new understanding is welcomed and seriously considered, and to belong to groups of people who enjoy exploring their faith together. My faith has changed significantly over the years, and no doubt will continue to do so.

Needed: Clergy With 'ticker' To Challenge Orthodoxy

Lesley Oakley

My connection with the church began from birth. I was born into a Methodist household in the 1940s where church attendance was a given and where family members played an active role in their church. I do not recall any questions about whether we 'go' or not, and in those days there were morning and evening services and Sunday school.

Church music played a central role in family life. I cannot recall theological matters or questions being discussed. The narrative and the theology (eg. incarnation, atonement) were accepted as gospel (!). In retrospect, it seems to me that theology was left to the parson and the congregation enjoyed church life and the sense of belonging that went with it. Of course in those days church life offered a social and sporting life as well as a spiritual one so belonging to the church provided 'a lifestyle'.

Belonging to the Methodist church brought with it certain prohibitions such as not drinking alcohol and not gambling. I believe now that this abstemious behaviour was seen as a social/religious responsibility and part of the Methodist culture in particular and Methodist 'theology'. It is interesting now to look back on this time as culturally and not theologically based, similar to the way deconstruction and contexualisation of the New Testament has provided new insights and understandings of how culture influenced theology. And how times have changed.

Youth Easter camps and summer schools brought with them a number of 'shoulds' for me—I should have a close relationship with Jesus Christ; I should experience prayer as meaningful; I should enjoy church services; when the Billy Graham crusade came along I should experience a wave of forgiveness for sins past and go forward feeling forgiven and 'give my life'.

I look upon those crusade meetings now as a travesty of true spirituality. Having a battered Bible waved at me, telling me that I was guilty of gross sinfulness, that Jesus died for my sins and I should 'come forward' and be saved from my sin and guilt, was something that left me quite unmoved.

Yet people from mainstream protestant churches, encouraged by their leaders, flocked to the Melbourne Cricket Ground (MCG). Looking back on it I think the draw card was not the theology, but the American razzle dazzle theatrics interspersed with George Beverley Shea, emotional choral interludes and the crusade circus. It was a theology of certainty—there was no mystery. Billy Graham knew it all and he was sure as hell going to share it with us. It was so un-Australian. Sorry Billy, but I just didn't get it. But I was not aware, even around that time, that there were serious scholarly challenges to the crusade's theological recipe so embraced by so many.

I first heard of Leslie Weatherhead in my late teens, and I remember he was praised and respected for his preaching among the clergy of the day. In his book, *The Christian Agnostic* the very title challenges certainty. Among many other matters, Weatherhead writes about the tenets that are central to the orthodox Christian belief system—incarnation, atonement and resurrection. He states clearly that he believes Jesus was fully human. "Any man [because of the culture of the day we may forgive him this terminology], to the extent to which he is good, reveals the nature of God". He describes Jesus as "a vessel full of God" but he argues that while Jesus reveals the nature of God he doesn't reveal all the 'activities' of God *(Weatherhead 1965:38).*

Weatherhead quotes the then Dean of St Paul's, Dr Matthews, saying, "We need to get clear on the point that no doctrine of the atonement is part of the Christian faith and that many different views are possible concerning the manner of Divine Forgiveness". Dr Matthews also said, "The mistake which 'orthodox' people make is to suppose that they have all the truth and that nothing more can be known" *(Weatherhead 1965:112).*

Weatherhead argues that the bodily resurrection of Jesus is, and has been, open to all sorts of theories from myth to reality. Weatherhead suggests that some mysterious process of metamorphosis occurred to the body and that what the disciples saw after Easter Day was an apparition. This underlines the notion that we cannot know everything.

This book of Weatherhead's was, as I said, published in 1965. What was being taught in theological college in Melbourne at this time? More to the point, what was being preached from the pulpits of the day at Christmas and Easter? How many congregations heard a challenge to orthodoxy?

Was it a matter of clergy being not so well-read on contemporary theology or was there cherry-picking, leaving out the challenging bits?

I know Bultmann was taught in theological college around this time. Who came out of the college and preached that a major theologian suggested that the resurrection was a myth? Were the Methodist Conference fathers so conservative and powerful that censure would have ensued? Were congregations also too conservative to hear any challenges to the narrative with which they were so familiar? Possibly, but either the theological students rejected the challenges, or they 'lacked ticker'. I wonder how many clergy today are closet progressive theology supporters but also 'lack ticker?'

I want to make the point here that challenges to the orthodox theology need to be handled carefully and sensitively, with a respectful attitude to those who hold dear the literal narrative of gospels. However, it is patronising to underestimate people's capacity to accept that there is more than one way to interpret the stories and parables in the Bible. For many people it is a doorway to new understandings of their role, and the role of the church in the world. I have had conversations with a number of people who say that in the traditional worship service there are certain things they will not recite or sing because they do not believe them.

My exposure to the progressive theology challenges to orthodoxy has opened up a whole new world. As far as I am concerned narrative can come and go, it is the message behind that is important. In fact I believe the narrative frequently gets in the way, and maybe for a lot of people the narrative is the message.

We try to understand the gospels within their cultural and political context, and see the contemporary mainstream church in the context of history, of its story and development over 2000 years. If we strip the accumulated theological and ritualistic layers away, I think we could argue that we are left with a more authentic church that has a greater relevance in today's world. Because, the focus is on the message of social justice, compassion towards those whose experience of life is one of pain, disadvantage, persecution, exclusion, etc., and the message directs us to advocate change to the structural things in our society that perpetuate their suffering. Imagine if the energies now taken up with maintaining religious institutions were redirected to fulfilling the message of the gospel, and in the process, revealing the nature of God.

I can hear the arguments already. 'We need some organisational structure, we like the tradition, the silly hats and funny dresses, the ritual, the theatre.' If we consider the life of Jesus to be the most comprehensive revelation of the nature of God, and then consider the bejwelled mitres, the finery, the elevation of men in the hierarchy of some church cultures, one has to ask how and why it all went so wrong. Human nature seeking power and glory in a church that deifies an itinerant preacher—paradox or unjustifiably incongruous?

I'm not suggesting a 'sandals and sackcloth' church because that is not a good fit with our culture, but so much time and energy are directed to things that are not central to the church's mission. The current inquiries into child sexual abuse and the way churches have responded in their own interest, are examples of so many resources and energies directed to protecting the institution and, in the process, turning their back on the victim.

Sam Keen, in an article in the *Washington Post*, wrote,

> If we want to explore the significance of religion we need to reject both religious literalism and dogmatic atheism and return to the root meaning of religion—'to bind, connect, or reconnect' in its original sense. Religion bears nearly the opposite meaning it has been assigned in modern times. It is not about cult, creed, ceremony, miracle, mystery or authority. Nor is it about occult knowledge of a transcendent God revealed by scriptures or religious institutions
> *(Washington Post, 8 March 2010).*

Having spent my career in child, youth and family welfare, and meeting social injustice every day in the lives of children, families and individuals, I have not always regarded my employment and volunteer work as an expression of faith. For me the notion of faith was inextricably bound to the theology I grew up with, and with which I failed to make a meaningful connection. Stripping away a lot of the 'bumpf' has meant I am more comfortable to relate to the idea of a faith in the message of the gospels and a Christian mission in the world.

My attendance at church is a sign of loyalty to the church community of people who are warm, friendly, and inclusive, and so many of whom work hard in the general community for the benefit of other people. My attendance is also a sign of a commitment to a regular role in the weekly service. For some years I did not attend formal church services because I felt they were irrelevant to my life, and one more obligation to fulfill when my life was at its busiest with family, work, and study. Today I rarely experience the sacred in church worship, in part, because I think I look more for intellectual rather than spiritual challenge. However, I wonder if the epiphany of intellectual awakening is not of itself an experience of the sacred. Discussions in a small group have been often far more stimulating where we can share and explore old and new ideas and sometimes say outrageous things in a safe and accepting environment.

At this time in my life when there is more time for reflection, I am finding the way progressive theology is all-encompassing of the spiritual and the physical, the written word and the historical, the meaning behind the story, is a better 'fit' for me. I have always found the sacred in the secular. For example, living by the sea offers every day the wonder of the natural world of vista and wild-life; being part of or observing acts of compassion and generosity; in the birth of a child; in relationships. Listening to Bach's *Cello Suites* can transport me to another plane of existence that is beyond the human. Progressive theology has confirmed for me that the experience does not need 'God' written on it to be a window into the sacred, the mystical.

A compelling phenomenon of the New Testament scholarship is that while the search for truth and the writing will continue, the mysteries will continue also. There is an interesting relationship between the rational and the spiritual that some people might perceive as a dichotomy because in our age of reason the head is expected to rule. But humanity is more than a physiological marvel. For thousands of years human beings have demonstrated a spiritual dimension that has not been quashed by scientific discoveries. So I am motivated to read more of progressive writings in a way I have not been interested to read traditional theological writings. It has encouraged me to think more about the nature of God rather than God as a figurehead with a name who has been saddled with a variety of human characteristics so our puny human brain can come to some understanding.

We should not be fearful of the unknown, of the mystery. I prefer to think of God as indefinable, the 'breath', the 'wind', the mysterious.

My journey, barely out of the departure station, leads me to ponder what being 'Christian' really means. In the face of the historical evolution of creed and doctrine I am surprised that for some people the essential building blocks of Christianity are set in concrete, not to be challenged. In the first few centuries I read that there were many competing views about the public ministry of Jesus, his divinity or not, the meaning of the crucifixion and whether there was a resurrection of the body. Charles Hedrick, in his article, 'What is Christian' writes that there were many other documents (some 34) from which the four gospels in the current New Testament were chosen. The understanding that church politics, the intended readership, and the deliberate connecting to prophecies in the Jewish tradition to confirm an assertion about Jesus, have really 'muddied the waters' for me. If the Bible is a product of human insight and also human frailty then I am not obliged to approach it with wide-eyed acceptance, and that is a relief.

So what does it mean to be a Christian? Does the *Australian Christian Lobby* speak for me? Do I tolerate what I perceive as prejudice because the speaker believes it is theologically based? When pronouncements from other people who call themselves Christian are not compatible with what I believe is the Christian message of hospitality, inclusiveness and non-discriminatory, then I reject the views and wish I had an equal voice.

So where does this exposure to new ideas and understandings leave me in terms of the traditional church? Mostly unmoved in church worship, interested and animated in formal and informal discussions; still enjoying and being uplifted by 'church' music because while I may not agree with the theology, much of the music is beautiful; not joining in with others to say the Nicene Creed (and I am certainly not alone there); acknowledging members who are active in the local community doing 'good works'; being touched by the care and concern of members for each other and people outside the church community.

I wonder if there will come a time when church members who hold dear the orthodox theological pillars of incarnation, atonement, and resurrection will tell 'progressives' to leave because they can no longer call themselves Christians. Conservatism in church administration and theological training does not augur well for any loosening of the theological straight-jacket we could call orthodoxy.

Preaching 'radical' theology from the pulpit is a challenge for clergy given they have, most likely, made certain orthodox vows at their ordination. I believe a large part of the responsibility falls on the grassroots church goer like me, to avail myself of the scholarship of progressive theology, to stay within the church and respectfully share the good news.

Notes

Hedrick, C. in 'What is Christian' in *The Fourth R*, 19, 4 2006.
Weatherhead, L. *The Christian Agnostic.* Abingdon Press, 1965.

Losing A Paradigm To Save A Life

Adrian Pyle

In 2010 social worker, academic and author Brene' Brown delivered a *Technology, Entertainment, Design* (TED) Talk entitled "The Power of Vulnerability" to a highly appreciative audience. The talk started something of a popular movement exploring notions of human vulnerability and shame in western cultures. It brought to greater attention the effects of an increasing trend towards perfectionism—the desire to conform to externally mandated norms—in those cultures. Among the symptoms of this trend, Brown noted an increasing need to *make the uncertain, certain.* She referred to both political and religious environments as the prime example of where this has occurred and is occurring. She specifically labeled as nonsensical, the idea that something called *faith* could have come to be about *certainties* and not about *questions.*

In 2006 the Progressive Christian Network of Victoria asked me to prepare and deliver *a minor memoir of faith.* I chose to call that reflection "Beyond Belief: When Faith is Something Deeper." That title, and the ideas presented under it, gives some clue to my developing relationship with certainty, or perhaps more correctly with uncertainty. Faith and belief have come to mean the mental assent that we give to a set of fixed propositions about a particular subject. By that definition, my faith journey has indeed been one of trying to explore *beyond belief.* It is indeed nonsense to me that I *get faith* by giving assent to a set of principles developed without regard to my own learning or experiences.

So, how did I get here?

My early years were spent in a family of cultural Christians. I am not trying to undermine the faith of some of my forebears by that statement. In several instances they would have seen their own faith as strong and true and not just a product of Christendom, the historical and cultural phenomenon that made the terms *Australian* and *Christian* almost synonymous. But there were significant aspects of our family situation (and I imagine that this was the case for most middle/late twentieth century Australian families with Anglo-Celtic backgrounds) that suggested we were connected to the church because that was what was expected of us. Certainly I remember my parent's orientation towards faith in this light. Consequently they were very clearly and certainly members of their local Methodist (and later Uniting) Church but they were irregular participants in the broader life and deliberations of the faith community. I also don't think it's unfair to say that my parents understanding of Christian faith retained very much a quality of Sunday school simplicity. I too was given that Sunday school formation in the faith. But while I was a studious and committed student in regular school environments, I found myself seriously distracted on Sundays. Often the lessons seemed to become spaces within which to hone my comedic talents, something I would never dare to do Monday to Friday. Perhaps this was a pointer towards my future yearning for a more exploratory faith environment?

I stayed connected to the church right through my teenage, university and early working years, though always in relatively tenuous fashions. I now understand that there was (and I know still is) an approval-seeking, conformist aspect to my character. It's partly that that made me a committed student in regular educational environments. Luckily in those spaces I was usually stimulated by the learning I was doing, which made the conformance easy to bear. However the often fatuous nature of Sunday school learning (as I saw it then) was beyond the pale it seems. And it seems there were relatively minor consequences for exploring the humorous side of faith which made that a more palatable option, even for someone with my personality. Yet something of that conformist streak applied even with reference to the church, and I continued to hang around on the edges (to, what now, seems like an extraordinary extent). It seems I was searching for some way that I could *do my duty* to be part of a faith community but equally understand faith in a way that resonated with my lived experience.

It was in this time of *hanging around* that I was introduced to the idea of progressive Christianity. And it was in that introduction that my patience started to be rewarded. I could start to let go of the idea that I *should* hang around the church as a notion of good civic behaviour. I could begin to actually belong to a faith community as a means of developing a healthy faith life.

In *Christianity After Religion: The End of Church and the Birth of a New Spiritual Awakening* Diana Butler Bass explores the notion that, within Christendom religion (representing that period between when Christianity was institutionalised within the Roman Empire and the mid twentieth century) the prevailing faith development paradigm was *Believe, Behave, Belong.* I'll call this *paradigm one.* In this paradigm the faith development experience is represented in three linear steps.

> Firstly a person affirms a set of externally mandated, mental propositions relating to the religion. In Christianity this has generally been a set of simplified propositions about the characteristics of Jesus and the effect that knowledge of Jesus has on *the believer.* This is the *believe* step within paradigm one.
>
> Secondly, somehow, these sets of mental propositions give rise to a change in behaviours. Perhaps the most common manifestation of this idea is equally the one I find hardest to understand. It is the relatively recent notion that affirming a set of statements about Jesus should or will give rise to a certain set of behaviours, simplistically labelled *family values*. This is the *behave* step within paradigm one.
>
> Thirdly is the idea that once I behave a certain way, I will be acceptable for admission into the particular religion. This is the *belong* step within *paradigm one* and relies on a rather tribal and hollow definition of belonging, it seems to me. It appears to look at the question of belonging from the perspective of how to maximise exclusions.

Butler Bass goes on to suggest that certain ancient and mystical religious experiences are being recovered in various contemporary, emergent religious expressions. These experiences turn the first paradigm on its head to create *paradigm two*: *Belong, Behave, Believe.* In this, the order is not only reversed but the elements of the paradigm take on more complex, less linear meanings.

> To *belong* here means that faith development starts through the process of finding a space (whether that is a faith community or more general community setting) where my unique understandings and experiences of the world are honoured and can be further

explored. In religious jargon, it is the place where my *indwelling divine* is acknowledged and celebrated. I often explain this idea of belonging by turning the word around: it is indeed the place where my "longing to be" is recognised.

The way we *behave* within this paradigm stems from the acknowledgement of the indwelling divine. Rather than a false connection of unrelated ideas (like *by stating these Jesus principles it means I must live out family values*) the way I behave reflects the best way to honour the divine in all members of the community. It is not an externally set thing but a contextual thing. I don't behave (have to be) according to some external script. Instead my behaviour develops in the context of honouring all souls within the community. The *have to* is a soft notion discovered together and not a hard notion mandated from outside.

What we *believe* in this paradigm comes about as a result of that set of behaviours (we might use the term *practices*) we have developed as a community. We give up the contemporary meaning that has been claimed for the word *believe*: *a set of mental propositions that I choose to regard as fact*. Instead we reclaim more of the earlier etymology of the word in its German form; *belieben*: *that which I can give my love or trust to*. So believing means that we begin to have trust in a way of life where we develop a set of community practices consistent with who we truly are.

Progressive Christianity was important to my faith development because it allowed me to see that *paradigm one* religion—something to which I had always struggled to subscribe—was not the only way. Without knowing it in those terms at the time, it alerted me to the fact that there was a *paradigm two* type faith available for discovery. It did this for me in two ways.

First I came to know of various members of the clergy who were reading and sharing the works of progressive Christian academics and authors. And through those clergy I came to read the work of those authors and academics directly. What these clergy, academics, and authors were often doing, was taking simple mantras of the religion (the mental propositions that became essential beliefs in *paradigm one* Christianity) and reframing them in broader philosophical and historical contexts. Suddenly these propositions were not statements of certainty to which one had to subscribe without question. If these mantras had multiple or contested meanings, the foundation of paradigm one Christianity was at question. Perhaps faith could mean something else.

As my exploration of the progressive case expanded, I realised that Christianity was a place of extraordinary and wonderful complexity. And while progressive Christians sometimes have a problem with *tradition*, I learned to regard that very word with wonder. I recognised that some splinter groups have at times had far too much say in influencing our understanding of *the tradition*. They've moved from *splinter* to *centre* and consequently mainstream denominational Christianity has followed along. For example, the thoughts and practices of many mainstream expressions of church are still influenced by a simplistic late-nineteenth/early-twentieth century American evangelicalism. This movement's basic faith tenets and Biblical-centrism became confused with traditional faith and were merged into the teachings of the mainstream Christian denominations. *Tradition* became *tradition 1950s style*. It has been both scary and liberating to realise this.

Revelations of this type have allowed me to sit more gently with *orthodoxy*, another term I've realised is highly contestable. "Whose orthodoxy and on what terms?" is a question that now occupies my mind when I hear the word. So this does not mean I have become slavishly committed to dogmas and doctrines in a *paradigm one* style. But in delving into the history of those dogmas and doctrines I've come to understand that at least some of their founders were exploring a mythic and metaphorical dimension of faith rather than simplistic linear faith statements.

By way of example, progressive Christian perspectives have helped me come to a much deeper understanding of trinitarian philosophy. I know many progressive Christians who are highly dismissive of trinitarian ideas. And, if the idea of Trinity is a literal god hierarchy, such a dismissal is easy to understand. To an educated, open-minded westerner, such a model of divinity with a god/human understudy is at best bizarre and at worst offensive to the Jewish faith from which Christianity sprang.

But what if that literal god hierarchy is not the only story? What if some of the instigators of the idea were simply trying to find a way to tell a different story about the way the world works? There is at least a suggestion that Roman theology already had its own trinitarian model, as a way of explaining the divine nature of the emperor. This Roman model seems to have had many hierarchical qualities. There are a number of Christian faith claims that take hierarchical Roman thinking, and put a different *political spin* on it. My explorations suggest that early Christians were trying to do the same thing with the idea of Trinity.

So Christian Trinity, from this perspective, was a very early attempt to describe divinity from a highly distributed, non-linear and power-sharing perspective. I see, in this perspective, understandings of the cosmos that are akin (and significantly so) to some of the most challenging, and enlivening ideas from contemporary quantum physics. This is where my explorations are leading me now, and all at the invitation of progressive Christian thinking.

The second way in which progressive Christianity alerted me to *paradigm two* faith, was through its concentration on historical Jesus research. Obviously this type of research has helped me look beyond the simple faith statements of *paradigm one*, as I have just explored. But it also has served a broader purpose in that it has re-orientated my understanding of the *way of Jesus,* aligning that concept with the *paradigm two* understanding of belonging, behaviour, and belief.

I have come to understand the *way of Jesus* through the Hebrew term *derek*. And I have come to understand *derek*, in the context of Jesus' life, to mean *that which I cannot, not do*. Another way to understand that would be *the way I respond when I can truly listen to the holy whispers; the messengers in the relationship between my life and the whole source of life.*

To me this is quite an open concept. I am aware of evidence that Jesus was a committed practitioner of his Jewish faith. But I don't interpret his *derek* as a set of rote, prescribed practices that everyone must follow regardless of context. Indeed, historical Jesus research has given me a stronger insight into how he resisted legalistic religious and political impulses, built relationships across demographic boundaries to understand other ways, and spoke about connection to source as being in the *Basileia of God* (a term often translated simplistically as *kingdom of God*, but which is actually in feminine form and hence suggests an exploration of our connection to source rather than a slavish dedication to Old Father God.)

So this idea of *derek* connotes for me the *paradigm two* definitions of belonging, behaviour, and belief. It feels to me like Jesus favoured the practice of making space for people to find their own orientation to source (rather than having that dictated by patriarchal religious or political systems).

With this understanding, my views about essential religious practice are obviously quite liberal—some may even say anarchic. And I tend to resist answering the question "Do I follow in the way of Jesus?" According to what I have written here, my answer could be a resounding "yes." But I find that people often have a fairly set idea of belief and practice in their mind when they ask that question, and I know that doesn't fit me. I remember someone once telling me that unless one took part in regular recitation of The Jesus Prayer, one could not consider oneself as living *in the way of Jesus.* Now we could have a significant academic argument about Jesus' own relationship to that prayer. But a more fundamental response is that I think Jesus' *way* was more about essence (finding the authentic connection to source for our context) rather than prescription. Perhaps my favourite quote in support of this comes from Canadian academic David Galston,

> We simply have to learn to admit and understand that we are all human. No one knows the answer. There is no correct way to follow the teaching of… Jesus and no correct way to do church with… Jesus. Jesus taken seriously is the permission to break the habit of Christianity. So go forward and be habit breaking.

Which brings me back to where we started; with an address entitled "The Power of Vulnerability" and a question as to why such a challenging topic would generate a popular movement? As I read some of the reactions to that presentation it occurs to me that people—particularly western people—are looking for a circuit breaker from a current of rigidity, perfectionism, expected clarity and certainty. We are cottoning on, it seems, to the fact that these expectations are superficially imposed and don't represent our authentic relationship to the whole. People are finding various ways to *save their real lives* by discarding an old paradigm of control. Progressive Christian thinking has been one of those ways for me; in fact it has been one of the most significant ways I have been able to shift paradigms. And in that way it really has been a life saver.

The Journey from Mythos to Logos and Back

Durham Smith

From ancient times the Greeks employed two terms to describe the kinds of knowledge we use to influence our decisions, and which give meaning to life and reality *(Armstrong 2000).* Mythos is the experience derived from our cultural history; it may be loyalty to a family tradition, or to a tribe, or to a belief system that conditions our response to life. Associated culture stories and myths are not always rational or subject to reasoned proof, but they seem to provide light and insight to eternal truths. Mythos provides the vision which persuades us to live in a certain way, because we are convinced that it contains something valuable, even if we do not understand its logic. Logos on the other hand, is the practical, rational and logical analysis of observable facts, and persuade us to function in real-life situations. Logos requires a reason for a particular course of action and unless there is a reasonable explanation of phenomena, it cannot be believed or acted on.

Many faith stories are of people who have lived predominantly by logos, pursuing a pragmatic way of life because it "works" for them, even if it lacks morality, even perhaps of crime or cruelty. Then there is an experience which brings a dramatic change of heart and radical enlightenment. John Newton, the eighteenth century author of the popular song *Amazing Grace*, who was known for his debauchery and cruelty, and later commanded a ship involved in the slave trade, had an overwhelming experience of the "amazing grace" of the forgiving love of God. In these faith stories mythos bursts upon logos with compelling force.

But they are not my story, which is much more mundane. There is no overt history of crime, no sudden light, no searing, bruising crisis which tore my life apart. It was more the slow realisation that mythos taught as a child simply made no sense in the real world.

I was brought up in a country town. My father was an Anglican minister, and the church was a central focus for much community activity. I had no pressure to attend church services, but did so. The message was "good", and

I accepted it quite naturally. By aged seventeen I had made the decision to become a doctor and a medical missionary. It was no big deal and seemed the most normal thing to do. I wanted to serve God. My faith belief was not totally blind as I remember being bored in Sunday School and wondering how a man dying on a Cross could take away sin, and, in any case, I did not feel particularly sinful! But they were not seriously challenging questions. My adolescent faith was mythos without logos. It empowered me to a commitment, and yet no serious questions were asked about its rationale. The mythos of belief was so strong that I just accepted that there were divine mysteries.

However, it was about to be sorely tested, because the year I left school at the end of 1940, WWII was raging. I briefly started medicine at university but, as a teenager, I was very disturbed with an emotional conflict between patriotic pressure to enlist and Christian conscience against violence, and with no clear conviction I opted to join the Services. In conscience, the adolescent subconscious mythos of a caring Divine Presence was still there, and in blind faith the suffering and evil of war were accepted as more of the divine mysteries. But later, this was seen as a cop-out. Although my personal Army service was insignificant, and in fact I later returned to continue the medical course, the pain and suffering of others was real and horrendous. Six of my closest friends from school died in service. I could no longer shelter behind blind faith in a mystery that God "out there" had it all under control. If God was not there in the midst of human pain, he was not anywhere. And if Jesus died to take away evil, we saw little evidence of it. There were serious questions and they continued throughout the war.

I immersed myself in the student life at university and completed the medical course in 1948. The heart of a university is the freedom of discussion in philosophy, politics, history, and rationalist and religious thought. I enjoyed the stimulation of the clubs of these disciplines, particularly the Student Christian Movement (SCM) which was liberal and stimulating. The leaders were leading academic scholars in history, philosophy, science and theology, prepared to ask serious questions about the relation of faith to contemporary challenges of science and society, about biblical interpretation, and about classical doctrines. Christian living was opened up to me as far more than personal morality. We were excited by the vision of a new world, seen through the eyes of idyllic student life.

We married on graduation and I commenced Hospital Residency but training was interrupted by a year out of action with TB—a tough time for my wife and newborn son—and two more years out of normal progression working in sanatoria. However, being perfectly well thereafter, specialist surgical training and postgraduate degrees were completed and consultant appointments followed. So began a lifetime in Paediatric Surgery.

Now with a family, we returned to the world of the local church. The theological questions, so openly discussed at the SCM, were foreign to the church community. It was sterile, replete with repeated clichés and unquestioned dogma, full of platitudes about biblical texts and personal morality, but with little reference to any biblical or theological scholarship, nor to the wider issues of contemporary society. My theological questions at first were no doubt immature, and centred around the person of Jesus—not his moral teachings, but the constant confusion of Jesus supposed to be God ("the Word was God"), but at the same time Son of God. To my simple mind that meant there were two separate entities, not one. We prayed to Almighty God "through Jesus Christ", again suggesting Jesus was separate. So who was he?

Then the questions became more difficult. The phrase "Son of God" was a problem in itself; in traditional theology it is a central concept of Jesus, said to confirm his Divinity. I was challenged when asked by traditionalists, almost in an accusatory tone, "Don't you believe that Jesus is the Son of God?"—challenged, not because I did not want to believe it, but because the question was fundamentally meaningless. The concept of God as "Father" and Jesus as "Son" is a human construction. God as "Father" is one particular image which, to our human minds, expresses something beautiful, loving and caring like we experience in a good father. It seems very appropriate for God so we use this image. With the image of God as "Father" it follows that one in a special relationship to God could be a "Son". But these are only human images, and as human images they prove nothing about the "divinity" of Jesus, only that there was a special relationship.

Next, it began to bug me that Christianity more and more seemed to be a self-indulgent religion of guilt, obsessed with sin and human failure, and our Sunday liturgies wallowed in it. The concept of humanity being basically depraved and in need of a rescuer seemed to me a decidedly unhealthy concept of life—and I still do. As a young paediatrician I found it abhorrent that holding a new-born baby in my arms, experiencing its incredible beauty and innocence, and then with any conscience claim it is "born in sin", and has to be "reborn", as confessed in the Baptismal Service. The whole idea is a monstrous distortion of the beauty and sacredness of life. In any case, the concept of a "fall" to an inheritantly flawed state, from previously being perfect and "made in the image of God", was illogical when all the biological and cosmological evidence was that there never was a time of perfection in man or nature from which we "fell"—we are just an evolving and incomplete species and world from earlier forms. Later I came to recognise that the institutional churches are steeped in this traditional and fundamental tenet of Christianity as a "fall-guilt-redemption" paradigm in which redemption comes exclusively through the atoning death of Jesus on the Cross. I reject it, as we will see. God may be calling us to a very different paradigm, a "Spirit-filled" paradigm where the Divine Presence, revealed in different faith traditions, is the in-dwelling sacred gift to every person, empowering us to love, and bringing humanity to its fullness.

Further, I found it morally highly questionable that an innocent Jesus was required to die ("to give his life as a ransom to many") as a substitute for us, because God demanded that the price of sin had to be paid for, and this was the price of forgiveness. It suggested a God for whom the satisfaction of his justice was more important than compassion for his Son, *which seemed quite inconsistent with the God about whom Jesus had been witnessing.* Nor could I understand how forgiveness was centred in the *death* of Jesus as the sole means of restoring an estranged humankind to a relationship with God. It was strange because the Bible quite clearly records that forgiveness did not commence with Jesus. The Old Testament is replete with references to God's forgiveness and establishing a new relationship, so redemptive action existed before Jesus. Further, "the Son of Man has authority *on earth* to forgive sins" *(Mk. 2.10),* that is, Jesus had the power to forgive sins *before* he died, (as he did with several sick people) so the death was not the necessary factor. And finally, none of these doctrinal arguments seemed to have much relationship to the moral values and way of life taught by Jesus.

These and many other questions swirled around as we tried to be loyal to the local church, but after ten years or so we became frustrated and had had enough. We stopped going to church for twenty-nine years, as it no longer had any relevance to our busy lives. The religious belief I had embraced as a youth was now seriously doubted because it simply did not make sense intellectually. We were living in a different world and what might have been inspirational in the fourth century was now irrelevant, if not positively obstructive to a re-interpretation in contemporary terms.

In these twenty-nine years one tried to live by the moral values of love, compassion, and respect for life as best one could, values shared with secular friends, but with no interest in affiliation with any religious institution.

So what brought me back? Even in those twenty-nine years of theological wilderness a basic faith in a Divine transcendence never quite went away. Ideas simmered away dimly beneath the surface, a kind of subliminal gut feeling, that there was a truth there somewhere, but it never became compelling. It was the witness of Bishop John Shelby Spong through interviews on TV who spoke a new language and at my then late age of 73, stimulated me to read some of his books *(Spong 2001).* It opened up a new world.

Essentially, his realism was to start with humanity, in real people in life and experience, and not with an incomprehensible God "out there". God had to be seen in the context of human experience, in the worth, value, and potential of humanity, and in its failures and blemishes, or else God is myth. To have the courage to say "no" to the repeated clichés and dogmas of institutional religion, even to the most central propositions considered to be fundamental, *if they made no sense.* As Spong said, "I cannot believe in my heart that which my mind cannot accept". It meant looking seriously at the biblical evidence again from afresh, as a human document, without any preconditions or presumptions of it being the "inspired Word of God", but honouring it by good scholarship. It meant relating faith to the real contemporary world of human relationships, science, political systems, gender and race issues, and the natural world. One may "move on" from Spong, or begin to fashion one's own interpretation, but undoubtedly he was the catalyst for a re-awakening for thousands like me and for which we are forever grateful.

Because the obstruction to faith was the credibility of doctrine, the search necessarily began with a re-examination of the two main propositions fundamental to the definition of Christian faith; firstly, a profound commitment to belief in Jesus *the Christ*, literally the Divine God in human form; and secondly, that Jesus' sacrificial death is the sole means of restoring a sinful and estranged humankind to a relationship with God. Several years of study have resulted in a book *(Smith 2011)* which analyses the biblical references and other evidence to add a rational logos to the mythos of faith. Space only permits the briefest summary of conclusions here. Readers are referred to the book for detailed analysis.

The obvious place to start was with Jesus himself. Jesus is the ultimate authority, not Paul, not John, not other letter writers, not Athanasius, not the Great Church Councils. What did Jesus himself say in the Gospels, the only source of his sayings and life experiences, even allowing for the constant textual problem as to which words are authentically from Jesus and which are the writers interpretation of what his words meant to them? *The remarkable thing is that Jesus himself never embraced either of the two fundamental propositions above!* There is no real evidence that Jesus himself ever claimed to be God; there are only four statements *by others* in his presence claiming his divinity and to which he gave equivocal answers, and not a single reference that he ever initiated any claim to the title himself. *Is it not remarkable that if the doctrine of Divine Incarnation is so central to Christian belief (and the consequential theology which derives from it) he never referred to it?* It was never an essential part of his mission.

Further, and conversely, there is a plethora of statements from Jesus that he clearly saw himself as quite separate from the "Father", *dependent on the Father working through him for his gifts and his power.* To quote just one reference among several: "It is the Father, living in me, who is doing his work" *(Jn. 14:11).* It is particularly significant that Jesus himself points to the gift of eternal life as coming, not from belief in himself, but from the Father—"I tell you the truth whoever hears my word and believes him who sent me has eternal life" *(Jn. 5:24).* The overall impression in the Gospels is not the conception of Jesus as God that is significant but that, as a human, *God is able to act through him.*

The second great proposition is that in the sacrificial death of Jesus on the Cross, sin is taken away from humankind, and it is *only through his death that forgiveness and "salvation" is offered.* There is no question that there was a sacrificial death, that is, he was executed for the values he had promoted in life, but this is a different question from the claim to forgiveness and "salvation" through his death. I have already commented that forgiveness did not commence with Jesus. Further, in the words attributed to Jesus himself only twice did Jesus ever assert that it was in his death that sin is overcome, and both are of doubtful authenticity. At the Last Supper "This is my blood of the covenant, which is poured out for many *for the remission of sins*", the fact is the words in italics only appear in Matthew's Gospel *(Mt. 26:28).* Is it not remarkable that if the sacrificial death to rescue us from sin is so fundamentally central in Christian theology, Mark, Luke and John apparently did not remember it as sufficiently important to be included? The second is the "ransom" reference, the basis of the so-called penal substitution atonement theory, entrenched in traditional theology, on which I have commented above. *Is it not remarkable that, if a redemptive act through Jesus' death is so fundamentally central, there are only two doubtful references from Jesus himself to support it?* Nowhere in the synoptic gospels does Jesus make any reference that the kingdom is dependent on any action that he has to do, in particular that it is dependent on his death.

Rather, there is a plethora of evidence that Jesus saw his death quite differently? Jesus predicted his death on several occasions, each time expressing complete faith that God would "raise him from the dead", but it is "*God my Father*" who will forgive us and who will bring us into a new reconciled relationship ("*so that your father in heaven may forgive you your sins" (Mk. 11:25)*). *All the action is God's action, not Jesus' action. That* is what Jesus was pointing to, *that* is where salvation lies, not in his death, nor in his sacrifice, but in *God's* continuing actions of forgiving, of reconciling and making new, actions always present from the beginning of creation, before Jesus, in Jesus, and beyond Jesus, extending into eternity, *because that is the nature of this eternal God.* Jesus accepted death *in complete trust that new life would follow*, and *this* is what he was promising his disciples and all of us. But not just after death. "Resurrection" is all about transformation to newness of life, to new values, new inspirations, new directions, and new choices. "Eternal life", "heaven", "salvation" are not some future promises after death, but are words to define a living relationship with the Divine Presence *here and now in this life* through the gift of the Holy Spirit transforming our lives. We are already "in heaven" and "in eternal life" *when we commit ourselves to that Presence.* I do not know what happens after death, if anything at all, but if something does continue, then death is a transformation into a new dimension of life, of which we cannot conceive scientifically, to continue that relationship in a more mature and intimate way.

So what was Jesus' central message? It is the coming of the Kingdom of God, the reign of God in our hearts, the call to respond to the gift of the Holy Spirit within, and so be empowered to build the Kingdom of God on earth. In all his loving actions Jesus himself is clearly filled with the Divine Presence, the Holy Spirit, which impelled him to these values. *His "divinity" is in his humanity*, not in his piety or some otherworldliness as "God". The uniqueness of Jesus is that in him the Divine Presence brings humanity to its fullness. Jesus lived out love in life and death, revealing to us the depth and breadth of what love can be; he was filled with so much love that through him we come to believe that God the Spirit is the source of love.

Just as Jesus was filled with the Divine Spirit, the gift of the Spirit to *all* people is a central recurring theme of the New Testament, and many texts could be quoted. *"We love because God first loved us", "if we love one another, God lives in us and his love is made complete in us" (1Jn. 4:12-19).* The wonder of creation is that *all* humankind is filled with the Divine Spirit as part of the essence of human life (and of all life itself in the biological world) irrespective of race, colour, gender or sexual orientation. Jesus had such love and trust in the potential of humanity to be brought to its fullness through the indwelling power of the Divine Presence in all people, that he calls us to build the Kingdom of God on earth, a kingdom where selfless love, limitless compassion, serene justice, peace and respect for life is possible. He was killed in defence of these values, and to the end trusted completely *in God's love* to bring forgiveness and healing for human failures, new life, transformation and wholeness to all people. The gift of the Spirit is an undeserved, humbling, almost preposterous gift, and yet that is the Good News promised by Jesus. The possibilities are truly unimaginable.

The centrepiece of the Gospel now began to expand for me beyond the divisive arguments of doctrine and dogma. We can move from a "fall-guilt-redemption" paradigm to a "Spirit-filled" paradigm. The centrepiece is the meaning of "wholeness" in human life (and in the natural world) through the Spirit. Right through biological life we see the direction to healing, to growth, to repair, in other words to wholeness—a thesis expanded elsewhere *(Smith 2012)*. In medicine we can explain and define many of the mechanisms in growth and healing, the interaction of physical and chemical forces, membrane potentials, genetic and other biological processes, but unless the damage of adverse conditions is overwhelming, nothing quite explains why the *direction*, the *intent*, is always to fullness of life and new growth. There are forces here perhaps beyond physics and chemistry. It seems there is a "life-force" built in to the very nature of biological life.

What shall we call this life-force? We can call it G-O-D, the Divine Presence. I believe life itself is the manifestation of the Divine Presence, present in every biological living organism, including humanity. We call it the Immanence of God, the Divine Presence within. Our humanity itself is divine in its very biological essence, and it works through the mechanisms of our physical and mental structures. The Divine Presence is, indeed, a gift of life, not determined by us, one we do not control. *Our* human task is to unravel and refine the mechanisms in every field of human endeavour and in the natural world, so this gives meaning and purpose to science, philosophy, education, learning, and creative art.

The Bible, of course, gives us evidence of the gift of life. In the ancient text of Genesis there is a remarkable symbolic statement that "God formed man out of dust from the ground, and breathed into his nostrils the breath of life; and man became a living being". And in the New Testament, I wonder if this is what John could have meant in the first chapter of his gospel. The traditional interpretation is that "the Word was God …in him was life… And the Word became flesh and dwelt among us", is referring to Jesus of Nazareth. Could it be that when the Word became flesh and dwelt among us, it has a much wider meaning? Maybe it is not referring to Jesus but to the Divine Presence entering all of biological life ("flesh") and dwells in all life, and is, indeed, the very basis of life. That truly is an Incarnation of wondrous proportions.

What does wholeness of life mean, and how does it relate to our daily lives? Wholeness means living abundantly in the engagement with life in peace and joy, and the capacity for love, compassion, justice, and respect for life in relationship with others. These values are the potential of all humanity, made possible by the gift of the indwelling Divine Presence. The presence of the Holy Spirit in every living being enlightens, inspires, motivates and empowers us to love. This is the uniqueness of Jesus, who responded fully to the gift of the Spirit, but the gift is for all people.

In human life wholeness does not mean perfection in every parameter of physical form and mental ability, perfect health—we are still subject to the constraints of human biology, our genetic history, environmental hazards, the process of aging, and our ignorance, as yet, of all the factors which impede health—but whatever our physical and mental state, with or without disability, wholeness is still to engage with life in peace and joy within those human constraints, and still be empowered to love and receive love.

Although the *ultimate* aim of God may be perfection, God never imposes it upon us. To do so would be to destroy our freedom and dignity, and this is the higher priority of his love. We are truly free, free to mess up—either wilfully or in ignorance—and suffering and tragedy can still occur. But God's extraordinary love is in honouring us by trusting in the potential of human life; God sets the objective of the intent of perfection, but waits and waits for us to choose to align ourselves with the Divine Presence and purpose. That is the depth of his love, even though the fulfilment of his own desire for a perfect world, his kingdom, is at stake, with our human failures and our incompleteness. Moltmann's phrase of the "waiting God" is profound.

How does this affect daily life? We are called to live with a consciousness of the real and living Presence of the Holy Spirit. We have to feel that Presence every day, bring ourselves into affinity with it, and *trust it*. We do not need to ask for its power. *It is already there.* When we need to love, the power to love is there. When we need comfort, the Comforter is there. When we need strength, the strength is there. When we need guidance, enlightenment is there. *The gifts and the power are given to us and are already within us by the indwelling Spirit*. It takes nothing away from the need or responsibility for us to mobilize our own resources and employ them to the full; but our job is to turn our direction *to trust God's Presence, to really believe it*, and then using our talents, such as they are, within our human capacity and limitations to engage fully with the world in our work, in our home, in our play, and in our community.

It is through prayer that we align ourselves with the Spirit, and the Divine Presence has all the power and love *already available* to us within ourselves and others, if only we open our hearts and minds to it in trust, to be executed through our physical bodies and minds to the degree possible within our capacity. When the prayer is specifically for others, just as God communicates with us in our own prayers, the same universal Spirit in all people will communicate with those for whom we pray. Trusting in the Spirit we become part of the spiritual ambience, which embraces the one, we pray for. Our prayer is not expecting a God "out there" to come and zap the universe to our bidding, but in shared love to bring the one prayed for into affinity with the Divine Presence already within *them*, and *to open their hearts and minds* to receive and respond to the gifts for their needs. This does not involve changing the rules of nature or asking God to manipulate change beyond what he already establishes in the human personality. I see no credibility in any prayers for God to manipulate changes in the laws of the physical universe or in our physical bodies: but in aligning with the Spirit wholeness is possible within the limits of our biological capacity.

Wholeness is thus to engage with life in joy and hope in all its abundance, in work, relationships, care for others, social justice, creativity in science and art, and respect and understanding of the natural world.

And so in this chronicle of one person's faith experience, we began with a childhood of trust in a mythos of a loving God, but without a supporting base of a logos which might have questioned its rationale. Then, for many years we had lives dominated by logos, consumed by the practicalities of life and work, and with it the rejection of a mythos of theological belief which simply did not make sense. We then looked again *at the primary evidence in the Gospels* to find a Jesus whose life and teachings bore little resemblance to traditional doctrines and institutional dogma; indeed, he pointed to the Divine Presence, "God", in much larger dimensions than himself, a presence as universally present in every person, inspiring, enlightening and enabling us to aspire to *the very fullness of humanity*, a Spirit with the potential to empower us to limitless love, infinite compassion, and serene justice and peace for all. The possibilities become unimaginable, if we choose to open our hearts and minds to respond, as Jesus did. Although challenging to traditional believers, the universality of the Divine Presence removes the specificity of Jesus as the sole agent for reconciliation and harmony with God. It is only for us Christians that he is the revelation for faith, but the same God speaks through other revelations and offers *the same redeeming power and gift of new life.* With all the deep blemishes in Christianity and in other faiths, and there are many, and our human incompleteness, that gift is still there. Finally, not addressed in this paper, is the majesty of all life and creation in the natural world, to which we bow in awe and wonder. God is not confined to humanity, all of creation is of God and we worship the transcendent Spirit vastly beyond our deepest imaging.

Faith has become a new logos in which both heart and mind can be reconciled. I can now believe in the mythos of my heart that which the logos of my mind can accept, even though we only know and see "in part".

For me, *the great 'good news of the Gospel' is not God made man in Jesus, nor is it salvation from sin through Jesus' death, but the empowerment to love by the gift of the Holy Spirit. This is what Jesus had, and to which he responded fully; in his humanity he showed us the potential of humanity, that loving is a human possibility, and by the power of the Divine Presence within us all can be brought to the fullness of humanity from which love, compassion and justice flows outward for all. "Wholeness" of life is God's promise for all people.*

Notes

Armstrong, K. *The Battle for God: Fundamentalism in Judaism, Christianity and Islam*. London: HarperCollins Publishers, 2000.

Smith, D. See www.pcnvictoria.org.au An address on "What do we mean by God?" given to the Progressive Christian Network of Victoria, July 2012.

———————, *Search for Understanding: The Fullness of Life. Wishful Hope or a Real Possibility?* (Second Edition). Gordon: Minipublishing, 2011.

Spong, J. S. *A New Christianity for a New World. Why Traditional Faith is Dying and how a New Faith is Being Born.* San Francisco: HarperCollins, 2001. (This book contains the references to nine other books and papers by Spong, the principle ones being *Rescuing the Bible from Fundamentalism; Resurrection – Myth or Reality; Why Christianity must Change or Die).*

From Evangelical To Progressive. My Faith Journey

Richard C G Smith

Early Years—Sunday School the Great Outdoors

My father was a Kentish fruit farmer. My mother from Norway. To this Anglican-Lutheran combination I was born in 1942, number two of four. All were christened in the Anglican Church, although our parents were not regular church goers, instead we spent our time on Sundays playing on the farm, in the surrounding woods, streams and ponds. Nature with its wonders was our world. All the magic of Christmas was played out on Christmas Eve in the Norwegian tradition. God beyond the sky appeared as Father Christmas and Easter as coloured eggs hidden in the garden. Easter and Christmas forays to church with the extended family usually terminated early for us kids with a quick toilet exit to the gravestones of our ancestors.

All this changed in December 1951 when my grandparents arrived by boat in transit from Norway to New Zealand where their other children had migrated in the aftermath of WWII. Grandfather was diagnosed with cancer and lived with us until he died six months later, but during this time Rev John Yeo, the local vicar provided much needed support. As a result grandfather's tomb stone was engraved "God is Love" (*1 John 4:8*), the summation of his lifelong struggle through two world wars to understand "God" in the twentieth century and his parting message to us all. This encounter had a profound effect on our family and has remained foundational in my faith journey.

Adolescence and Rev John Yeo's prophetic wisdom

To progress from primary to secondary school I needed remedial coaching and Mrs Yeo provided this. After my lessons, I had many theological conversations with Rev Yeo. At Sutton Valence Public School, I enjoyed chapel each morning and was confirmed by the Bishop of Croydon, who preached on "Behold, I stand at the door and knock: if any man hear my voice, and open the door, I will come in to him, and will sup with him and he with me" (*Rev. 3:20*). He told us when we took the wafer at communion to pray "Come, Lord Jesus, Come", (*Rev. 22:20b*). Words that still echo in my mind when I take communion.

As I headed off to university I remembered Rev Yeo warning that reading the Bible was not easy. He would not recommend it for beginners unless I was prepared to get something of the background and acquire the knowledge that would put the whole thing in proper perspective. To do that I had to have a knowledge of the true purpose of the book and the men who wrote it and the purpose for which God inspired it.

University—Evangelical Theology

At Wye College, London University, all that was on offer in this country village was an Evangelical Union, no Student Christian Movement. The positive benefits of the EU was three years intensive Bible reading, extemporary prayer, and lasting friendships. A Plymouth Brethren contemporary grounded us in evangelical and later pentecostal theology. Occasionally we went to London to hear leading evangelical preachers such as Dr Martyn Lloyd-Jones (1899-1981) and Rev John Stott (1921-2011) and to Inter Varsity Fellowship camps. On Sundays I attended the Baptist Church or Plymouth Brethren. I was rebaptised by emersion and later, in the Holy Spirit. Rev Yeo who obviously knew me well from our many discussions, advised my perplexed parents that I would soon move out of this phase. Following similar evangelical exposure, my siblings and I now span the theological spectrum from fundamentalist to progressive, which always creates interesting family gatherings and theological discourse, at least for me!

Agricultural Science at Wye taught me to "grow two ears of wheat or blades of grass where one grew previously". At this time, with only two billion people to feed, the notions that the world was finite, many agricultural practices environmentally destructive, highly dependent on fossil fuels and a significant contributor to greenhouse warming had not entered the curriculum. Computers were on the horizon, the internet not yet visible.

At Oxford University for a Diploma in Agricultural Economics I attended an evangelical Anglican Church on Sundays, but avoided EU type bible studies. Economics gave me insights into the centrality of human competition for wealth creation, that economic growth follows population growth, role of government fiscal stimulus in times of depression and progressive taxation for the redistribution of wealth from the rich to the poor. Investment required forgoing of current consumption, but innovative credit creation turned this concept into the Global Financial Crisis (GFC) of 2008.

Australia, Marriage and the God of Miracles Fails to Deliver

While at Oxford I applied for the position of Farm Management Consultant with the Broomehill Farm Advisory Group in South Western Australia to manage over one million acres of agriculture. Late 1965 I was on the tarmac at Perth airport as a £10 pom to be met by the chairman of the Group, Alf Barrett, a keen Methodist, so I would often attend church with his family.

Some months later, to find a dance partner from the new intake of nurses at the Katanning District Hospital, I chanced upon a lovely RN. We were married six months later in a Presbyterian Church in Perth where her parents attended. While a PhD student at University of Western Australia in 1970 our second son Phillip was born and later diagnosed with hydrocephalus due to birth trauma. The minister counseled that prayers of faith might deliver a miracle. After weeks of intense prayer but no miracle, we placed our faith in neurosurgery. The miracle of medical science trumped the miracles of a supernatural God. My wife, who had been a (sceptical) Baptist Sunday School attendee from an early age, had already instinctively rejected evangelical theology and substitutionary atonement and was dubious about supernatural miracles; she was after all a nurse. She has forever been a corrective to my religious naivety and Phillip a stabilising joy in my life.

Within weeks following Phillip's two operations, we departed for the USA on a CSIRO Post-doctoral scholarship at the University of California, Davis, (UCD) where we attended the Uniting Methodist Church. I became captivated by a TV show, "I Believe in Miracles" by Kathryn Khulman (1907-76), then one day her faith healing ministry came to Sacramento. Hoping for a miracle we joined the crowd, among them other parents of disabled children. As the service progressed we observed the "healings" were adults making decisions to exit their wheelchairs or discard their crutches. Existence of a supernatural God able to suspend the natural processes of the universe was not evident.

At UCD my application of "Systems Theory" to the modelling of ecological systems revealed to me the amazing ordering of the natural world through the interconnection and interdependence of all species and processes of life. The sacredness of this ordering seemed more significant to me for human welfare than orthodox Christian theology.

New South Wales, the Aftermath of Donald Mackay's Murder and Liberation Theology

On return to Australia in 1972 we moved first to University of New England, Armidale NSW where a sabbatical took me to Israel to study irrigation, then Syria to advise the new International Centre for Research into Dry land Agriculture (ICARDA). At weekends I visited the archaeological world of Jesus and early Christianity.

In 1980 I joined CSIRO, Griffith, NSW to lead their irrigation research. We attended the Uniting Church where Barbara Mackay was a member. Her husband, anti-drugs campaigner Donald Mackay had been murdered in 1977 and as his body had not been found, the Government was refusing an inquest causing distress to Barbara and her four young children. Don's estate could not be settled and most members of the church and community felt powerless. I responded to her cause by heading the Concerned Citizens of Griffith to lobby Government for action.

Against the backdrop of my public activity to achieve justice for the Mackay family and citizens of Griffith I was invited by Rev John Butson to study to be a Lay Preacher. Our theological text was Dr Gordon Dicker's *Faith with Understanding* which gave me a good grounding in theology. Thirsting to read more widely, I soaked up other texts, particularly Willi Marxsen's *The Resurrection of Jesus of Nazareth*, much to the next minister's concern that I should question this Christian fundamental.

Living the Questions: In the Systemic Corruption that led to the rise of the Drug Trade and Murder of Mackay, where was God?

Except for the Rev Fred Nile, there appeared to be a general silence in the UCA about these issues. Our church studied the Bethel Series, memorising Bible verse upon Bible verse. To my wife's question who was this God who does these marvellous deeds, the minister looked aghast and answered, "He is your Heavenly Father". Later he cited research from the USA that evangelical Christianity had to be embraced if the church was to survive. We found ourselves heading in the opposite direction, seeking God in the "historical Jesus" and the concrete situations of life.

Barbara Mackay hoped someday that divine intervention would resolve the corruption in Griffith. She died on 24 February 2001 still hoping, a few weeks after Frederick Bazley who had been convicted of Don's murder had been released from prison. My past experience in seeking a miracle had led me to an alternative understanding of how God works in history. The stock market crash in 1987 saw much of our meager retirement investments reduced to dust. For as Jesus said: "He causes his sun to rise on the evil and the good, and sends rain on the righteous and the unrighteous." (*Matt 5:45*).

Seeking to live with the questions, Rev John Smith (no relation to the editor of this collection) of "God Squad" Melbourne, introduced me to books such as, *Jesus before Christianity: The Gospel of Liberation* by Albert Nolan and Gustavo Gutierrez, *A Theology of Liberation*. This helped me to understand that justice in the Mackay case could only be achieved through the power of "truth and goodness" being greater than the power of "evil". Or in a summation of Edmund Burke: "All that is necessary for the triumph of evil is that good men do nothing". My theology was captured in an interview with Alan Harvey published in *On Being*, July 1986 entitled "Piercing the Heart of Evil".

Church Alumni 1989 to 2005—Observing the Devastations of the Earth from Satellite

Pressure was building on me from within Griffith. Fortunately a Research Associateship at NASA Goddard Space Flight Centre, Maryland USA, enabled us to leave in late 1988. Returning to Western Australia in 1990, I took a position to develop the State Government's capability in Satellite Remote Sensing. For the next twenty years I worked on the impact of humans on the earth's surface using satellite observations and became increasingly conscious of the disconnection between religion and the reality of the interdependence of all life forms on earth. Something was amiss as the Abrahamic religions largely ignored the destruction humans were heaping upon God's earth. In fact often the reverse, with James G. Watt, Secretary of State in Reagan's Administration proclaiming that: "After the last tree is felled Christ will come back".

Living the Questions and an Epiphany in the Savannah and Rainforests of SE Asia

Wildfires in the tropical savannahs of Northern Australia and rainforests of SE Asia were adversely impacting biodiversity, greenhouse emissions, and the fate of indigenous people. In Indonesia the devastation was a result of the West's insatiable consumer demand for palm oil, and in Australia aboriginal dispossession from their land. Problems that science could quantify but not solve. This was the rightful province of religion.

My ecologically driven spiritual awakening coincided with our eldest son and his family arriving back from the USA in 2003. They attended a UCA to maintain continuity with their Presbyterian Church in Utah to provide their children an alternative to Mormonism. Matthew invited me to the *Living the Questions* series (LtQ) on Progressive Christianity, led by the minister. The "historical Jesus" of the Jesus Seminar scholars captivated my imagination and I was invited by the minister to chair the Mission and Outreach Task Group, All Saints, Floreat. With other similarly motivated members two innovative initiatives were born to assist dispossessed indigenous people. One to Aboriginal people of the former Uniting Church Mission at Mowanjum near Derby, the other to Papuans in Eastern Indonesia.

To engage with progressive Christianity I attended Common Dreams1 Conference, World Parliament of Religions, and Jesus Seminar (USA) 2009, Common Dreams2 (2010), the John Dominic Crossan Lectures in Sydney (2012) and Common Dreams3 (2013). My lay preaching was re-activated by Wembley Downs Uniting Church, encouraged to explore "progressive worship" and George Stuart hymns sung to traditional tunes. Being on the Common Dreams3 2013 Planning Team has further expanded my range of contacts and dialogue with progressive thinkers.

I have attempted to make LtQ and other progressive studies more widely available within the WA Uniting Church Synod through membership of the Lay Preachers Association and Commission on Education, Discipleship and Leadership (CEDAL). To facilitate progress, four lay members of the UCA formed the Perth Progressive Network WA Inc in 2013. But it is salutary to remember that it took the early Christian paradigm three hundred years to take root in the Roman Empire!

St Paul and Roman Imperial Theology

In May 2013 I joined a pilgrimage to study St Paul and Roman Imperial Theology in Naples and Rome. Led by Marcus Borg and Dom Crossan, two pre-eminent Jesus Scholars who devote their retirement years to sharing modern biblical scholarship with the wider world. It was the most stimulating fourteen day faith journey of my life. Each night Crossan would summarise the significance of the archaeology viewed that day, then Borg would speak on the implications for the way we read Paul's letters.

I began to see in the New Testament reflections of the encounter between the Roman Empire (where most people were ruthlessly exploited for the material gain of a few) and the Jewish commitment (to a world to be shared for all God's people). That such oppressive but often well-disguised 'domination systems' continue in our current world makes this insight of Borg and Crossan particularly potent for progressive Christianity.

Conclusions

Insights from "historical Jesus" scholarship correlates well with my scientific perspective that the supernatural world is progressively being subsumed by our expanding understanding of the natural world. This dialectic is causing pre-enlightenment religious beliefs in a parallel heavenly universe to become obsolete if not positively toxic. Therefore my image of God over the years has evolved from supernatural theism to pan**en**theism through to non-realism. However, since feedback is intrinsic to all complex biological systems, will not non-realism reflect the reality of God? Is not our changing understanding of God our link to the "historical Jesus" and early Christianity? My progressive journey continues.

Writing My Life Journey Through Books

Val Webb

I was a God-intoxicated child from the moment I could step back from basic toddler needs and reflect on things. My parents were evangelical Christians from Presbyterian and Plymouth Brethren stock. My father was a university lecturer and my equally bright mother was removed from high school during the depression while her three brothers enjoyed tertiary education. You can see why education and religion were defining priorities in my family.

It's interesting to me how some people simply accept the God-idea and go on with whatever else they are doing, while others, like myself, are gripped by it. I keep stumbling across such God-obsession when I read autobiographies. I was in love with God and longed for some dramatic experience—to see or feel God in some way. I would lie on the grass for hours staring up at the clouds and willing a sign, a face in a cloud, or a shaft of sunlight beamed intentionally down on me. My religious groups had altar calls. I lost count how many times I rededicated my little life to God, either going down the front or in my mind, but later would plead with God into the night to *feel* something. If anyone wanted God, I did.

Thus began my struggle with doubt, even though I dared not admit it to myself, or anyone else. While I desperately wanted to believe, questions kept bubbling up, "How do we know the Bible is true? ...Did Jesus really rise from the dead? ...Was Jesus God?" These were life and death questions because wrong belief would land me in hell. They were also important for a teenager whose brand of Christianity shunned school formals and university socials, anywhere drinking and dancing might lurk. Given such teenage sacrifice, it had better not be for nothing!

I also remember the stress of witnessing. On the bus to school, I needed to engage the person next to me to convert them by stop 21. Otherwise, if they died that day and went to hell, it would be my fault. As I write this, anger washes over me at such deeply engrained manipulation and guilt.

I also developed a smile as my face's default position, because good Christians were happy. That turned out well because my husband of forty-seven years declares the smile first got his attention.

My doubts isolated me. I could spot inconsistencies in dogmas, but no one else seemed to have a problem or, if they did, suppressed their doubts as successfully as I did. Even at university, our religious group offered water-tight arguments for everything and doubt was never seen as a sign of intelligence but as not enough faith or too much pride. I remember venturing a different opinion once, only to be told "we'll pray for you". We constantly "opened up the Bible" as if shucking oysters and thought ourselves very scholarly, but certain beliefs were never open to question and these were the ones I doubted.

In my first year at university, the resurrection was my big struggle. Every night before sleep, I had to convince myself afresh that it happened, yet my first thought each morning was, "What if it's not true?" I was doing a science degree that taught me to investigate everything, yet in this most important area, good Christians "just believed."

Why didn't I walk away? It was bigger than that. My family, friends and identity were in that tradition, so it was walking away from them as well. Such religious groups have a gang mentality. People stay, switching off to discrepancies rather than lose the camaraderie of the faithful. If the compromise with reason is minimal, it's bearable, but when the compromise becomes too great, the choices are to abandon your reason or leave. I did not want to abandon God.

After years in research, I married and we moved to England and then the United States. My outer life still revolved around church while my inner life struggled with doubt. Fortuitously, we joined an open-minded church where I first tackled the minister for not using the right religious words, but something held us there. I had never experienced such love and acceptance among Christians. They emphasised people's gifts and creativity rather than beliefs and, for a while, my doubts could be tucked under the rug.

We returned to Australia ten years later to the newly created Uniting Church and I became involved at state synod level. With more maturity under my belt, I decided to confront my doubts. I could no longer be at war within myself, even if my search led me away from Christianity altogether. Our Uniting Church College at that time only accepted students bound for ordination, so I enrolled in religious studies at Queensland University, another fortuitous move. This secular environment freed me from the constraints of "correct" doctrine. I discovered my professors had *also* asked my questions, as had the theologians we studied. Doubt was recognised as a path to more authentic thought.

On discovering so many biblical characters and theologians through the centuries who also doubted the truths of their day, a new thought began to ooze into my mind. What if doubts were positive.... from God, even? The more I thought about this, the more it made sense. Isn't doubt a natural part of life? Without doubt, the earth would still be flat and diseases sent from a devil. Every major evolution in history happened because people doubted current knowledge and refused to be silenced. And so, on returning to America in 1988, I sat at my desk and wrote *In Defense of Doubt: An Invitation to Adventure.*

At that time, Christian books on doubt told how to get rid of it, but I celebrated it as part of being human. I described how Christianity, beginning with "doubting" Thomas, had loaded doubters with guilt and fear. I called this abuse—replacing someone's personal authority with another's. I told stories of lives ruined by such condemnation and also tales of survivors. I described doubt, not as the opposite of faith or belief, but as the healthy discrepancy between what we are taught to believe and what we experience. Doubt was not something to get over, like puberty or a cold, but divine nudges urging us to richness of life.

The book offered readers permission to doubt and also marked my future mission—to use my theological knowledge to dismantle doctrinal walls that trapped people into beliefs that did not make sense and often destroyed their lives. I vowed, whatever the cost, never to be a theologian who remained silent.

The book was published in 1995 and an expanded version in 2012. It has been very popular with people who sit in church pews struggling with questions but blaming themselves. As one person said after reading it, "my chains fell off, my heart was free" took on a whole new meaning, the freedom to doubt.

At this stage of my life, I was completing my PhD. at Luther Seminary in Minnesota. At Queensland University, I had been exposed to biblical criticism, debates about Jesus' divinity and about other religions. Feminist theology excited me, as did Process Theology which images God, not as an external manipulating ruler, but as Energy within everything in the universe nudging towards transformation, an image that sits with contemporary scientific knowledge and is also inclusive of other religions. In this seminary, however, I encountered new forms of theological oppression. Lutheranism has its own language, ethnicity and theology and, for some faculty, if Luther did not say it, it was wrong. While some professors were marvelous teachers and mentors, others were overtly opposed to both feminist theology and process theology and did everything to denigrate these positions.

Having survived doctrinal pressure in the past, such opposition made me more determined to own my questions, which made for interesting moments of defiance in class, but left me crying for the two-hour drive home. Thanks to Professor Paul Sponheim, who encouraged me to hang on, I earned my PhD and received a thorough traditional education while internally formulating my own ideas. As my feminist theology lecturer told me, "Jump all the hoops and learn all you can; when you finish, claim your own voice with confidence."

Having now accepted my right to doubt, I realised that many childhood doubts came from growing up as a woman in the 1950s and 60s. While encouraged to achieve in school and university, the underlying message was that this was a fall-back position in case I did not marry. When I did marry and have children, I watched male colleagues with lower grades take prime research jobs and still be fathers and husbands.

Biblical scholar Marcus Borg calls feminist theology the most important theological development in his life-time because it gave another standpoint from which to view Christian traditions. Rather than begin with biblical rules about women, it begins with women's experiences and challenges doctrines that offer bad news for women. For centuries, women have been named subordinate, less intelligent, less reliable and a host of other deficiencies wound into their DNA, claims created by men reinforced by biblical texts. Yet this did not reflect women's experiences. They had borne children at great risk and held family and communities together when men went to war, yet not allowed into university because their "natural" makeup could not stand the rigors of learning. When enough women scholars entered theological colleges in the late 60s, however, they found other women questioning the same ideas and applied a hermeneutics of suspicion to biblical study, asking whether any texts about women from a culture that saw them as disposable male property were applicable today.

Feminist theology gave me permission to address my experiences as a woman and claim my personhood. Out of this came my book, *Why We're Equal*, where I trace how the Adam and Eve story has been used to control, subordinate, denigrate and even kill women, simply by making Eve the origin of sin and thus condemning all her daughters for posterity.

The World Methodist Council produced four study books on the gospels for the Millennium. I was asked to write on John's Gospel which was a challenge, as this gospel is most used to argue Jesus' divinity and, by this point, I saw Jesus as a human being transparently filled with the Divine spirit. There is a big difference between saying "Jesus is God" and "In Jesus, we see God." However, the opportunity to read this gospel through new theological spectacles convinced me it portrayed Jesus as God's emissary—a human being dispatched, as it were, to represent the family business and promote the product. The resulting book, *John's Message,* represented my evolution as a theologian informed by the evolution within my own self.

As a follow-up to my feminist theology book, my editor requested a book about women in history who contributed to theological change but were not recognised for it, or their ideas were attributed to a man in their life. I had read Florence Nightingale's autobiographical fiction about a gifted woman who preferred death to a woman's life in an upper-class Victorian drawing room, but I was stunned to find her unpublished eight-hundred page hand-written manuscript in the British Library offering a new religion for the poor. After pages of notes, I called my editor and said, "Florence needs the whole book." What an exciting journey to write the first full book on her as theologian, *Florence Nightingale: The Making of a Radical Theologian*, who voiced liberation, feminist and process theologies before their time.

Much of the struggle with traditional theology revolves around descriptions of God. My next book, *Like Catching Water in a Net,* was urged on by my surgeon husband Maurice. He wanted me to write a book that "told it like it is," not tiptoeing around church sensitivities or the feelings of conservative friends and family. In this book, I let my theology all hang out. The biggest doubts people have are about God—"what is God like?" to "is there a God at all?" What comes to mind when we say the word God *matters* because it determines how we relate to the divine and whether we can believe in a God at all. Much of my childhood doubt stemmed from a God-image of an external Blueprint Planner before whom I must act correctly and believe in sincerely in order to go to heaven, even though it seemed odd that a loving God would create us to fail. Yet anything we say about God is a metaphor and, since metaphors are borrowed from within cultures, they make the best, and sometimes only sense, in that setting.

Today, certain ancient divine metaphors have become literal descriptions—a human-like King, Judge, or Father, offering salvation through a literal conflict with the devil. Pew-sitters simply assume these are the dominant biblical images, yet we first meet God as Wind brooding over water, Life breathed into humanity, Voice, Cloud, Spirit, Comforter and Wind and Flame at Pentecost.

Contemporary theology is reclaiming formless God-metaphors *within* the universe rather than an external deity manipulating the world from outside. Such formlessness is common across religions, which is why I wrote this book exploring many religious traditions and all humans as part of the cosmic dance of the universe. Divine Energy within everything, or the universe as God's body "in whom we live and move and have our being" (*Acts 17:28*) sits comfortably with science's organic, interconnected universe. The problem, however, with divine formlessness is the slim line between this and God as not-at-all.

This book demanded a sequel—*Stepping Out with the Sacred.* How have humans across religions tried to make contact with, attract or appease the divine; and has this worked? There are many silly things done in the name of religion and also many amazing rituals about which many do not know. By pulling these together and taking a closer look, we can better evaluate what we do and why; and also find inspiration from the rituals and actions of others who also seek the sacred.

In 2011, my book on doubt went out of print after a long and helpful career. Mosaic Press has published an expanded edition, *In Defence of Doubt* which sums up where I am at this moment.

While this trail of books demonstrates how my life and theology have evolved, theology is not something only scholars do. We all need a working theology that can function in our lives, making sense for *us*, rather than clinging to ancient dogmas into which our experiences must fit. The question is always, "What is good news for *me* here and now?" In the past, systematic theology by its very title was about cohesive systems into which all ideas must fit with nothing embarrassingly hanging out. But theology has now moved to contextual theology to include peoples' various experiences. Rather than re-frosting a doctrinal cake baked in ancient language and worldviews, we begin with our contemporary world and concerns and, from that perspective, reflect on how to speak of God today. The questions I have asked over the years have come from *my* life experiences and concerns—your struggles and questions will be different.

Today, I identify with the progressive Christianity momentum around the world, not as a new set of beliefs but as the base from which to build sacred stories for today. The search for the sacred is ongoing, even for those who have rejected such a possibility, because that conclusion is open to future contradiction just as certainty is open to future disillusionment. It is about the journey more than about "once I was blind, but now I see." This is the adventure of being alive.

Notes

Webb, V. *In Defense of Doubt: An Invitation to Adventure*. St. Louis: Chalice Press, 1995.

———————, *Why We're Equal: Introducing Feminist Theology*. St. Louis: Chalice Press, 1999.

———————, *John's Message: Good News for the New Millennium*. Nashville: Abingdon Press, 1999.

———————, *Florence Nightingale: The Making of a Radical Theologian*. St. Louis: Chalice Press, 2002.

———————, *Like Catching Water in a Net: Human Attempts to Describe the*

Divine. New York & London: Continuum, 2007.
———————, *Stepping Out With the Sacred: Human Attempts to Engage the Divine.* New York & London: Continuum, 2010.
———————, *In Defence of Doubt: An Invitation to Adventure.* Second Edition. Melbourne: Mosaic Press, 2012.

Part Four: Progressive Christianity: Embracing A Faith In Action

From Evangelical Religion To Something Quite Different

Gerald Christmas

In looking back over my last sixty years, I can now see the broad pattern. It commences with 30 years of orthodox religion. There followed a period of ten years of theological turmoil and radical changes in my basic life assumptions. Then a third stage emerged. It is this stage which I am currently working on.

This pattern will be common in the experience of many men and women who spent their adolescent years in the Western World of the 1950s.

As I will explain below, the catalyst for my change was in essence, a disagreement on a matter of biblical interpretation. For me, this led to a fundamental re-think in relation to my approach to the scriptures. This, in turn opened up for me, totally different concepts of everything important in my life, of religion, of God, of humanity, of Jesus, of nature and the cosmos.

I am still a work in progress, still traveling and not quite sure when, if ever, I will really arrive. How will I know when I have arrived? May I now try to explain what has been happening with me for the past sixty years?

Having given the skeleton outline and rather commonplace version of my "journey", I will now attempt to flesh out the details and my experiences along the way.

My Life in Orthodox Institutional Religion

I wonder at the events that have happened, the changes that have occurred, since the very different world of my early school and university days in the 1950's. The priorities and the people were then very different. Life since then has changed. We live amid change. The world has changed but it seems that institutional religion has not. More of that below.

I am not sure whether I would call my journey a "progress", which implies improvement? I am not sure that I would call it a "journey", which implies a destination? It is more like a random series of experiences, decisions (usually ad hoc without full information or any understanding of consequences) and memories that, in retrospect, have formed themselves into a sequence, which I could call "my life".

I don't recall thinking in my adolescent years very much about God, humanity, nature, or the cosmos. I never attended Sunday School, but came into my first contact with a nearby parish church in my early teens and there I grew into an Anglican believer within the Sydney Diocese as a member of the Youth Fellowship with responsibilities quickly imposed to talk, lead and be actively involved.

The prevalent available theology was not questioned because there was no alternative offered. This was the world of correct beliefs. If we had any doubts or questions as to biblical authority or infallibility or any matter of correct doctrine or belief, there was the Bible or a relevant textbook available. For example *Fundamentalism and the Word of God* by J. I. Packer was published in 1958. If we doubted the historicity of the trials, crucifixion, death and bodily resurrection, then there was Frank Morison's *Who Moved the Stone?* published about the same time. I remember giving many talks to and leading discussions with younger fellowship members, under the watchful eye of the Curate in charge at the time. It was an "attend, agree and admire" community. My path in those fundamentalist days was secure and I was nourished by good company and, for me at the time, stimulating growth in understanding.

After my marriage to my wife Rosemary in 1961, we moved to another suburb and became heavily involved in more committees and Sunday Schools. I developed interests and an involvement in organisations such as Scripture Union as well as the Diocesan Synod which led me into membership on a multitude of diocesan committees, filling my spare time when not working as a partner in a city legal firm of solicitors.

I was introduced to Synod politics and then the General (Australian) Synod, and further committees, through my membership of the Anglican Church League of which I was lay chairman for some years. I was appointed Diocesan Registrar by Archbishop Loane in 1977. It was a part time appointment involving one day each week, in conjunction with my legal practice. I was thus totally immersed in what was the religious fundamentalist world of conservative Anglicanism. It provided theological answers for all adherents and a secure stable fellowship community in which I was accepted and secure.

My Christianity survived the challenges of *Honest to God* and all that followed. Being a lawyer and a churchgoer I was a member of the two most conservative institutions in society: the legal profession and the church.

However, in the long term, it was not to last. The storm clouds had started to gather in the early 1980's. The catalyst for religious change for me was the push for women's ordination that had started to be felt in Sydney. It was a highly emotive and divisive issue throughout the diocese and the Australian church.

I had always understood the genius of Anglicanism to be the concept of unity in diversity. This would allow for differences of opinion in relation to many issues but united on essentials. This approach enabled me to continue as I did as an Anglican in a state of tolerable disagreement with my fellow Anglicans who, on theological grounds, opposed women's ordination tooth and nail, as firmly as I supported it. However, gradually the tempo of the debate increased, and it became clear that, for a Sydney Anglican, upon strong advice from its theological pundits, opposition to women's ordination became an essential belief for card carrying Anglicans in Sydney.

My Period of Turbulent Change

I saw the diocese becoming less Anglican and inclusive, and more sectarian and, sadly divisive, not only in relation to the rest of the Anglican Communion, but also within its own boundaries. My position as Diocesan Registrar was becoming more difficult and conflicting. I was a minority believer in a world where "religiously correct beliefs" were everything.

When I was personally embroiled in the debates, meetings, and committees on the subject, there were many clergy who told me confidentially that they would like to side with me and others in favour of women's ordination, but they were unable to do so publicly. On the other hand, as a layman, I had the liberty to speak out and not jeopardize my livelihood. I wept tears for those clergy in bondage for their beliefs.

Slowly, my time of hitting my bruised head against the doors and walls of the diocesan embattlements was coming to an end. That happened in the year 1990. I was informed by the then Archbishop, Donald Robinson, he needed a full time Registrar rather than the one-day per week arrangement. Politely and graciously, I was extracted from the diocesan structures.

I moved slowly towards the fringes of Anglicanism. Many of my former colleagues and acquaintances continued to be in touch, and for that I am grateful. The drift away was not sudden or dramatic. It was gradual, civil, and formally courteous, even if a little lukewarm or even cold at times.

I had enjoyed my thirteen years as Diocesan Registrar and my longer time in the ecclesiastical and Christian community, as one actively involved in a collection of committees not only in Sydney, but also at the General (Australian) Synod level. I met and befriended and learnt much from clergy and lay people, all engaged in promoting in various capacities, the Anglican religious franchise. I never have regretted my time then. Do I not regard my religious thirty years as a mistake, later to be corrected? No, not at all.

However, I was appalled that my colleagues at the time, on the basis of their chosen interpretation of some words in the New Testament, on the basis of their intellectual religious belief, could regard women as somehow less than human. On the basis of a religious belief, quoting the Bible as God's Word, they were degrading women as something less than fully human. It was similar to the support of slavery by parts of the Church in the eighteenth century. I remember saying this in the course of a Synod debate. I began to doubt that this New Testament was really God's infallible Word at all. The credibility of the Scriptures was being seriously undermined.

Orthodox institutional Christianity is, in essence, a creedal religion. This was creedal religion at its worst. Creeds and entrenched beliefs—at the heart of most religious systems—clearly divided people one from another. Jesus clearly thought this. In contrast, the early church community, following the teaching of Jesus, would not have experienced this division, which comes from some believing themselves to right the wrongs of others to such an extent that leads to division, separation, expulsion and rejection.

Jesus of Nazareth was not only opposed to religion as a belief system, but was more concerned with behaviour than beliefs, creeds and dogmas.

Anglicanism, although a creedal religious body (with some exceptions), is and has been, generally tolerant of diversity of belief. Hence, I continued to maintain fellowship within the Anglican fold because my minority beliefs on the ordination issue were not inconsistent with authentic Christianity, and could be embraced by an inclusive Anglicanism. Hence, although I argued with my evangelical friends for my belief and against theirs, in relation to women's ordination, I did not consider it a matter that should affect my basic membership of the Christian community.

But it was clear that Anglicanism in the Sydney Diocese was at that time becoming less liberal and was losing its precious quality of liberal tolerance. Tragically it was becoming an anti-women's ordination sect of the Anglican Church. Sadly this position persists today.

My Present Phase

So, in the net result, I had to vacate evangelical fundamentalism. I ceased attending a local parish church because I could no longer with integrity, recite the creed, or sing the hymns or pray the liturgical prayers.

I had a good deal of relearning to take on board in this period of transition. I read widely in areas that were new to me and which had been off limits to fundamentalist Bible believing Christians. Once I had a new approach to the interpretation of Scripture, my entire theological landscape completely altered.

Once I had ceased to be Registrar, over ensuing months I not only extracted myself from church and committee involvements, but also actively promoted the cause of women's ordination, which had taken me out of diocesan life. Arising from my concerns for Anglican unity, I initiated a meeting of synod members that led to the formation of the group of clergy and lay people now called "Anglicans Together". My wife and I also initiated a movement in Sydney called "Men Women and God" and organised for visiting theologians from the United States and other places to visit Sydney to promote our cause and to speak at meetings in sympathetic churches (including some Anglican), to present the biblical case for women's inclusion as priests and bishops in the church. They were interesting and busy times for my wife and I. Rosemary had been studying theology for many years and graduated with a BD and an MTh from Sydney University. It was through her personal contacts in the United States and other places that these visits from overseas became possible.

I had not only rejected evangelical fundamentalism. I also rejected Sydney Anglicanism in its present form, and furthermore, I see organised institutional creedal religion of any form as being unhelpful to one's spiritual being. So I had by then, burnt three bridges behind me.

I also as a consequence, left behind me beliefs adopted and defended for years. Slowly, I worked my way into my new ways of thinking. My new insights as to how to read the Scripture metaphorically led to a marvelous liberty and new attitudes to my fellow humans, new understanding of God, new insights which control our care for the world in which we live, a reassuring feeling of oneness, at-one-ment with the cosmos and its mysteries, which science is only now beginning to understand. These matters are too great for any one person to grasp. God is too complex to be understood just by theologians. The cosmos is too great and mysterious and needs the philosophers, the scientists, the theologians, the botanists, the physicists, to pool their knowledge. The astrophysicists should talk to the botanists. The geologists should share their findings with the theologians, and so on. We need to be polymaths in cooperation.

We also need to see the cosmos beyond Mother Earth, which is our backyard, as one. All humanity is one with all living things. The whole cosmos consists of the same basic elements. Such a view of things has a wealth of exciting implications for Christians. It would take a few books by persons far more qualified, experienced, and equipped than myself, to expound them all.

I have a new set of views about all those things, issues, and concepts that matter. I will not go into detail. I will spare you that. None of them are original. There is nothing new under the sun it was once said.

In the old days I had beliefs I believed to be the truth and contrary beliefs were not only wrong, they were "contrary to God's word".

I hope I have been able to shed this intellectual religious arrogance. I now have beliefs, but I do not have to assert them as God's infallible word. They are my beliefs that I will run with until I am persuaded otherwise.

I enjoy speculation and discussion with others, of our beliefs. I belong to a small group of likeminded people who meet regularly and we talk about everything from God to motorcars. We have been meeting for years. We have disagreements, but we respect the views of the other. We have beliefs and we try and persuade each other to our point of view. In the process we learn and gain insights that are gifts to each of us from the other.

I recently joined the Centre for Progressive Religious Thought (CPRT) Sydney where I find freedom to think aloud and share, discuss, disagree and debate the issues of Christian faith in an atmosphere of mutual acceptance. That is what the church should be like.

I have a fresh liberated creative approach to Scripture now free of burdensome infallibility and authority. From this base, I think of God no longer as supernatural, omnipotent, and judgmental. God is more a source of life being present not in one place but in all humans and living things, and all the elements of the cosmos. From this flows new understandings of our world corroborated by the understanding of our new physics and new understandings of neurology which take us into new insights and often further insoluble questions.

I more readily have begun to understand and appreciate mysticism, paradox, and ambiguity, as something to be embraced and trusted. I have come to accept doubt as part of faith. These matters I find difficult. I am but paddling in the shallows…

This then, is the life of a former orthodox, very conservative Bible believing Christian, now in the process of being transformed into something else. The process continues day by day.

A Newer *Post-modern* Reformation

Ruth Doobov

I am reading my grandson *The Lion, the Witch and the Wardrobe.* Aslan is approaching death. The lion is sad, the children are puzzled, and the mood is sombre. My grandson knows it will turn out all right, because there are six more books. I find myself thinking, "Yes, that's what this is. It's a story for children. How can any thinking adult imagine God acts like this?"

Yet I could, and did. I grew up in a typical traditional Presbyterian church in a country town in Queensland. I must have had a religious gene, I suppose, for I eagerly adopted all I learnt there, because I knew of no other way to approach the sacred. Going to university certainly made me aware that other people, whether Christian or not, thought differently. But I studied English literature and, like C. S. Lewis, I buried myself in the past where traditional Christianity was the norm. The pressures of adult life, work, and family, left me with little thinking time. Two decades later I was still going through the motions of being an active church member but beginning to wonder if I was wasting my time.

A light bulb moment for me came when sitting unsuspectingly in the pew one Sunday, and a visiting Uniting Church minister conducted the service. He preached on the doctrine of substitutionary atonement. He said it was nonsense. He said no reasonable person could believe it. Suddenly I saw he was right, and I had to restrain myself from cheering out loud. That was enough for me for the moment, but things were soon to change dramatically.

The church I attended appointed Rex Hunt as its new minister, with very little idea of what we were letting ourselves in for. He started us off cautiously with Marcus Borg, but before long we were devouring the writings of Spong, Holloway, Crossan and our own Australian Val Webb. A friend lent me Bart Ehrman's book on the New Testament. It was a whole new world.

I have thought resentfully, along with many others, why weren't we told sooner? But to be fair, there are many reasons why progressive Christianity took so long to filter down to the ordinary church member. When Bishop

John Robinson's books *Honest to God* (1963) and *The New Reformation* (1965) were published, this latter title was absolutely apt. While his ideas were not totally original even then, it was, I think, the first time such ideas had been put before the public in such an accessible way. On the other hand, his more academic books on the New Testament contained what we would now consider quite conservative thinking. At that date he lacked access to some of the discoveries that have informed the work of more recent scholars. We were, in fact, only part of the way. No other such popular books followed for quite a while, and it has taken the movement the best part of fifty years to gather momentum. On the other hand, the old Reformation took more like 250 years to work itself out.

It could be argued that by 1900, progressive religious thinking had begun to gain a foothold, at least among intellectuals in English speaking countries – people like Florence Nightingale, John Greenleaf Whittier, and William James. Indeed, it was in the wake of these ideas that the term "fundamentalism" was born, to counter such subversive thinking. Two world wars and the Great Depression served to send people back to the old certainties. Other factors were also at work. Much new thinking in theology was coming from German scholars, whose lives were greatly affected by world events. The English speaking world was understandably unwilling to embrace ideas coming from Germany, and in any case, who wanted to read turgid English translations of indigestible German prose?

Then Billy Graham arrives and fills every conservative Christian church in Australia with new converts or revitalised old ones. He took us back to the eighteenth century and only in the last couple of decades has this influence faded away. Let us not be too hard on clergy whose livelihood depended on not offending people without whom, it seemed, their churches would barely exist.

Meanwhile, something else was happening in another war-torn part of the world, the Middle East. Since the late nineteenth century, archaeology had begun to unearth ancient manuscripts with biblical and other religious content that had not been previously known. The most famous of these were the Dead Sea scrolls, but there were many others. Because of the poor preservation of the texts and in some cases the obscurity of their language, work on deciphering these was painfully slow. The slowness of work on the Dead Sea scrolls became an academic scandal. While the *Gospel of Thomas* had been known previously, it was at first dismissed by scholars as merely another gnostic text. When a complete text of it was discovered in the Nag Hammadi library (unearthed in 1945), scholars had to take it more seriously.

Finally the Jesus Seminar began to make serious work on ancient texts more widely available, and our whole perspective on the Bible changed. Now the intelligent layperson could understand that the meaning of scripture was much more variable and uncertain than that which came from a naive dependence on the exact words of the King James Bible. Indeed, the whole composition of the canon of sacred texts was called into question. I believe the advances that have been made in the understanding of ancient canonical and extra-canonical material have been crucial in changing our view of Christianity.

By the 1970s women were entering theological colleges in significant numbers, and bringing with them inevitably a less literal approach to the Bible (otherwise they would not have been there at all) and a more nuanced approach to the sacred, which embraced both meditation and social justice. The charismatic movement seemed to be giving the ultra conservative side of Christianity a major boost just as it was beginning to lose momentum, but its appeal to Australian churchgoers already seems to be on the wane. Meanwhile, gentler approaches such as the Iona movement were showing us that we could find in the past a time when spirituality which emphasised kindness to people and respect of the natural world had been practiced.

Towards the end of the twentieth century, circumstances arose which made a profound difference to the world as we knew it, and in particular to religion and how it is perceived. One of these was a change in the way we think philosophically, now known as post-modernism. I think it is no accident that the first Reformation coincided with the Renaissance and the New Reformation we are currently experiencing, with post-modernism. Early Christianity quickly abandoned its Jewish roots to adopt a style of thinking consistent with that of Greek philosophers, particularly Plato, which made more sense to the increasing proportion of Gentiles in the church—just compare the supernatural visitor from the spirit world described in John's gospel with the very human Jesus of the synoptic gospels. The Reformation saw protestant churches dispense with the medieval overlay the church had developed, but to embrace even more strongly a theology birthed in Greek thought. As a university student I wrote a thesis for my Masters degree in

English literature on a monumental work written in the sixteenth century by the poet Edmund Spenser. This profoundly protestant Christian work was expressed almost completely in terms of the mythology of Greece and Rome. While I could see how this arose out of the Renaissance culture of the period, I completely failed to see at the time how much our religion was still caught up in the same mindset.

Another influential factor was, of course, the result of computing and the internet. Books have become much easier to produce, cheaper, and easier to obtain. We have not seen such a profound change in the dissemination of knowledge since the invention of printing—another factor which coincided with the first Reformation.

We are also much more aware of people from other places and of other religions. We see their common humanity and their suffering on our television screens every day and reasonable people find it difficult to any longer believe they are all bound straight for perdition. It is no accident that mainstream churches have given up trying to convert the heathen overseas and concentrate on humanitarian aid.

Besides, if we want to convert people of other religions there are plenty of them here in Australia. Migration from a wider pool of people than the British has led to Christianity being only one of many religions practiced actively in Australia, and we have learnt from other religions. Buddhism, for example, has contributed much to our understanding of meditation.

For me, my encounter with another religion began when I met and married an Orthodox Jew. My Christian friends said it would not last, or if it did, I would "lose my faith". After forty-three years, I think I can safely say they were wrong on both counts.

The fact is, these days in Australia, most of us encounter people belonging to non-Christian religions in our daily lives, and have the opportunity to learn from them. I kept trying to understand what Jewish theology was, and kept being confronted with a blank stare and "what's theology?" I finally worked out that it was possible to have a religion that did not have a complicated theoretical explanation for interaction between God and humans, and that traditional Christianity was the exception rather than the norm in this respect.

Reading writers like Geza Vermes, Amy-Jill Levine, and Spong (in his book *Liberating the Gospels*) led me to understand the essential Jewishness of Jesus, and to ask myself, what view of God would Jesus have had? Of course, I suppose this is a question that you do not need to ask if you think that Jesus is God. I was gradually forming a clearer view of what I thought the religion founded by Jesus' followers ought to be like:

It is something which needs to be practiced in a community, so that we can encourage and care for each other. It should not, however, be an exclusive community, nor should it feel threatened or embattled. Its members should support each other, while acknowledging that others are pursuing the same ends but along different paths. It should always be open to new possibilities.

It should place its greatest emphasis on concern for others, both within our own community of like-minded followers of Jesus, and, perhaps more importantly, as far outside it as we can reach. Concern for the spiritual welfare of others is part of this, but concern for people's physical well-being is at least, if not more important. I heard someone recently express a worry that the UnitingCare tail was beginning to wag the Uniting Church dog. Wag away, I thought, this is how it should be.

It should believe that people have a sense of a sacred presence in the world and a desire to connect with the sacred. We can call this sacred presence, by way of shorthand, God, as long as this does not lead us back to an idea of a great puppetmaster in the sky, pulling strings. We need to develop this sense of the sacred by meditation or whatever related activities work for us personally (music? contemplation of nature?). Shopping lists of requests for divine intervention do not have much value for me.

I think that there is hope for Christianity in the future when I read the following extract from an address by the then Archbishop of Canterbury, Rowan Williams, to the Synod of Bishops at the Vatican in 2012:

> Contemplation is very far from being just one kind of thing that Christians do: it is the key to prayer, liturgy, art and ethics, the key to the essence of a renewed humanity that is capable of seeing the world and other subjects in the world with freedom—freedom from self-oriented, acquisitive habits and the distorted understanding that comes from them... The human face that Christians want to show to the world is a face marked by... justice and love.

My Journey Has Made Me Question A Lot Of Things…

Ken Fletcher

It has been an interesting journey from being born into a devout evangelical fundamentalist protestant family to being able to question the nature of God, the authority of scripture, the doctrine of the atonement and who was the real Jesus verses the Christ image subsequently attributed to him.

This upbringing resulted in the predictable instilling of the stories, ideals and theology of fundamental evangelical Christianity. Much emphasis was put on the sinfulness of man, the guilt of falling from grace, and the ideals of the fundamentalist's God who required us to seek forgiveness for our sins—which had been provided by Jesus Christ through his death on the cross and the atonement. The reward and hope for the future was the promise of eternal life, in heaven, if we turned to Christ, confessed our sins, accepting him as saviour.

We were continually challenged about devotion and dedication to the cause of spreading the gospel message. There was strong peer pressure with continual reminders of the consequences of not being saved or worse still, the consequences of questioning the proclaimed doctrines of God, the Trinity and the gospel story. Much emphasis was put on having a personal God, having the spirit inside us to guide us, and be our comfort and support.

This all sounded very idyllic but I found it did not translate to the reality of living. I realised an image of God had been built in my mind of a perfect person who watched over and controlled everything. This image was as real to me as were my parents and other people. I also realised my concept of God had become a parent figure from which I was expecting a form of parental guidance.

I found I was unable to distinguish between my thoughts or those inspired by a Holy Spirit. I could see the danger. If I took notice of the god thoughts my mind was telling me, I could believe they were divinely inspired so must be the will of God and that as an agent of God I was expected to act according to these thoughts. This feeling of inspiration coupled with human ego could tempt us to think we are god-like. I concluded that for many Christians a thought was interpreted as a direction from God when in reality that thought was an emotional idea stimulated by the continual indoctrination of the peer group's expectations.

The church I attended had a large congregation and was very active with youth groups, social, and recreational programs. It encouraged living as Jesus Christ would have lived, providing a supportive atmosphere and good fellowship. A message of love, compassion, and care was evident, and expected from all. It reflected the positive qualities that Christian groups can offer when meeting the needs of its congregation.

But the good can be contradicted by the negative aspects of a judgmental and vindictive attitude some church groups can display when confronted with doubting questions and ideas different from their own. Many church going Christians consider that their brand of Christianity is the only truth, and everyone else is wrong and must change. Yet if they are accepting their beliefs on faith, are they so uncertain about the validity of their beliefs that they must reject anyone who may challenge them and be different?

The crunch time came as I ventured outside this protected, confined environment, entering university and the workforce, to learn there were different explanations and truths. I realised I was ill prepared to handle the challenges of a less protected and a more self-interested secular world. I began to see the different ways individuals handled the fundamentalist evangelical dogma. Some did not take the fundamentalist message seriously or personally, such was their personality and attitude to life, but for me the guilt and ideals to live up to and conform with smothered the person.

I also observed that the behavior of some individuals in the church, many of whom claimed they were filled with the Holy Spirit, was no different from and sometimes worse than, non members. The pecking order of personalities and the assertion by dominant individuals within a group is the same the world over. Within the church groups it was these dominating individuals asserting their interpretation of "Holy Scripture" and their conclusions of what was their God's will, that was being expressed, not any divine inspiration.

Further research of the biblical stories of the creation, the virgin birth, and the varying accounts of the crucifixion and resurrection, made me doubt their accuracy. I realised the emphasis on guilt and punishment was to coerce and force followers to submit to the expectations of a church group for fear of punishment.

I felt I needed to break away from this influence and start to build a life in the wider world. This may not be the path for everyone but for me it appeared the best way.

This did not mean I abandoned the moral standards I had been taught but that I would not be limited by the peer pressure and practices of the past. Nor did it stop me from thinking about God and the Christian message, as I continued doing this as I sought a better explanation of life than the traditional myths.

It took many years to break down the guilt and work through the emotional bondages I had been taught and taken upon myself. I was interested to learn of new insights into the Christian story and the influence other philosophies had on Jewish and Christian theology. Christianity had its origins during the harsh repressive social and living conditions of Roman times. The revelation that the Christian story, as inherited through the Church of Rome, was not the only interpretation of Jesus' life, and opposing views that had been ruthlessly exterminated by the dominant militant Roman Church made me question the truth of the Christian story, especially as it contradicted the peace-loving, forgiving message that was taught by Jesus.

I no longer attend church now. It is not an environment I enjoy. I still feel the disappointments of the past and find there is too much hypocrisy, inconsistency, contradiction, and intolerance of other people who express their faith and beliefs differently. Most churches still adhere to out-of-date creeds, liturgies, and belief in stories that have been superseded. The lack of integrity to find answers keeps it behind the times to the extent of possibly becoming irrelevant.

It is the basic message of Jesus' teachings that needs to be lived without legalities and guilt. How the church or a Christian group handles individuals who are not compatible with its ethos is the major issue each group must sort out, but it should be with love and compassion, accepting that although individuals may have different beliefs it need not make them a lesser or unacceptable person.

I have found fulfillment in nature and communicating with others in various groups in a variety of environments. I feel I am more aware that we are all part of the wider community and as such should be active participants in it. I can understand there are those who, although they may have their doubts, still attend church as they enjoy the tradition, it is where their friends are, and they find social and spiritual fulfillment.

I feel I have and am addressing the hollowness of my previous spiritual life, and that with the continuing enlightenment that comes with new knowledge and understanding, I am closer to nature and feel part of the whole of existence. We are all part of nature, which for me is the sacred. It is the continuing communion or sharing with others and feeling part of a group and nature, that brings fulfillment.

I had been taught that Christianity had all the answers and that we need to commit to a set of answers. But now I am happy to have no specific commitment or expectation of finding definite answers. The gaining of knowledge and relating this to our connection with nature is the exciting journey. I expect my conclusions to be continually changing as I learn new facts and think through the implications of life's experiences.

As I said at the beginning, my path has made me question a lot of things, the most significant being: what is God and whether there is a God or not? It seems to me our human understanding of God is a combination of the wonderment of the workings of nature itself and the processes of the human mind as it seeks to make sense of the world we live in. Attributing human qualities to an imagined "king/god" entity that controls everything has been a model humans constructed and through which they explained the processes of nature they were observing.

We have no definite proof either way of God's existence. I find is very hard to find any other explanation than that we are experiencing the workings of nature and its processes. The human mind, with its intellect and decision making abilities, is a product of nature. I can conceive that the raw energy, our whole universe and existence is said to have developed from, has the potential to become anything in existence, including human intelligence, emotions, talent, and thinking. But this raw energy need not have intelligence of itself, only the potential for intelligence, and all other things to develop from it.

The idea of a just and omnipotent God controlling everything is an enigma, and is contradicted by the injustices and hurt innocent people suffer for no other reason than that by chance they were in the wrong place when something disastrous happened. To remove the God image and let the processes of nature be the determining factor better reflects reality.

Instead of believing there is a God who will guide me, I am happy to feel I am an independent individual who can make decisions which adhere to the standards of love and compassion as taught by Jesus. In this sense I feel I can still call myself Christian even though I no longer accept a lot of the Christian story.

The process of growing and maturing is one of trial and error as we learn from life's experiences. To strive to treat everyone as we would like to be treated, to admit and set wrongs right when we have behaved poorly, is an important principle in becoming a better and more mature person. It is not something that happens automatically or directed by spirits but is a continuing living process we can actively work at.

The greatest act of human love and sacrifice is to give one's own life so others may benefit. This love and concern for others that was the core of Jesus' teachings, was built into the atonement doctrine to explain his crucifixion and symbolically takes the place of the practice of animal sacrifices. What initially started as symbolism was transformed into the atonement doctrine with all its power to enforce reliance on, and adherence to, the faith.

I am fortunate to associate with a progressive religious discussion group (Centre for Progressive Religious Thought—Freedom to Explore) that provides the opportunity to investigate recent ideas, and work through the issues that concern us, in a non-judgmental environment. Here I realised I was not alone in my journey, that there are many others on their own similar but different pathway. We are all trying to reach our own individual understanding of our existence.

My evangelical upbringing makes me want to share this new understanding. I feel I have been liberated from the emotional and restricted thinking imposed by the dictatorial mentality of the mistaken beliefs of self-righteousness assumed by many religious people. I feel too many people are frightened to step outside their boundaries for fear they are the only ones with doubts, and they will be rejected by friends or punished by a vindictive God.

For me Jesus was a person who understood people and taught the essence of being human, having fulfillment through communion with others. It is the connection that humans feel when there is bonding and communion among us that reflects the connectivity within nature, which for me, relates to what is expressed by Christians as the workings of the Spirit.

The authority and authenticity of the Bible is another red herring. Recent scholarship indicates the texts in the bible were selected and altered to fit the theology of the Christian Church at Rome. Stories were inserted to supposedly fulfill Old Testament prophecies. While many of the stories have political implications as well as moral messages. There are so many contradictions we can only question its historical accuracy. Still there is value in the moral lessons and the emphasis on love, communion, and compassion, which its accounts portray. The biblical stories reflect human nature, its trials and tribulations. Human experiences throughout history are similar even though the environment in which humans live can vary greatly.

It is regrettable the New Testament scholarship regarding the historical Jesus that has been around for some time now, has not been taken up by many of today's clergy, but suppressed in favour of the old mythology. Often the congregations want to dictate to the clergy/theologians what they should preach and how they should behave. Resistance to change is a characteristic of conservative personality types making acceptance of change a slow process.

The challenge is complicated because so much of the new scholarship involves differing and often contradictory opinions of the researchers and theologians presenting them. I no longer expect to find a single answer or that anyone will present a completely correct view. Now, I am looking for an overall picture of what could have been the important facts and historical events, or who were the personalities involved, and what political or social agenda they may have had. In other words what was the other side of the story that may have been suppressed up until now?

I can relate to the outcomes Rex Hunt has listed as being the fruits of recent New Testament scholarship on the historical Jesus, such as:

Discover an authentic/essential Jesus
Establish a faith that has intellectual integrity
Throw off the bonds of guilt
Embrace life
Experience a renaissance in my faith
Feel proud of your humanity
Experience sacredness in the ordinary
Experience the living reality of the spirit of Jesus of Nazareth.

May I also suggest:

- It is our responsibility to do the research, to find the facts, and make decisions in life. I need to understand and keep coming back to the basic truths of Jesus' message. I can see how our lives are governed and have evolved through human decisions and actions not under the influence of mysterious spirits.
- We should resist glorifying or deifying significant individuals or events as this usually distorts the truth.
- The biblical stories need to be continually reinterpreted to relate to today's world. Humans and their personalities have not changed much despite major changes to the comforts in which we live, the social and political systems we have developed, the advances in technology/science and our expectations of life. And…
- There is much we can still learn from the biblical accounts.

It’s In the Ordinary ‘ebb and flow’ of Life I Find Myself Immersed In The Sacred

Gai Nowland

My first visit to Nightcliff Uniting Church was in February 2004. I was drawn by the recommendation of my in-laws hinting that there was something radical to be found among this group. I felt at home with familiar elements immediately, the un-churchy building, significant Lay leadership and the Seasons of the Spirit resource materials. Other elements intrigued me as well.

While hymns and pipe organs had been left very happily in the distant past, I had spent the previous decade bouncing along to catchy choruses beamed into vision by a data projector. But this music was very different; with wordy thought provoking lyrics to difficult tunes, I found I was being reminded about the edgy social justice mission of Jesus.

I had only just arrived in Darwin but my new husband, Paul, had lived in the Territory since a toddler. Paul didn’t attend church as an adult but given his childhood experience with missionary parents he was known by many in the congregation and was reasonably comfortable with the Sunday morning process.

New to town I was seeking a community, a life long engagement with the church made it the logical place to begin. Paul caught on immediately, and then to my surprise encouraged the members of our newly formed blended family to come along on Sunday mornings. Paul and his teenage children had been quite socially isolated for a number of years and he could immediately see a healthy set of social interactions for his kids. We were all seeking community.

During those early weeks I noticed that there was an opportunity to form some new small groups. This opened a life enhancing experience for us. We joined with two other families, with children spanning the same age group as our own, for a journey of sharing together that still contains a web of connections a decade later.

It came to pass that a member of our small group, Rev Felicity Amery, was the Chairperson of the Presbytery, and the Presbytery minister. I spent a short time as the Presbytery Secretary working with her, and during that time stumbled across a promotional flyer advertising the release of a DVD based study program called "Living the Questions" (LtQ). I was already familiar with the work of Bishop John Shelby Spong and knew vaguely of the Jesus Seminar. I became really excited about the potential of this material. The Presbytery agreed to purchase a copy and together, Felicity and I embarked on running the program in the Nightcliff Uniting Church congregation.

We embraced the whole program as suggested in the material, printing flyers, running information sessions, advertising in the newsletter and during announcements for weeks prior, and even buying a large tea-set for the tea ceremony—the whole deal!

Out of a congregation of sixty regular adults we hosted seventeen at our first session. Over 12-weeks numbers fluctuated but we always numbered at least twelve people. Sometimes we found the format difficult and the sessions a little long. It wasn't a perfect package but it *had* opened up the questions. The worms were out of the can, people were talking, but not everyone was comfortable.

Our minister, Rev Kate Fraser, handled the difficult moments with skill. I remember especially the time a member of the congregation put up her hand to question the starting point of Kate's sermon. The anticipation was palpable. I've never heard the congregation so silent! Kate gracefully acknowledged the concerns, took a deep breath, and mentally wound up her sermon a notch.

The LtQ experience created momentum which we built on with a book by Marcus Borg *The Heart of Christianity*, and using the work book *Experiencing the Heart of Christianity* by Tim Scorer. This leg of the journey connected with several folk who had struggled with LtQ but were able to really grab hold of Marcus Borg. A retired minister in the group re-read the book numerous times as he worked through a lifetime of theology from a new perspective. Others who had missed out on LtQ joined in enthusiastically, building on the conversations that were already buzzing around the congregation.

With interest and excitement still growing so we next decided to re-run LtQ, but this time we'd do it our way. A small lay group who'd participated in the previous sessions decided to lead collaboratively. This involved a generous time commitment with sessions held fortnightly, and with the leadership group also meeting on the off week to prepare the format for the coming week. Together we'd watch the DVD and then toss around ideas. We kept a basic rhythm for the evening but every week was quite different. The overall change was to share more deeply with each other, foregoing discussing some of the input.

We were very quickly responding with action as new ideas spontaneously emerged from the congregation. A new level of trust seemed to carry us forward.

Quite recently, while in conversation with a 'companion on the journey', I suggested that our regeneration as a congregation had begun with sharing together around biblical scholarship. She agreed, stating that finally we could all be honest with each other and realise that we were all on the same page.

During this period I noticed the attendance at and participation in, our open Church Council meetings to be strongly represented by members who'd participated in the LtQ and Borg groups—a group with the majority in the 25-50 year old bracket.

Our first big move was the relocation of our Op-Shop into the worship space for both sales and storage. All the clothing was stored at the front of the church during worship. It looked awful but we were committed to change anyway and had leased the previous space to the local indigenous people's community development arm the Larrakiah Nation.

The new look Op-Shop ignited a smoldering passion to offer hospitality to our Saturday morning shoppers. Instead of getting complicated we decided 'to just do it', to use what we had and see what happened. With ease, four small teams were formed from the congregation to cover monthly shifts, serving Fair-trade plunger coffee and tea. The volunteers also baked cakes and built tables. We borrowed chairs from the church, tablecloths from the Op-Shop and Sunday's mug and cup supply. The following Saturday we were running under the banner of *Frilly's* named in honour of the frilled-neck lizard population in our garden.

With that simple beginning and vision we had hoped to cover the input costs by donation. Now, three years later, at least half our volunteers aren't part of our Sunday congregation; we serve 50-80 espresso style coffees every Saturday, plus tea, and often, new customers are surprised to find an Op-Shop!

We have served a number of grass roots community organisations during their formation stage and watched them progress to other venues as their needs evolved. These secular community groups are mostly engaged in social justice activities that I reckon Jesus would have blessed.

Volunteers still bring along their home baked cakes, and our donations have become a sizable line on the income side of the ledger.

At the same time as launching *Frilly's* we began developing a Community Garden called *The Mulch Pit.* From a red dirt car park we now share tropical food, shade, and a story with broad community connections. Many of *Frilly's* volunteers joined us through the garden, while others found our church community through the garden's FaceBook site. Top End permaculture courses are run on site using the worship space as well as the garden.

Our Friday evening working bees include a monthly cooking workshop usually led by people who have lived for countless generations in the tropics from places like India, Sri Lanka, Indonesia, Timor, and the Pacific Islands. Darwin is home to a wonderfully diverse population and all involved at *The Mulch Pit* benefit from learning about the tropical foods we can grow and cook here, alongside the multicultural sharing and relationships that flourish in a community garden.

Very recently *The Mulch Pit* began to host groups of Asylum Seekers from local detention centers for morning permaculture workshops, which facilitates experiences with friendly Australians. *The Mulch Pit* has also received Northern Territory Government Climate Change funding for a proposal to build an outdoor kitchen and run a series of cooking workshops, with the aim of teaching participants how to cook the food grown locally. Construction commenced mid year, 2013.

As I reflect on this journey I remember being convinced that the church still had a contribution to make in our society. Engaging in the scholarship and the congregation's progress, provided me with hope that the church might re-discover 'the way'. I came to admire the brave theologians and biblical scholars who freed us from the constraints of a first century understanding of Christianity and from repressive doctrine, thus opening the doors to the real or human Jesus of Nazareth who confronted repression and sought justice.

Personally, I was delving more deeply into the process of unlearning, clearing out the religious detritus. There were times when I felt duped by clergy, when I questioned the games they were playing with people. If I was young I might call them hypocrites, but life and time reveal complexities. I can now see they can be trapped by a myriad of expectations and many attached strings. The church spent a millennia or so in a powerful position. It probably has two millennia worth of unlearning to do!

I've struggled long with the reality of the institutional church, particularly its tired slowness, but more recently I've grown in my appreciation of the benefits the institution can bestow. Well located property, education, and tradition can all be positive resources if tapped into by the creative people. There are many possibilities awaiting discovery. These give me hope that the church will continue to evolve and change; and that 'struggling' good-hearted people will keep emerging and bring their varying perspectives into the process. For in the tensions and the struggles it is likely 'the way' may be found, or indeed refound.

My process of unlearning has stripped my faith back to simplicity. I trust the stories of the historical Jesus announcing that the Kingdom of God is here now and available to all. I endeavour to express my faith by living in the present moment and responding to that moment. The arrival of our first grandchild has served as a very timely reminder for me about the future. The prospect of climate change reshaping the earth into an unfriendly place for human habitation is now even closer to my heart.

I find much of my hope for the future in the three guiding principles of permaculture: care for earth, care for people, enough for all. This growing passion for permaculture led to us as a family moving to a rural property 60km from Darwin. The distance has affected my attendance at Sunday church, but distance is not the only factor. I found that through irregular attendance I was much more alert to the words spoken and sung in the worship service. I found now there was much in the liturgy I could not consent to. However, I am saddened to miss the opportunity to be stimulated by the reflection, and to share in the awe and mystery of participating in the simple symbolic rituals, which are usually part of the service.

I maintain my close connection to the Saturday community through *Frilly's* and *The Mulch Pit*, in part because I was intimately involved in their creation, but also because I want to stay connected to the church community. My felt responsibility however is to the wider community: to those connecting beyond Sunday morning—the good-hearted folk who have bypassed the church—and who give fully of themselves to others thus doing God's work in the world.

When moving through the cycle of the Lectionary I have long been a lover of 'Ordinary Time'. Christmas with its materialist hype alongside an unbelievable narrative has long left me cold. Over time Easter also lost its relevance. But Ordinary Time is about ordinary stuff—real things, life's struggles, journeys, laments, adoration—inspired by ordinary stuff in the hands of ordinary people. It's rich and it's deep and it's what fills my heart.

So it's in the ordinary ebb and flow of life I find myself living immersed in the sacred: the croaking frogs, the phone ringing, the chickens cackling, the friends visiting, the long awaited cool breeze, a silent thought, the daily chores, a new green shoot, commuting to a meeting, the rumbling of thunder…

In that 'being-ness' I hear the call to stay connected, sometimes against what I think to be my better judgment. But I no longer feel like I need to save the church. It will be what it will be, and so will I. I also hear of tiredness in the congregation and wonder if we have come back to a place on the spiral of again needing to deeply engage in a process of sharing together: around progressive biblical scholarship, sharing our stories, remembering who we are, and why we gather and do what we do.

Staying Connected With Intellectual Integrity

Ian O'Reilly

I was born and raised in the church. My father has spent his whole adult life serving the Methodist then Uniting Churches as an ordained minister. Sunday school, worship twice on Sundays, assorted youth groups and camps, moving every four years or so—this was my upbringing. Dad and mum served in country areas, and built strong friendships and great respect everywhere they went. I rebelled a bit in my young adulthood, but when I moved out of home mum cleverly linked attendance at morning worship with a baked dinner for Sunday lunch, so I stayed 'connected'.

The formation of the Uniting Church, for which I happened to be in the right place and time, led to a new approach to youth work in my region, the Hunter Presbytery. I was an up and coming youth leader who benefited from visionary work that established a new movement based around Easter Camp. This led to the formation of the Hunter UYF. Within three years I was on the Order of Saint Stephen working as the first presbytery-level youth worker in NSW. Really, there wasn't much to rebel against.

During this time I got a reputation for personifying an 'Australian' faith—using Aussie accents, expressions, humour and cultural references to express and engage with the Christian story, particularly the life and parables of Jesus. But the theology inherent in this was basically mainstream. We worked through some ructions about baptism/re-baptism and charismatic worship, but not the historical accuracy of the New Testament or the pillars of the incarnation, Jesus' death for us all, the Trinity... I was concerned about faith in action, doubtless inherited from observing my parents' lives, which added a social justice weight to my faith pendulum.

I accepted a position as Synod Youth Worker in the Northern Synod, starting in 1984. In that capacity I led worship at Darwin Memorial Church, close to Christmas, I think in 1985. I preached a sermon on the obedience of the youthful Mary in accepting God's news of her impending (miraculous) pregnancy and all it entailed. I challenged those present to consider following Mary's extraordinary example when it came to responding to the message God might be bringing to us today. I was particularly attentive to the Christmas proclamation of "peace on earth"—it was the mid-1980s, and the Peace Movement with its anti-nuclear, anti-militaristic message was fairly strong in Australia. A few months earlier was the fortieth anniversary of the atomic bombing of Hiroshima, and friends of mine had painted the outlines of human bodies in the streets of Darwin, representing the civilian deaths. Peace was a pretty constant theme in my work at that time.

Anyway, I asked a respected colleague, Rev Chris Budden, for some feedback on the sermon. He surprised me by saying "I thought the delivery was alright, but I don't accept the exegesis." Of course I wanted to know more and for the first time I heard a clearly expressed rationale regarding a faith that didn't accept the New Testament stories as fact. I had never taken the position of the whole Bible being a history book. I accepted the creation stories in Genesis as myth. But the Gospels were a different kettle of fish. I was a strong admirer of Jesus, particularly his defying the religious authorities and their hypocrisy; his challenging of the cultural mores of his day. The Christmas narrative and other supernatural events appeared to be part of an indivisible package.

The conversation with Chris opened my mind to new possibilities. At about the same time I read some cultural analyses of Jesus' parables and used some of this in my work, unpacking the cultural meanings of the *Good Samaritan* and the *Prodigal Son* (really about a *Father and Two Sons*) for young people.

Throughout this time I was a member of the wonderful community at Nightcliff Uniting Church. I was able to more deeply connect there once I stopped working for the church, because I ceased the large amount of travelling inherent in that job. A small group (the ingeniously named *Tuesday Night Group*) was an intrinsic part of my exploration and growth in understanding. The congregation itself was tolerant, open, experimental—willing to explore together what it meant to be 'church' while grappling with what others labelled 'liberal' or 'progressive'. Over time we stopped singing songs that referred to God and humanity as exclusively male, prayed with our breath, disbanded Sunday school and intentionally catered for our children during worship. We welcomed gay people, performed street theatre and music at combined-faith peace events and demonstrations against Darwin's militarisation, marched for Indigenous reconciliation and agreed to 'pay the rent' to local Indigenous organisations in perpetuity. We were lay-led—ministers were facilitators, not authoritarian or personality-based leaders.

In time I came into contact with the work of John Shelby Spong and later 'The Jesus Seminar'. This stuff was exciting. The *Tuesday Night Group* explored these and other scholars alongside movies and articles and real people who visited and shared their wisdom and experience. These new insights emerged not as part of dedicated study but a gradual, organic process. In this period I changed employer from church to local government, got married, bought property, had children, started a Masters—I had plenty on my plate.

I particularly remember the impact Marcus Borg's 'new paradigm', conveyed in his book *The Heart of Christianity*, had on me. He so clearly articulated what I had been fuzzily working towards for ages. I purchased multiple copies and gave them away to friends—the first time I had ever done such a thing.

So here I am, still on a journey, still in the church. There were (and are) times when the institution deeply frustrated and alarmed me. However I chose not to leave, because the church was part of my culture. I think one rejects this at one's peril—you risk losing your identity. I observe this loss of identity in many Australians, and it deeply concerns me.

I have questioned why the scholarship that has opened the new paradigm up to me is not more readily discussed in many churches. I suppose it must be at least partially related to leadership. I am not conversant enough with the education theories and practices that exist in theological colleges to be able to comment. But clergy are like the rest of humanity: they are on their own journeys, they possess a range of skills and foibles, and they have a range of beliefs. In their role they all face opposition—overt or covert—from those whose position is threatened by another view.

But I've also been very lucky in that my church community has enabled me to stay in the broader church. My sense of connectedness to my church community is strong and vibrant. My sense of connectedness to the broader church has probably diminished somewhat. I haven't attended a Presbytery or Synod meeting for more than twenty years. Opportunities to converse with like-minded thinkers outside my immediate community are fairly rare. Visiting scholars brought to Darwin by the then local Anglican Dean have enabled me to maintain contact with scholarly approaches. I always find these stimulating, though sometimes I struggle to engage with their books afterwards.

I was never an evangelical in the narrow sense of 'bringing people to know Christ'. My priorities now have distilled to creating community, applying what I understand are Jesus' values in my own society and culture, and practicing spirituality.

Creating community is about finding common ground, and these days for me this isn't limited to the common mode of religious belief or culture, but via values such as passion for justice, sustainability or creativity. So our community is able to welcome people who don't share the standard Christian belief system, to join and belong. Worship is an integral part of sustaining many members, including myself, but not all. People still feel connected to the community through their participation in other activities generated by the community. This is my current understanding of the role of the church—to create a community of acceptance, connectedness, mutual support and social justice.

Borg describes the Celtic concept of 'thin places', where the spiritual and the human somehow draw closer. I think we can create our own thin places through creating spiritually open relationships within hopeful, active communities.

I have lost my fear of 'the other', particularly in the face of militant Islam, as I have supported Muslim refugees and conversed with courageous Muslims who have gone public after events like 9/11 and the Bali bombings. I have also spent time with Buddhists and Hindus, and they have been welcomed at Nightcliff church. I am much less tolerant of the gracelessness of so many Christians who are judgmental, gratingly closed-minded, isolated and isolating. They embarrass me. I now find I have much more in common with enlightened practitioners of other faiths, or humanists of no faith, than I do with noisy conservative Christians. I usually choose not to engage with their carping. I suppose some in the church need to keep leading the church out of the darkness, but I'm over them. For this reason I don't use the term Christian to describe myself much anymore.

I seek ways to express the mystery of the sacred—in worship, in spiritual practice, in relationships, in my own spiritual practice. I expect my relationship with the sacred to be a never-ending journey in this life. My cultural approach to this is Christian via the Abrahamic faith tradition, but I recognise and am open to other approaches. I am much more comfortable than I was with mystery, questions, messiness. I am much less comfortable with rigidity and assumptions of certainty. When I prepare worship I now avoid such prayers and litanies. I would struggle to belong to a church where expressions of uncertainty and openness to new expressions were not welcome or encouraged.

'Progressive' theology informed by New Testament scholarship has enabled me to make sense of my own upbringing and stay connected to my culture with intellectual integrity. It has allowed me to discover a more authentic Jesus, and to experience and contribute to community sustained by the mysterious spirit of God.

Conclusion: 'Where To From Here?'

The 1962 film "The Loneliness of the Long Distance Runner", traces the story of a youth, Colin Smith played by a young Tom Courtney. Colin has been incarcerated in a Borstal reformatory for stealing from a bakery. He has brought with him some emotional baggage in the form of concerns about his father's recent death and his mother's desire to move on to another relationship. On top of all this he reacts negatively to people and systems of authority. During his time in the institution he discovers the passion for long distance running which the Governor of the institution encourages.

Colin is given permission to take long runs into the countryside, outside the walls of the reformatory. He discovers that running releases his anxiety and this allows his mind to deal with the concerns plaguing him. He is able to put these matters into perspective and this leads to a re-evaluation of his life.

In reading the life journeys conveyed by our storytellers you, the reader, will be made aware that for the vast majority the journey has allowed them to put their lives and their understanding of their spirituality into perspective. A perspective that makes sense for that individual and allows them a particular form of freedom and sense of liberation. For people such as *Christmas* and *Tacey* it is embarking on a quest, in some sense almost a crusade, to bring justice and gender equality or enlightenment to hierarchy of a religious institution.

These stories also remind us that not all people see the value of such a journey. Some begin but simply give up because they feel isolated or they despair at the enormity of the task.

It is our fervent hope that all of these honest and brave stories will bring hope and encouragement to people considering embarking on a similar journey. We trust that people will find comfort in the understanding that they are not alone when they set out on a quest to find what is real for them, because others have provided a guiding light.

A number of our storytellers discovered, to their delight, they were not alone with their doubts and questions. Their message to those who are questioning the traditional orthodox view of Christianity is to own and embrace your questions and doubts. *Val Webb* and others proclaim this could be the beginning or 'launching pad' for the discovery or rediscovery of a vibrant life.

Our authors paid due regard for the support and encouragement they received from the many New Testament scholars, especially those from the Westar Institute/Jesus Seminar. Writers such as Spong, Crossan, Borg, and Vosper were mentioned, as were the 'Living the Questions' DVDs developed by Felten and Procter-Murphy. This material was highly valued for its content, but more importantly because the information contained in these resources was aimed at communicating, in non-academic language, the most recent scholarship. In the United Kingdom we have a parallel development in progressive literature from Ward, Swinburne, Churcher, Armstrong and others.

Over the last twenty-five years Australia and New Zealand have witnessed a significant increase in similar resource material from people indigenous to our region—theologians, practitioners, and biblical scholars such as Geering, Jenks, Webb, Leaves, Tacey, Morwood, Parkinson, Bodycomb, Hunt, Preston, and Ogden to name just a few. Like their counterparts in North America they have provided easily readable material to give guidance to 'progressive sojourners'.

In considering the need for readily available resource information for those journeying into spiritual alternatives to Christian orthodoxy, we have become aware of an interesting developmental process. The question raised earlier that still needs to be explored is, 'what came first for those embarking on this journey?' Did the doubts and questions, brought on by one's own practical experience and knowledge lead people to seek alternatives, or did they discover alternative understandings of spirituality from the writings of scholars that led to a questioning of their beliefs?

A closer examination of these personal stories reveals a general pattern begins to emerge and we have determined that there are three developmental stages in this pattern. We have called this development *"A Journey from Doubt to Deconstruction to Discovery"*. We would also claim that much of the material recently produced by scholars of the historical Jesus school is an attempt to respond to this developmental process.

The vast majority of our storytellers began their journey in progressive Christianity by questioning or *'doubting'* the orthodox explanation of the life of Jesus, including his virgin birth, his resuscitated body after his crucifixion and his miracles (particularly the nature miracles). The interpretation of these events either through a literal understanding of the Bible or in the institutional affirmation of creeds and doctrines of the established Christian church, could no longer be accepted. These traditional interpretations also impinge on an understanding of the character and nature of the divine presence we call God.

These doubts and questions then led to an attempt to understand the message of the person of Jesus and a consistent image of the source of sacredness we in the past have referred to as God. To achieve some credible understanding of these matters people began to use their knowledge and experience to *'deconstruct'* the traditional interpretation by seeking to understand the metaphorical message hidden within these stories. This stage of spiritual development has been greatly assisted by the work of John Dominic Crossan through his ability to imbed the story of Jesus within the political, social, economic, and religious circumstances of the day. By understanding the 'matrix' as Crossan suggests, we can put the metaphorical message of Jesus within an historical context.

The process of '*deconstruction*' can be a painful one for many, because it entails the letting go of images of the person of Jesus and the image of a personal God that previously had brought comfort and support. Many atonement hymns, which cannot be logically justified, still hold us to a belief that we are so loved by Jesus that he is willing to die for us. Letting go a comforting image of a God that personally knows and cares for each person is challenging. However, by deconstructing the traditional message *about* Jesus, we reveal the message *of* Jesus by concentrating on what he said and did.

The third stage, called *'discovery'*, comes through in the stories of our contributors as a stage of relief, joy, liberation, and excitement. Perhaps the term *liberation* expresses this sense of discovery more than any other. *Garnett* expresses that *'discovery'* for her is a wonderful sense of *freedom*, freedom from no longer having to believe something she had found intolerable and morally incoherent. It is only when the realisation hits home that guilt, fear, and self loathing are no longer a prerequisite for a healthy relationship with the source of life that the joy of *discovery* can be experienced and shared. This does not absolve the individual from accepting responsibility for their inappropriate responses or their need to continue to seek wholeness of being; but it does remove the stumbling block of the feeling of wretchedness that stems from a belief in 'original sin' and which hinders positive growth.

So what then are the implications for the church from our research into the lives of people on a progressive Christian journey? Our research recorded in *Why Weren't We Told?* and in the earlier more intensive work of Hal Taussig, indicates that many people are now seeking to journey down the path of progressive Christianity. For some this has meant leaving the traditional congregational structure and becoming associated with a small support group to openly explore spiritual matters. Others have stayed within the church institution, while yet others have left altogether. Bishop John Shelby Spong refers to this latter group as the 'Believers in Exile', or the 'Church Alumni'. The majority of our authors wish to remain within the church institution, but to do so they need the freedom to explore their spirituality outside the confines or demands of Christian orthodoxy. We need to recognise that these storytellers are really just the tip of the iceberg within the Christian faith. They are people who are more concerned about spirituality than organised religion.

The stories in this collection provide a valuable insight into the importance of the spiritual dimension of people's lives. They also alert us to the difficulties experienced by people who dared to step outside the orthodox square of Christianity as they sought to make sense of their personal spirituality. Our plea is for the orthodox Church not just to tolerate this ever increasing population of Christians, but to embrace and make space for them to continue within and even to influence orthodox Christianity.

What do these people require to make a contribution to the life of the church?

A significant majority wish to stay within a church based community of faith. The reasons presented are that within the environment of the Christian church they are able to experience a sense of a sacred presence that most refer to as God. They experience the evidence of the Spirit of God not only in their own lives, but also in the lives of the members of the faith community. Many, but not all, welcomed the traditional aspects of the liturgy and the lessons they have learnt from members of the community. Some like *Tacey* discovered a real sense of the unity of the community in the sharing of the Mass, which for him is a profoundly spiritually moving event.

Considerable information was presented testifying to the value of a caring community. For many such as *Oakley* it was the single most significant reason to remain within the church. In this environment they were able to experience the presence of God; people caring for one another and the wider community revealed a sacred spirit. All felt most comfortable with people who were not judgmental and who were open to alternative ways of experiencing and responding to the sacred spirit we name God. That is, a community that welcomes and embraces diversity, accepting the possibility of change through an embrace of new paradigms, as *Pyle* suggests, and engaging in life with a vitality. This is what is being sought by many progressive Christians.

Faith communities have power through the unity of their action, to be a powerful force for change. As Margaret Mead says "Never doubt that a small group of thoughtful, committed citizens can change the world. Indeed, it is the only thing that ever has." A number of our authors welcomed the opportunity to pursue the spiritual dimension of their lives while working together with companions to make the world a better place.

Embracing the 'historical Jesus' is perhaps the key element in empowering the journey for progressive Christians, because to embrace the human or historical Jesus is to reject Jesus the divine being, who has equal status with God. The figure of Jesus then becomes the very human 'wisdom sage' rather than the second partner in the doctrine of the Trinity. Once we accept the true humanity of Jesus we automatically 'demote' him from the lofty position of the creeds, for it is the human Jesus who calls us to embrace *life* and not *religion*.

To understand the historical Jesus our authors needed to come to terms with the information available about him and to place this information in its historical context. More importantly they needed to discern how to interpret the Jesus stories not as literal facts, but as messages about the nature and character of him and what his particular message is. As *Carter* says, it was this approach that changed his understanding of the nature of God and caused him most discomfort. Generally speaking, they have depended on the work of such New Testament scholars and theologians, as Borg, Crossan, and Funk (who refers to his own journey as seeking to find 'a credible Jesus') for their understanding of the historical Jesus.

It is apparent from these stories that the work of these scholars needs to be more publicly available, not only to theological students and clergy, but to all people seeking a Christian path to enlightenment. It is a real concern that the scholarship surrounding the historical Jesus has not been systematically taught in theological colleges around Australia, except in a very limited way. The scholarship that enlightened the search of our authors needs to be made available and taught to the theological students in our 'halls of learning', if only so they can respond honestly and openly to the questions they will be asked by a growing number within their faith community. It will also give them a resource with which to guide people on their individual spiritual journeys. All clergy should be trained to never underestimate the intelligence of the faith community or their ability to accept change! This is a responsibility of theological colleges and all involved in continuing education.

What advice are these storytellers offering the established faith traditions? The main issue these stories raise is, does the Christian church, as we know it today, have a future and if so will it be in its present form?

Evidence collected from the Australian Bureau of Census statistics and the Christian Research Association show that there has been a steady decline in the numbers of people attending mainstream Christian churches. However what is interesting is that there has been a steady increase in the number of people who refer to themselves as being 'spiritual'. This information corresponds to the findings of Harvey Cox in his book *The Future of Faith* that leads him to suggest that we have entered the 'Age of Spirituality'.

Religion is no longer culturally or ethnically determined through family ties and further defined by gender roles and class. The evidence of these stories appears to support this conclusion. Religious adherence in a pluralistic society is no longer determined by tradition; it has now become a personal lifestyle option and not something we do because our parents expect it of us. As evidenced by these stories, people are determining their own unique spirituality, which is not necessarily dependent on Christian orthodoxy. Belief for many is now based, not on creeds, doctrines, or infallible proclamations—be it the Bible or a Pope—but on the experience of what works, and this is not simply dependent on a knowledge base. How we live is driven more by our unique understanding of our spiritual experience and not some article of faith.

It also appears that small supportive communities will flourish, providing the opportunity to develop mutually caring relationships and the chance to work together on time banded projects. The stories also indicate that these small groups will not necessarily be committed to a life long arrangement but will be more transitory.

The role of support networks, such as those established by people travelling the progressive journey, will be to nurture and provide resources for the development of this 'subjective' spirituality. Many of these networks have occurred as a result of chance relationships and they in no way resemble the rigid organisations of the past. For many in the traditional orthodox church this will be a painful transition, but for those who have already embarked on the journey, like our storytellers, it is music to their ears.

Further Reading

Bass D. B. *Christianity After Religion. The End of Church and the Birth of a New Spiritual Awakening.* NY: HarperOne, 2012.

Bessler, J. A. *A Scandalous Jesus: How Three Historic Quests Changed Theology for the Better.* Salem: Polebridge Press, 2013.

Bodycomb, J. *Aware And Attentive. 'Worship' in Evolving Christianity.* Richmond: Spectrum Publications, 2012.

Borg, M. J. *Speaking Christian: Why Christian Words Have Lost Their Meaning and Power—And How They Can Be Restored.* NY: HarperOne, 2011.

Cox, H. *The Future of Faith.* NY: HarperOne, 2010.

Crossan, J. D. *The Power of Parable. How Fiction By Jesus Became Fiction About Jesus.* NY: HarperOne, 2012.

Crossan, J. D. *The Greatest Prayer: Rediscovering the Revolutionary Message of The Lord's Prayer.* NY: HarperOne, 2010.

Cupitt, D. *A New Great Story.* Salem: Polebridge Press, 2010.

Dewey, A. J. (ed) *The Authentic Letters of Paul. A New reading of Paul's Rhetoric and Meaning.* Salem: Polebridge Press, 2010.

Galston, D. *Embracing the Human Jesus. A Wisdom Path for Contemporary Christianity.* Salem: Polebridge Press, 2012.

Geering, L. G. *From the Big Bang to God.* Wellington: Steele Roberts Publishers, 2013.

Habel, N. *Rainbow of Mysteries. Meeting the Sacred in Nature.* Canada: CopperHouse/Wood Lake Publishing, 2012.

Hunt, R. A. E. & Smith, J. W. H. *Why Weren't We Told? A Handbook on 'progressive' Christianity.* Salem: Polebridge Press, 2013.

Hunt, R. A. E. *Against the Stream: Progressive Christianity Between Pulpit and Pew.* Preston: Mosaic Press, 2012.

Jenks, G. C. (ed) *The Once and Future Scriptures. Exploring the Role of the Bible in the Contemporary Church.* Salem: Polebridge Press, 2013.

Jenks, G. C. *The Once and Future Bible. An Introduction to the Bible for Religious Progressives.* Eugene: Wipf & Stock, 2011.

Leaves, N. *Religion Under Attack. Getting Theology Right.* Salem: Polebridge Press, 2011.

Macnab, F. *Discover A New Faith. Energy for a Better Life.* Richmond: Spectrum Publications, 2011.

Morwood, M. *It's Time. Challenges to the Doctrine of the Faith.* South Bend: Kelmor Publishing, 2013.

Parkinson, L. *The World According to Jesus... His Blueprint for the Best Possible World.* Richmond: Spectrum Publications, 2011.

Sanguin, B. *The Advance of Love. Reading the Bible with an Evolutionary Heart.* Canada: Evans & Sanguin Publishing, 2012.

Scott, B. B. *The Trouble With Resurrection. From Paul to the Fourth Gospel.* Salem: Polebridge Press, 2010.

Spong, J. S. *The Fourth Gospel: Tales of a Jewish Mystic.* NY: HarperOne, 2013.

Taussig, H. (ed) *A New New Testament. A Bible for the 21st Century Combining Traditional and Newly Discovered Texts.* Boston: Houghton Mifflin Harcourt, 2013.

Vosper, G. *Amen! What Prayer Can Mean in a World Beyond Belief.* Canada: HarperCollins, 2012.

Webb, V. *In Defense of Doubt. An Invitation to Adventure.* Revised & Expanded Edition. Preston: Mosaic Press, 2013.

Wolsey, R. *Kissing Fish: Christianity For People Who Don't Like Christianity.* Xlibris Corporation, 2011.

Appendix 1: Narrative Questions

Has this journey changed my opinion of the role of the church and if so in what way?

Has it changed my own understanding of my faith and if so in what way?

Has it changed how I express my faith?

Has this journey affected my attitude to church attendance?

Is anything different and does this difference influence why I come or why I do not come to church?

Is attendance at church a sign of the strength of my faith or is it an opportunity to recharge my batteries?

Why I didn't walk away?

Has it changed the way I see my responsibility to the wider community?

Have I discovered a hollowness in my spiritual life and am I seeking something that is more meaningful?

Am I seeking a more intimate relationship with the sacred?

Am I seeking a greater understanding of the work of God's Spirit and the person of Jesus of Nazareth?

Why did I commit myself to actively encouraging the spread of progressive Christian thought and action? (You did not just make a change within yourself you have actively promoted a state and national change)?

What impact has this movement had on me personally?

New Testament scholarship regarding the Historical Jesus has been around for some time I am concerned/annoyed that it has not been more readily available to lay people generally.

Since discovering this information has my opinion of clergy/theologians changed?

The New Testament Scholarship on the historical Jesus has allowed me to:

Discover an authentic/essential Jesus

Establish a faith that has intellectual integrity.

Throw off the bonds of guilt.

Embrace life.

Experience a renaissance in my faith.

Feel proud of my humanity.

To experience sacredness in the ordinary.

To experience the living reality of the spirit of Jesus of Nazareth

Other.

Appendix Two: About the Storytellers

Elizabeth Burns was born in England into a farming family who were practising church goers for generations. A few years after marriage she and her family migrated to Western Australia in 1970, settling in Albany "where I still live today".

Elizabeth writes: "I was a keen horsewoman, becoming a judge in the disciplines of Dressage, Show Jumping and Hacking and am currently a commentator for Showjumping.

"I undertook the UCA Lay Preachers course through Coolamon College and became Accredited.

"I was chair of Stirling Presbytery for two periods—the first for six and one half years, the second for two years. I was appointed Chaplain to the Presbytery for several years. Later I was appointed Regional Pastor, following the reshaping of the Synod."

"I was elected Moderator of the Western Australian Synod UCA from 1999-2002. Over almost 30 years I served on many Synod Committees, including Standing Committee, and Pastoral Relations Committee. I have been privileged to attended seven National Assemblies, and served two trienniums on the Assembly Standing Committee, which gave me a broader view of the Uniting Church in Australia".

Richard J (Dick) Carter is a retired Melbourne based company director with special interests in the minerals industry, board leadership, corporate governance, strategy formulation and occupational health and safety.

In non-commercial life Dick is active in lay leadership roles in the Uniting Church in Australia as a member of the Standing Committee of the Synod of Victoria & Tasmania, Chairperson of UCA Funds Management, and Chair of the Church Council at Ewing Memorial UCA, East Malvern where he worships. He is also President of The Progressive Christian Network of Victoria (of which he was a co-founder).

In the commercial sphere he was a director and, in several cases, Chairman of a number of stock exchange listed companies in the mining and mining services sectors. His executive career spanned thirty seven years with the BHP Group (now merged into BHP Billiton) from which he retired in 1997 as BHP Minerals' Chief Executive Officer.

Dick has also had wide experience in industry and professional representative groups (including The Australasian Institute of Mining & Metallurgy of which he was President in 1998) and government bodies concerned with regional development. He was Western Australia's Citizen of the Year in 1996 and he was awarded the Centenary Medal for services to technological industries.

Gerald Christmas was the Sydney Diocesan Registrar (Anglican) from 1977-1990 and a Pracitising Solicitor, 1961-1998. He retired in 1998.

Neville Davidson was for 35 years, employed as a Clerk of Courts, culminating in his appointment as a County Court Pre-Trial Conference Mediator and a Deputy Registrar, retiring in 1997.

He has spent a lifetime of active involvement in the Heatherton Methodist, Wangaratta Presbyterian and Vermont and Heathmont Uniting Churches and is also an accredited Lay Preacher. In 2000, he graduated BTheol. from the Melbourne College of Divinity. From 2001-2006, he was part-time Uniting Church Lay Minister at Monbulk.

He is a member of the Heathmont Uniting Church Faith Explorers' Group and the Progressive Christian Network of Victoria. Committed to actively encouraging the spread of progressive Christian thought and action, sadly, he has found a distinct lack of overall progressive thinking within the institutional church, both in worship and the exposition of the Christian message. Disheartened and disillusioned, in 2009 he ceased attending Sunday worship, preferring to be a "Christian in Exile."

Ruth Doobov is a member of both The Centre for Progressive Religious Thought, Canberra, and The Uniting Church of St James, Canberra. She is a retired senior public servant, and worked mainly on programs of assistance to students and higher education funding.

Before joining the Public Service, she spent a few years as a teacher of English Literature at the University of Queensland and the University of Canberra. She has an MA in English Literature from the University of Queensland. She is married to Allan, an Orthodox Jew, whom she met as a result of a shared involvement in the Aboriginal Rights movement. They have two children and two grandchildren.

For recreation, she likes bushwalking and cryptic crosswords.

Sue Emeleus studied physics and psych at University of New South Wales (UNSW). She taught physics and high school science for 30 years, and Christian studies for 20 years, in Sydney, Tanzania and PNG. Sue has also undertaken counsellor and chaplaincy training, served on the Editorial committee of *Eremos* Magazine, been Secretary of Women's Interfaith Network, and completed a DMin (CSU) in 2010.

Sue is married with four adult children and ten grandchildren.

Ken Fletcher was born and raised in Sydney, and educated at Fort Street School and Sydney University. He is married with three children, and operated a Pharmacy business in partnership with his wife for 30 years.

Ken is interested in all things mechanical and scientific, attended continuing education courses in communication, improving skill levels, philosophy, psychology, history and comparative religions.

He has travelled extensively in Australia and overseas particularly enjoying time in national parks which "we can do now we are retired".

Desley Garnett started her working life as a microbiologist, but later, after spending several years as a stay-at-home mum with her three girls, moved into working as a coordinator of a Family Day Care Service. She currently works part time as the Resource and Advisory Officer for the Family Day Care Association Queensland.

Desley is passionate about children having wonderful childhoods and significant respectful relationships in their early years that give them the best start in life.

Desley has been an active member of the Methodist Church and Uniting Church all her life, fulfilling various lay leadership roles. She has a commitment to her local New Farm community where she has lived for over 40 years and is very involved in the local Historical Society. A particular area of interest is ensuring people with disabilities have valued roles in the community and contribute to the development of community to their full capacity.

Being grandmother to three young children is a significant role which gives a lot of pleasure.

Aaron Harper is currently an advisor to the Defence Minister and has been involved in Defence budgeting for 20 years. He enjoys playing piano, writing contemporary progressive Christian songs, and composing music. He regularly speaks at The Uniting Church of St James, Canberra, and is interested in creating new forms of liturgies and prayer.

Aaron has a love of all things to do with wine but most of all drinking it, and has made his first shiraz this year with a friend.

He also enjoys reading both fiction and non-fiction and regularly going to the cinemas.

Lorna Henry is a retired teacher of German and Religion in secondary schools. Living for a year in Germany in the early '60s enabled her to experience a wider, more diverse world of thought than might have been available in Melbourne at the time. As a result she has constantly questioned the assumptions of Australian society and religious experience.

She divides her time between community involvement, playing in music ensembles, and leading discussion groups about faith and life. She is a mother and grandmother, and lives in Melbourne.

Fiona McDougal is a Scottish New Zealander, born and brought up in Aberdeenshire, Scotland and emigrating to New Zealand in the late 1990's. She is a member at St Andrew's on The Terrace Church, Wellington, joining the Parish Council in 2009 and contributing in the areas of worship and pastoral care.

Fiona is currently studying theology by distance learning through EIDTS (Ecumenical Institute of Distance Theological Studies). She works as a Registered Nurse on a Surgical/Gynaecology ward at the Hutt Hospital and is a NZNO workplace delegate.

In her spare time she is also a keen amateur musician, playing the flute and singing in various local groups.

Gai Nowland has had a 10 year involvement with the Nightcliff Uniting Church in the Northern Territory. In addition to her leadership within progressive study groups she has been involved in the congregation's community projects such as *Frilly's* Op-Shop and *The Mulch Pit* —a community garden.

Ian O'Reilly is married and is the father of two young adults. He has worked as a youth worker, youth sector network coordinator, school counsellor, consultant, client and program manager and most recently with *Anglicare Northern Territory* as an Operations Manager in Darwin, NT. Some of this work has taken him onto remote Indigenous communities.

In 2013-14 he took a year's leave without pay to volunteer in Solomon Islands through *Australian Volunteers International.*

Lesley Oakley worked in child and family welfare and youth justice for 30 years. She trained as a family therapist and the major part of her working life was in management. Her last position was as a regional director with Connections UnitingCare in the south-east of Melbourne.

Since retirement she has worked with refugees and is a member of Rural Australians for Refugees on Phillip Island in Victoria. Lesley is a member of St John's Uniting Church, Cowes, Phillip Island.

Frances Porter was born in Hawera, South Taranaki, New Zealand in 1925 and educated at the local high school, at WEA classes, and at Victoria University College. She credits two remarkable teachers in Victoria's history department – Fred Wood and John Beaglehole –as being the formative influences in her later career as an historian. She began writing in her 40s. Whatever the subject, social context – particularly women's place in that context – has remained pivotal.

Publications include: *Turanga Journals (*1974); as editor, *Historic Buildings of New Zealand (*1981, 1983); *Born to New Zealand* (1989): this biography won the NZ Book Award for Non-Fiction 1990. *My Hand Will Write What My Heart Dictates* (1995): a collection of 19th century NZ women's letters and diaries co-edited with Charlotte Macdonald; *Away from Home* (2002)

In 1993 she received an honorary doctorate from Victoria University of Wellington.

Adrian Pyle is, chiefly among other things, a husband, father, innovation and relationship development worker for the Uniting Church in Australia, Synod of Victoria and Tasmania, emeritus chair of a major Melbourne community service agency, founder of an awards program for young people tackling the challenge of poverty and an energy reduction and ecological sustainability advocate.

He has a deep interest in community development, particularly as it relates to increasing grassroots connections between neighbours and the link between community and spiritual development. Responsible travel is a new interest of Adrian's as, in his professional and personal life, he examines ways to help people turn travel activity into localised, contextual learning journeys.

Pam Raff writes: "I was a wife for just over 50 years, a mother of five and grandmother of ten. For the whole of my marriage I have lived in the Rockhampton Diocese (Anglican, Queensland), mostly in Rockhampton itself. I have worked in an office, taught sewing, been an announcer with the ABC, prepared tax returns and taught English as a second language.

"In the diocese, I have served as a parish councillor, parish treasurer, synod representative, parochial nominator, member of diocesan council, secretary of the Diocesan Thanksgiving Program. I have also prepared the lectionary for both *An Australian Prayer Book* and, later, *A Prayer Book for Australia* since 1979.

"I am now organising myself to move to Brisbane, QLD to be closer to family. I love retirement and the leisure it gives me to travel, to read, and to do all the things I enjoy."

Lynne Robertson has worked for 15 years as a school chaplain and ten years in the training and management of chaplains.

She was the founding Director of the Council for Christian Education in Schools Centre for Clinical Pastoral Education, and has conducted Clinical Pastoral Education programs in several hospital and community centres, currently working with Uniting CPE, The John Paver Centre. She has recently completed a role on the Faculty of the Uniting Church Theological College in Melbourne as Field Education Coordinator and is currently writing a Supervision Training Package for the Assembly of the Uniting

Church in Australia to resource supervisory training for Uniting Church ministers and lay leaders.

Lynne lives in Melbourne with her partner of 25 years.

Kathleen Rowe is a member of the Community of Saint Luke in Auckland, New Zealand where she is currently Parish Clerk of this Presbyterian congregation. A secondary school teacher of Technology and of Studies in Religion she has taught at leading Auckland and Sydney schools.

Contributions within the wider church have included a period as parish liaison for the Auckland Methodist Mission assisting congregations to relate to the needs of their neighbourhood and three years within the office of the Uniting Church Frontier Services with a primary focus on support of outback padres.

Kathleen is strongly committed to a future for the church shaped by inclusion, care for the needy, and room for people to do their own believing within a supportive community.

Betty Shore was born in Bakersfield, California, USA. She has graduate qualifications in education and has worked as a primary school teacher as well as teacher training and community studies at tertiary level.

Betty and her family moved to New Zealand in 1973 because her husband lost his job in the economic recession. She has continued her concerns and activities in Christchurch, working for a quality education for everyone.

Durham Smith AO, is a retired consultant Paediatric Surgeon from the Royal Children's Hospital, Melbourne, Victoria. He is the author of several books on surgery of children, and has travelled extensively as a guest lecturer.

Durham was involved for many years in the Royal Australasian College of Surgeons in the setting of standards in surgery, in the training of young surgeons, as an Examiner for the Fellowship (FRACS) and as president of the College in 1987-89. In 1991 he was awarded an AO in the Order of Australia Awards.

He is married to Dorothy, a graduate of music, in a continuing partnership of 64 years, and they have four sons. He has been active in sport and has had a life-long interest in history, current affairs, ethics and theology. They attend St John's Anglican Church, Camberwell, Melbourne.

Richard C. G. Smith has been a farm management consultant, University Lecturer, CSIRO Research Scientist and Leader, NASA Research Associate and most recently Manager, WA State Government's Satellite Remote Sensing Centre. In this period he has worked overseas in the USA (3x), Netherlands, Saudi Arabia, Syria, Vietnam, Malaysia and Indonesia.

With his wife Claire he has three grown sons and two grandchildren at high school. He is a Lay Preacher and Chairperson Mission and Outreach at All Saints Floreat Uniting Church. He is a volunteer guide on Rottnest Island and with the West Kimberley with the Mowanjum Aboriginal Community helping to run a Centre providing Computer and Internet access.

Richard is Chair of the Perth Progressive Network WA inc.

George Stuart was born in Melbourne, Victoria. He writes: "I married Wendy in 1960 and we have four lovely daughters and six delightful grandchildren."

"Initially I worked as an industrial chemist, then as a youth worker. I was ordained as a Presbyterian Minister of the Word in 1965, my first church appointment being Whyalla, SA. After much negotiation both locally and in Adelaide, the church eventually gave me permission to become a 'minister in secular employment'. I began full time employment with BHP in Whyalla in 1969. This situation continued in both Whyalla and Newcastle for a total of about eight years."

"With my family I moved to Newcastle in 1972, continuing my employment with BHP and work in the Presbyterian Church. After Church Union I took responsibility for the Kotara/New Lambton/Lambton Uniting Church parish in Newcastle for a few years until I resigned from 'the ministry' in 1975. I retired from BHP in 1990."

"I continue to write new lyrics to traditional church melodies and have now written over 500 sets of lyrics."

David Tacey teaches courses on the crisis of meaning in Western culture, depth psychology and postmodern theory at La Trobe University, Melbourne. Professor Tacey studied literature, psychology and philosophy at Flinders and Adelaide Universities, and completed post-doctoral studies in psychoanalysis in the United States. He is a public intellectual who is often invited to address contemporary issues, including ecological awareness, mental health, the future of faith and Aboriginal Australia.

He has written extensively on spirituality, religion and society. His most recent book is *Gods and Diseases: Making Sense of Our Physical and Mental Wellbeing* (Harper Collins, 2011). He is the author of thirteen books, including *Edge of the Sacred* (1st ed., Sydney, 1995; 2nd ed., Zurich, 2009), *ReEnchantment: the New Australian Spirituality* (Harper Collins, 2000), and *The Spirituality Revolution* (Harper Collins, 2003). He is working on two new books on religion, *The God You Don't Believe In*, and *It's a Metaphor, Stupid: Beyond Literal Thinking in Religion and Life.*

David's books have been translated into Cantonese, Korean, Spanish, Portuguese and French.

Val Webb is a theologian now living in the New South Wales country town of Mudgee. Born in Brisbane, her professional life began with a graduate degree in Microbiology and a research position at the University of Queensland.

After an 18 month stint in England, Val and husband Maurice moved to Rochester, Minnesota, USA where the family spent almost thirty years. Maurice was a surgeon and head of the Department of Gynecologic Surgery at the Mayo Clinic and, during the 1970's, Val owned and operated Val Webb Galleries which featured the work of some eighty national and international artists, including Val's sketches, etchings and prints. She had two books published on the art and history of Minnesota, *Rochester Sketchbook* and *Twin Cities Sketchbook*. For eight years back in Brisbane during the Eighties, Val was heavily involved in the Queensland Synod of the Uniting Church and its hospital, The Wesley Hospital. Val then completed a PhD in theology in the United States and has taught religious studies and world religions at universities in America and Australia and written ten books.

Bishop Jack Spong says of her: "Val Webb is one of the most exciting Christian voices in the 21st Century".